Rethinking Our Centralized Monetary System

Rethinking Our Centralized Monetary System

The Case for a System of
Local Currencies

Lewis D. Solomon

Foreword by Bob Swann

Westport, Connecticut
London

Library of Congress Cataloging-in-Publication Data

Solomon, Lewis D.
    Rethinking our centralized monetary system : the case for a system
of local currencies / Lewis D. Solomon.
        p.   cm.
    Includes bibliographical references and index.
    ISBN 0–275–95376–9 (alk. paper)
    1. Money—United States.   2. Currency question—United States.
3. Banks and banking—United States.   I. Title.
HG540.S65   1996
332.4'973—dc20   95–34441

British Library Cataloguing in Publication Data is available.

Library of Congress Catalog Card Number: 95–34441
ISBN: 0–275–95376–9

First published in 1996

Praeger Publishers, 88 Post Road West, Westport, CT 06881
An imprint of Greenwood Publishing Group, Inc.

Printed in the United States of America

The paper used in this book complies with the
Permanent Paper Standard issued by the National
Information Standards Organization (Z39.48–1984).

10   9   8   7   6   5   4   3   2

For my son, Michael,
and our conversations about the future.

Contents

Foreword *by Bob Swann*   ix

Acknowledgments   xi

1. Introduction   1

2. The Evolution of the U.S. Monetary and Banking System:
    An Overview   5

3. The Current Context and Objectives of Local Currency
    Issuance   17

4. Barter: Evolution into a Modern Economic Tool   37

5. Discount Scrip: Creating a Local Currency Pegged to the
    U.S. Dollar   53

6. Local Currency Not Pegged to the U.S. Dollar   67

7. Legal Aspects of Local Currency   95

8. Conclusion   129

Notes   131

Bibliography   153

Index   163

Foreword

That the present monetary system does not suit the economic needs of communities is increasingly acknowledged today. Just a few of the system's failures are:

- that over 95 percent of all foreign exchange transactions are of a purely speculative nature, against less than 5 percent for investments and trade for goods and services around the world;
- that most national currencies are devaluing at widely fluctuating rates, making trades between them difficult or almost impossible (even the so-called First World countries are suffering from such "inflation pressures");
- that world debt (private and public) has been increasing at an exponential rate—in the United States alone this debt is 16 trillion dollars or $62,000 per person.

Perhaps the most important concern for the world today, then, is to plan a new system that will replace it. How will this new global system work and how will we start to build it? Although the overarching need is for a global system that is stable and universally acceptable, the first step in that direction will have to be taken by small communities or at the regional level. These small steps are already being taken. We are fortunate that Professor Solomon provides a history of small steps, beginning with prerevolutionary scrip, toward a decent monetary system, and an outline of the practical steps that can be taken in almost any community.

Few people realize how important a good money exchange system is, not only for community welfare but also for the health of the natural environment. A local currency can have an incubator effect—it encourages local production and responsibility to one another and the local ecology. Even fewer people are aware that they can create such a money system—"it's illegal, isn't it, to create a local exchange system?" Professor Solomon, with the help of his students at The George Washington University, has put to rest this superstition that "only the government can create money." This book lays out many possibilities for local economic renewal that can be immediately realized in any community or neighborhood—"life boats" which will increase local trade of local goods and services. It is important to deemphasize national currencies and trade that distance us from the production process and take from us the control of our local economies. This book suggests many other money systems which will devolve economic control and can absorb the shock waves of financial collapse.

Anyone who lived through the Great Depression of the 1930s knows how destructive financial shock waves can be. But it was precisely because of the Great Depression that experiments in the use of local scrip, like those described in this book, were initiated and are now being revived. We are indeed grateful to Professor Solomon and his students for updating us on the history of scrip in the United States, and for pointing the way out of the present financial morass.

As someone who has been involved in local currency experiments, I know how rewarding it is to participate in a successful local currency program. The new local currency movement makes me feel that something genuinely new and liberating is taking place and, with it, hope is reignited.

Bob Swann
E. F. Schumacher Society
Great Barrington, Massachusetts, 1995

Acknowledgments

This book was supported by The George Washington University Law School Summer Research Stipend Program. I acknowledge the research assistance of Steven J. Kim and Dwayne Stuart Eichenbaum, students at The George Washington University National Law Center and Patricia A. Tobin, Reference Librarian, Jacob Burns Law Library, The George Washington University National Law Center. I want to thank Paul Glover for his helpful suggestions. Last, but not least, I want to thank Bob Swann and Susan Witt of the E. F. Schumacher Society for their encouragement of this project. The time I spent at the library of the E. F. Schumacher Center offered me access to a unique collection of books, pamphlets, and newspaper clippings dealing with local currencies.

Rethinking Our Centralized Monetary System

one

Introduction

The time has come—indeed, it is long past due—to recognize that economic and political institutions honored by time must be altered, and substantially so, if the United States is to achieve a more sustainable pattern of economic growth and reduce the dangers of an increasingly centralized economic system. Moreover, these institutions *will* be altered, if only by the force of circumstances, and the question thus becomes whether change can be guided.

It is the belief of humanists that they can remake the world (David Ehrenfeld has coined the term *The Arrogance of Humanism*),[1] rectifying old wrongs and bringing a measure of justice and equity to all Americans. Whether or not this is possible, however, is not really the question. Only those who are willing to let society drift from crisis to crisis would deny that it is crucial to find solutions to our current social and economic problems. This handbook is such an effort. It is an inquiry into the extent to which the institutions of our political economy can help in resolving the increasingly complex problems facing our nation.

The questions we face are these: Where do we go from here? How? Can change be managed? It is easy enough to envision an ideal society; many, indeed, have done that. But one must deal with the world as it is, rather than as one would like it to be, and this adds immeasurably to the problem. That social changes will come is certain. Rather less certain are the direction the changes will take and to what extent they will go.

There is no doubt that the world is undergoing major change, although we cannot be sure that humankind can determine the direction of change. I see no alternative, nonetheless, to acting as if what is being done by people not only makes a difference but also can influence the direction and rate of change. But with any process of change the chance of success is uncertain, and we do not know which values will be retained in the process.

What will shape our future economic and political institutions? A system of local currencies would pave the way for a network of viable regional economies—one that *can* be established, given the necessary will and energy. I admit that the notion of a local currency seems quaint. So many take for granted not only our existing system for the issuance of money but also (and even more fundamentally) what life means and where we want to go. Many can only conceive of minor reforms of institutions as they presently exist—whether it is our currency system or, more generally, the political economy. Somehow we think that the creation of a national currency (and more broadly, the nation state) "represents progress and promotes the stability of economic life."[2] In questioning the necessity for or the advantages of the acceptance of a national governmental prerogative in producing money, this handbook presents a challenge to the prevailing notions of "progress" and our "economic life."

The argument in support of a system of local currencies unfolds as follows in this handbook. Chapter 2 presents a brief overview of the evolution of America's increasingly centralized money and banking system. In a centralized system, people are controlled by and subject to an economic system over which they have little or no control and which they really do not understand. In many ways the foundation of the federal government's power rests on its prerogative to create and manipulate money—the medium of exchange. As one proponent of local currency notes, "[t]he entire machinery of money and finance has been appropriated to serve the interests of centralized power."[3]

Chapter 3 treats both the values implicit in and the rationale for a local currency approach. The chapter stresses the importance of scale, specifically the decentralization of economic and political power and the construction of viable units in which people can participate in shaping the economic, political, and social decisions that affect them. We need to overcome our inability to participate effectively in decision making that affects our lives. The scale of our present political and economic institutions limits effective participation. On a smaller scale, these institutions would provide wider, more effective participation.

Building on the need to encourage a greater degree of participation and local self-reliance designed to promote a noninflationary economy of ecological permanence, human development, and fuller employment, Chapter 3 shows how a system of local currencies represents one of the key levers to help us get from here to there. Briefly, an alternative currency will stimulate local economies and employment. It will provide incentives to resolve existing economic and social difficulties, thereby enhancing local self-reliance and getting away from vast bureaucratic schemes based on federal governmental intervention. Local currencies will help return power to smaller societal units and encourage ecological sustainability.

Next, Chapters 4 and 5 discuss two contemporary approaches to issuing a local currency. The first is based on barter—the exchange of goods and services. The second uses local currency pegged to the U.S. dollar as a means to offer bargain purchases—discounts for consumers.

After examining one local currency experiment not pegged to the U.S. dollar—the Constant project in the 1970s—Chapter 6 discusses in considerable detail the business aspects of implementing a viable local currency system. Among the topics considered are: (1) how to back a local currency, that is, the benefits of a redeemable currency system; (2) who will issue the currency; and (3) the relationship of the issuer and the local currency to the existing banks. Having a community-based issuer will democratize the issuance of money and focus on giving top priority to the human and ecological concerns developed in Chapter 3. By placing the control of money issuance and lending at the local level, initiative is freed to create diversified small businesses that can become the basis of sustainable regional economies. The chapter concludes by examining some of the potential issues critics of a local currency may raise.

Chapter 7 analyzes the legal aspects of the various types of local currency systems—barter, discount mechanism keyed to the U.S. dollar, and community currency not pegged to the U.S. dollar. The chapter establishes that these three types of local currency can legally be issued under federal and state laws (with the possible exception of Virginia and Arkansas). In addition, the chapter examines not only the currency-specific issues, but also related banking, securities regulation, and federal income taxation questions, thus providing a road map for the organizers of a community currency system. It concludes by offering recommendations for federal legislation which, if enacted, would promote the widespread acceptance of local currencies throughout the United States.

Chapter 8 presents a brief summary of the handbook.

As we approach the twenty-first century, we must rethink not only our existing political economy but also our centralized monetary system. Local currencies may become a necessity, perhaps sooner than we think.

two

The Evolution of the U.S. Monetary and Banking System: An Overview

This chapter begins by providing an introduction to the basics of money and banking, focusing on the benefits and attendant risks of a fractional reserve banking system. The remainder of the chapter surveys three periods in U.S. monetary and banking history: (1) the pre–Civil War free banking era; (2) the 1863–1913 national banking era; and (3) the modern central banking (Federal Reserve System) era.[1]

THE BASICS OF MONEY AND BANKING

Money and banks are such a basic part of our everyday existence that we do not reflect on the evolution of paper money and the commercial banking system. As this chapter demonstrates, the contemporary American money and banking system emerged over many decades.

Money came into existence to replace bartering in the buying and selling of goods and services. Money served as a convenient way to exchange goods and services by creating a medium of exchange, establishing a common unit of account, and creating a store of value allowing transactions to be deferred into the future. Money is what people in a community will accept to carry out these basic functions.

Looking back to the early history of the United States, the eighteenth century witnessed the development of paper money. Public warehouses—in Virginia, Maryland, and the Carolinas—began issuing certificates representing that a specified volume and quality of tobacco had been weighed and graded. These certificates, as well as other experiments with grain and cattle as reserve commodities, passed in circulation, from hand to hand. The certificates, promising to pay the bearer in specie, gained acceptance as money.

These bearer certificates, an early form of paper money, avoided the need for each owner to sign over a note for the payment of debts. The number of people using certificates as money was not limited by the number of signatures a certificate could accommodate. The commodity backing of the certificates became a reserve currency which did not pass from hand to hand, but could be delivered on demand, if required. The growing acceptance of paper money, as opposed to hard currency or the commodity the paper money represented, provided greater convenience and the opportunity for banks to create money at will.[2] In contrast to a pure, commodity-based monetary system, a paper money approach economized the use of the reserve commodity.

With independence from Great Britain, commercial banks began to flourish in the United States. The conceptual origins of commercial banking are quite simple. Individuals with surplus stocks of gold "lent" their commodity to others (banks) who paid interest. The "lending" took the form of individuals depositing their gold in banks.

Banks then provided borrowers with a note having a claim on a reserve commodity, namely, hard currency. Two notes—one held by a depositor and a second held by a borrower—would circulate claiming ownership to a bar of gold.

Commercial banks created both assets and liabilities on their balance sheets by creating and issuing bearer notes (money) to borrowers who, in turn, issued interest-bearing notes back to the bank in the form of a loan agreement. For a bank, the notes became a liability and the loan agreement an asset. Conversely, for the borrower, the loan agreement represented a liability and the notes, which the borrower exchanged for goods and services, assets. Commercial banks got their notes circulating in the form of hand-to-hand money.

The pyramid grew ever higher as one depositor's deposit of gold was used to back a note issued to a new borrower without the consent (or knowledge) of the depositor. Bank-created credit notes for borrowers were secured by the reserve commodity (for instance, gold) as well as alternative assets. Given sufficient time, banks could extend full value to all depositors. However, a bank could not convert all of its outstanding notes into the reserve commodity at the same time.

Despite the attendant risks, the conventional wisdom in the nineteenth century was that banks could prudently create paper money on their physical reserve or hard currency of about five times greater than they actually possessed. Thus, the total amount of money in the system became much larger than the gold used for monetary purposes. The United

States received its monetary services at a lower cost, reflecting the will-ingness of banks to pay interest (or higher interest) to their depositors.

Also, the additional monetary demand resulting from an increase in demand for money due to economic growth could be satisfied with less gold. However, the system was more sensitive to changes in the non-monetary demand for gold which made up part of the total demand for gold.

Fractional reserve banking thus came to characterize America's com-mercial banking system. A bank could fulfill its obligations even if its reserves were much less than its total obligations. A fractional reserve system thus means that a bank's reserves equal only a fraction of its obligations.

The money multiplier effect flourished because one bank could borrow gold (or by a paper claim on the reserve commodity accumulated in another bank) to cover any excessive demand by the public to convert its own paper currency. Also, a bank could sell nonreserve assets, such as a loan (or part of its loan portfolio), to obtain hand-to-hand currency or a reserve commodity. A bank might suffer a loss if a purchaser of its nonreserve assets wanted a discounted price. To repay all of its depos-itors 100 cents on each dollar deposited, a bank needed to possess equity and reserves greater than the discounts suffered in liquidating loans and other assets. Problems arose from having insufficiently liquid assets; as-sets having a market value measured in money which plummeted in a panic; or having total assets less than its total liabilities.

Economist John Kenneth Galbraith aptly put the magic of money in the context of America's commercial banking system:

The marvel of banks in relation to money—the wonder of creating deposits or issuing notes that so served—was suspended on one silken thread. That was the requirement that the depositors or noteholders come in decently small numbers for the hard currency that the bank was under obligation to pay. If all came at once, the bank could not pay. And when the thought spread that the bank could not pay, then, often in much haste, all came. When that occurred, the depositors notes serving previously as money ceased to be serviceable. The deposits and notes of the firstcomers could be cashed; for the depositors or notes of the late-comers there would be nothing. Theirs were worthless deposits or the worthless paper of what was now a failed bank. As such, it was money no longer. The miracle of the earlier creation of money was now matched by the despair of its sudden erasure from existence.[3]

FREE BANKING ERA

Prior to the Civil War, the United States did not have a central bank after the charter of the Second Bank of the United States, which in some ways functioned as a central bank, expired in 1836.[4] Each state had its own banking regulations. Some states outlawed note-issuing banks. Elsewhere, legislative chartering limited the number of banks. State laws preserved reserve requirements and regulated the type of investments and loans banks could (or were required to) make.

By the mid-1830s, legislative chartering, which permitted state governments to extract financial favors from privileged banks, resulted in mounting dissatisfaction with the prevailing "spoils" system. Free banking laws were enacted beginning in Michigan and New York, and were later adopted by many other states. Free banking statutes brought banking into the prevailing arena of general incorporation laws so that a new bank could open without a specific charter from the legislature.

However, many states included bond deposit provisions in laws regulating the issuance of redeemable notes by private banks. The bond deposit regulation required a bank to secure its notes issuance with government bonds, particularly bonds of the state where it was incorporated. Bank funds went into the states' coffers. However, the bond security often depreciated in value or was unsalable. Banks attempting to sell the bond security to pay noteholders could only make good a fraction of their debts. Also, the supply of bank-issued notes fluctuated according to the supply of bonds declared "eligible" as security by state governments and the cost to banks of acquiring "eligible" bonds on the open market.

In New England, free banking laws existed without bond deposit requirements. Bank chartering resulted in healthy competition. The Suffolk Bank of Boston established a private, free-market-oriented institution, which functioned as a clearing system/central bank for New England (Suffolk Bank System).[5]

A private clearinghouse, such as the Suffolk Bank System, served two functions, namely, generating strong incentives to maintain a sound currency, and creating efficient, two-way information flows about the quantity of notes the public desired and the quality of notes issued by banks. The clearinghouse ensured the safety and soundness of notes. It created incentives that compelled bank managers to issue only that quantity of notes the public held willingly, given its demand for liquidity and the commodity reserves. The threat of (or the actual) redemption for specie also forced country (non-Boston) banks to curtail note issues and prepared these banks to redeem notes on demand.

Thus, banks joined clearinghouse associations to sustain each others' notes and secure payment from nonmember banks. The Suffolk Bank System provided these services from 1818 to 1866 and redeemed on demand the notes of banks that did not maintain a balance with member banks of the Suffolk Banking System.

In other areas of the United States, apart from New England, the quality of bank-issued notes varied from "fair to miserable."[6] The lowest ranked bank notes were those issued by the "wildcat" banks in the West and Midwest, encouraged by lax state bond deposit provisions that allowed banks to secure their currency using junk bonds purchased at big discounts from face value.[7]

By the time of the Civil War, state banking was in disarray and contributed to the turmoil in the nation's financial system. The problem with pre–Civil War, nineteenth-century banking, a system of free banking, stemmed, in part, from state regulations that hemmed in the system. Free banking, as previously noted, meant a system that eliminated the need to obtain a special charter from a state government to organize a bank. However, to open a bank, the entity generally had to buy state bonds. Free banks basically served as a scheme to sell state debt to banks. Banks were forced to hold state government debt as a share of their assets (and bank note issues) rather than being able to diversify their portfolios. Commentators recently have found that most of the bank failures occurred during periods of declining state government bond prices. When that asset depreciated in value, the banks became insolvent and suspended payments.[8]

NATIONAL BANK ERA

The Civil War resulted in a redesign of the monetary and banking system of the United States. The Civil War brought about four pieces of monetary and banking legislation: (1) the 1862 legal tender laws; (2) the 1863 National Banking Act; (3) the 1864 act outlawing private coinage; and (4) the 1865 act imposing a prohibitive 10 percent tax on state bank note issues. The last three acts placed the entire currency supply under the jurisdiction of the federal government.[9]

The legal tender laws authorized the U.S. Treasury to issue greenbacks—notes printed in green ink—which put the United States on a fiat monetary standard. The issuance of greenbacks, an irredeemable currency not backed by gold but by the federal government, facilitated the Union's ability to finance the Civil War without resorting to direct taxation. From 1862 to 1879, the United States used a fiat monetary standard. In 1879, greenbacks were made convertible into gold.

The 1863 National Banking Act[10] provided, among other things, for the establishment of federally chartered note-issuing banks. In essence, the law created privately issued notes, a feature of free banking, but at the federal level. Notes issued by national banks were uniform in design and accepted at par by all other national banks.

The notes of the new national banks had to be secured by deposits of federal government securities. Thus, for each $90 of notes they issued, the 1863 Act mandated that national banks purchase $100 in government bonds to be deposited for safekeeping with the federal comptroller of the currency in the Treasury Department. More specifically, the total value of notes issued by a bank could not exceed 90 percent of the face value or market value, whichever was lower, of the U.S. government securities on deposit.[11]

This arrangement provided a margin of safety for the note issuance. If a national bank collapsed, the bonds it had deposited could be sold and, under ordinary circumstances, its notes redeemed. Not coincidentally, the bond deposit requirement was designed to create a forced market for federal debt and provide another means to pay for the Union's military activities during the Civil War.

The 1863 Act, as reenacted by the National Bank Act of 1864,[12] also established federally mandated requirements for bank reserves. Each national bank had to hold federal government securities equal to at least one-third of the value of its capital. The 1863 Act had specified reserve requirements with respect to deposits for all banks in the national system—25 percent for banks in central reserve cities and 15 percent for other banks (so-called country banks).

The 1865 Act imposing a 10 percent tax on state chartered bank note issues,[13] effective from July 1, 1866, assured that state chartered banks could no longer deprive the federal government of potential revenues from bond sales to federally chartered banks. Note issues by state chartered banks became a theory of the past after mid-1866.

The 10 percent prohibitory tax on state bank note issues had two other results. First, a temporary flood of rechartering occurred as more banks became national banks. Second, institutions that wished to remain state banks used demand deposits to finance loans and investments.[14]

Following an initial decline after the Civil War, state chartered banks boomed, fueled by the increasing popularity in deposit and checking accounts. Less stringent chartering, reserve, and capital requirements, in contrast to the more onerous requirements imposed on national banks, contributed to the popularity of state banks, which swelled in number from 325 in 1870 to 17,376 by 1910.[15]

State chartered banks, in providing funds for a borrower, put a deposit instead of a bank note at its disposal. But this substitution had unintended consequences. As noted by a historian of Appalachia:

Before 1865 just as afterwards, the relatively rich (or at least enterprising) received most of the loans made [by state chartered banks]. But loans made in cash directly benefitted nonborrowers (the general population) because cash changed hands not only in large transactions, like checks, but changed hands at all levels of economic exchange. The beauty of plentiful cash had been that some of it had trickled down to everyone in its vicinity. Checks changed hands only between the relatively rich, whereas cash had changed hands between virtually everyone.[16]

By 1866, the U.S. currency supply consisted of greenbacks issued by the U.S. government and notes issued by national banks and secured by U.S. government bonds purchased on the open market. The amount of greenbacks was fixed by statute as, initially, were the national bank notes. In 1875, Congress abolished the government-imposed limit on the aggregate amount of national bank notes issued.[17] This step followed the enactment of legislation in 1874[18] which eliminated the required reserves national banks were to maintain on hand for their circulating notes, but maintained the reserve requirement on deposits. Instead of the on-hand reserve requirement for notes in circulation, the 1874 legislation required each national bank to keep a redemption fund with the treasury of 5 percent of its notes outstanding to redeem its own notes. The redemption fund also served as part of the required reserves against deposits.

In large measure, the post–Civil War supply of national bank notes followed the supply of U.S. bonds as collateral. In other words, the supply of U.S. bonds collateral determined the absolute limits on the issuance of notes by, and their profitability for, national banks.

From 1866 to 1871, the expanding federal debt ensured an adequate supply of currency issued by national banks. The year 1871 marked the beginning of a long period of contraction in the amount of the outstanding U.S. government debt. Thereafter, the U.S. Treasury, which consistently ran a surplus, bought up and retired government bonds. As the supply of federal government debt instruments declined, their market value increased. National bank note issuance became prohibitively costly as a result of the low rate of interest on U.S. government bonds and the significant premium (i.e., the difference between market price and face value) enjoyed by U.S. bonds available in the open market. The national banks found it increasingly difficult and expensive to acquire collateral needed for new note issues.

Especially after 1882, national banks were hampered in issuing notes by the growing scarcity of U.S. government securities, required by the 1863 National Banking Act as collateral for note issues. These circumstances precluded the secular growth of currency supply and prevented cyclical increases in demand from being met. This was the setting for the financial crises of 1884, 1893, and 1907. Each of these crises coincided with the heightened currency demands to finance the movement of crops. In 1893 and 1907, the seasonal credit stringency degenerated into full-scale financial panics.

In response partly to the loss of reserves during seasonal credit crunches, banks curtailed credit extensions. Banks also restricted payments, which meant that deposit holders were unable to convert their balances into currency. As a result, the public hoarded outstanding currency even when the supply of money in circulation might have exceeded normal trade and business requirements. Deposit holders learned to anticipate currency shortages. The slightest indications of a currency stringency set off large-scale bank runs and currency-hoarding panics.

To deal with the money panics and the accompanying drains of critical reserves, the marketplace demonstrated great ingenuity. In northern tier states, Canadian bank notes appeared in circulation. But the most creative developments occurred in private clearinghouses.[19]

Clearinghouse associations arose in the nineteenth century as a market response to the problems of providing reliable information and coping with uncertainties in the timing of interbank payments. In a clearinghouse association, member banks debited items that were cleared against their credit items. After the balance was struck, debtor banks paid creditor banks the amounts owed on the clearinghouse accounts.

Beginning before the Civil War, the New York City Clearinghouse Association in 1857 permitted irredeemable notes of country (nonmember) banks to be included in the clearinghouse settlement accounts. The New York City Clearinghouse Association also issued clearinghouse loan certificates against these redeemable notes.

From 1857 to 1913 private clearinghouse associations issued temporary clearinghouse loan certificates as well as clearinghouse certificates. Clearinghouse loan certificates—demand obligations—were held by banks. These certificates functioned as supplements to gold in the settlement of clearinghouse balances among member banks and as emergency reserves so that suspensions of the conversion of bank deposits into currency could be avoided. Market factors, such as interest rate charges as well as the requirement of acceptable collateral, constrained the issuance of loan certificates by private clearinghouse associations. Banks issued clearinghouse notes in small denominations thereby satisfying the general public's currency needs. The clearinghouse notes were issued in a multitude of localities throughout the United States on the perceptions of numerous bankers.

In many communities, checks of well-known individuals and firms were also issued in small, round denominations and passed from hand to hand until they were filled with endorsements. Banks issued cashiers' checks and negotiable certificates of deposit in small, round denominations. As a result of the use of clearinghouse loan certificates, clearinghouse certificates, and checks issued by individuals, firms, and banks, the extent of the potential for economic destruction that occurred during the various panics "was greatly reduced."[20]

THE MODERN CENTRAL BANKING ERA

In 1913, proposals for governmental reform of the nation's monetary and banking system culminated in the enactment of the Federal Reserve Act.[21] This act was designed to create a special, centralized public sector reserve agency that would provide the nation and its banks with emergency currency reserves by acting as a lender of last resort to forestall panics and illiquidity in the banking system. With the creation of the Federal Reserve System (the Fed), especially after 1932, the federal government also came to assert control over the alleged excesses of banks and the frequencies of their failures. Banks were forced to rely on deposits at the Fed for their stability and liquidity. Richard H. Timberlake, an economist, succinctly summarized the eighty-year evolution of the Federal Reserve System, as follows:

In the beginning (1913) Congress designed the Federal Reserve System to be a system of supercommercial privately owned banks. But the Banking Act of 1935 and the Monetary Control Act of 1980 formally changed the Fed from a system in which the Federal Reserve Banks were autonomous and the Federal Reserve Board a refereeing committee, to one in which the Board in Washington is all-powerful and the Federal Reserve banks not much more than administrative units; from an occasional discounter of real bills [i.e., notes, drafts, and bills of exchange arising out of actual commercial transactions] at the initiative of member banks, to a constant and momentous monetizer of governmental securities at the initiative of the Federal Reserve Open Market Committee; from an institution specifically subordinated to the gold standard, to one that has a monopoly with no vestige of a gold standard remaining; from a lender of last resort for banks, to a perpetual motion machine of money creation; from an institution with an avowed interest in providing liquidity in support of sound banks, to a cloak-and-dagger operation that has often bred uncertainty in financial markets.[22]

The issuance of paper currency soon became a monopoly of the federal government. The last of the post–Civil War national bank notes were retired from circulation in 1935. The currency supply has basically remained a monopoly of the Federal Reserve System ever since.

The U.S. dollar is no longer tied to any commodity, such as gold. In 1933, the U.S. Congress passed the Joint Resolution of June 5, 1933[23] that abolished all gold clauses in all public and private contracts. This meant that contracts could not require payment in gold. The Gold Reserve Act of 1934[24] went further, withdrawing all gold coin from circulation to be formed into gold bars.[25] Even the treasury could not hold gold coin unless it was in the form of gold bullion.[26] The Gold Reserve Act was intended to abolish gold coin as a component of our monetary system.[27] Gold was thereafter not money, but rather a commodity. The public could not get gold in the United States. Coin collectors were able to hold gold coins but only those of numismatic value.[28]

Gold lingered for international transactions involving the federal government. However, in 1971, the U.S. government ceased supplying gold to foreign central banks. In short, hard currency no longer exists in the U.S. monetary system except in the form of coinage. The U.S. government systematically, from 1933 to 1971, obliterated any notion of a value standard by refusing to permit the conversion of its paper money into gold and forcing the acceptance of its inferior paper currency. By putting an end to redeemability, policy makers eliminated an effective means for imposing discipline on government-issued money. The way was opened to abuse on a grand scale.

The Federal Reserve System now possesses virtually unlimited capacity to meet the public's currency demands. The United States has two types of currency: (1) basic cash or hand-to-hand money (so-called outside money, i.e., issued outside the banking industry) in the form of Federal Reserve notes, and (2) bank liabilities—deposits (or deposits created by bank loans) which are transferable by check or electronically. Deposits represent privately produced currency (so-called inside money). Their value derives from their redeemability in the hand-to-hand currency. About 31 percent of the U.S. money supply takes the form of circulating paper currency or coins.[29] However, part of the money supply which appears as paper currency began as bank credit.

We have a system of fiat money, not backed by any commodity. Dollar bills are just printed pieces of paper. Deposits are nothing more than accounting numbers. Coins have some intrinsic value as metal, but it is considerably less than their value as money. The scarcity of money, relative to its demand, fixes its value. The supply of money is determined largely by the Fed's monetary policy. Congress has mandated that the basic objectives of the Fed's monetary policy are to "maintain long-run growth of the monetary and credit aggregates commensurate with the economy's long-run potential to increase production, so as to promote effectively the goals of maximum employment, stable prices, and moderate long-term interest rates."[30]

To achieve these goals, the Fed has three principal means of controlling the money stock: (1) establishing reserve requirements for depository institutions; (2) engaging in open market operations; and (3) setting the discount rate.[31] The reserve requirement requires depository institutions to maintain reserves against the demand deposits of their customers. Reserves are composed of currency held by a bank and deposits of the bank with the Fed. Increasing or decreasing reserve requirements reduces or enlarges the money multiplier effect and causes banks to extend fewer or greater loans.

Open market operations, the most important tool the Fed uses to control the money stock, involves the buying and selling of U.S. securities in the open market. Sellers of U.S. securities receive checks drawn on a Federal Reserve Bank. When checks are deposited in banks, those banks acquire a credit with the Fed. Because deposits with the Fed, as well as currency on hand, count as reserves, banks can now extend more loans.

Moreover, the Fed increases the money stock directly by simply creating the money to pay for U.S. securities.

The discount rate is the interest rate at which the Fed will loan funds to commercial banks and other depository institutions. Banking institutions borrow from the Fed primarily to meet temporary shortages of reserves. An increase in the discount rate will discourage borrowing, causing banks to build up their reserves and extend fewer loans. Decreasing the discount rate will have the opposite effect.

For instance, if the Fed adopts an expansionary monetary policy, characterized by a rapid rate of growth of the money supply, it might reduce reserve requirements, purchase additional U.S. securities, and lower the discount rate. Reducing reserve requirements would free excess reserves and induce banks to extend additional loans. Purchasing additional U.S. securities would not only expand the money stock directly but also increase the reserves of banks, which can then extend more loans. Finally, lowering the discount rate would encourage banks to borrow more from the Fed and to lower their reserves (because of the lower cost of borrowing from the Fed if their reserves run low).

The Fed is distinct in purpose and function from the U.S. Treasury.[32] Whereas the Fed is concerned primarily with the availability of money and credit for the entire economy, the U.S. Treasury is responsible for the revenues and expenditures of the national government. If there is a budgetary deficit—where government expenditures exceed tax revenues—the U.S. Treasury issues interest-bearing bonds as a method of financing the deficit. When the Fed purchases U.S. securities, it purchases part of the national debt, and it has the power to write a check upon itself without having its own deposits, gold, or anything else to back up the check.[33] The Fed simply creates money by writing a check, and if the recipient of the check wants cash, the Fed can simply print Federal Reserve notes.[34] Thus, in effect, the Fed can monetize the national debt by purchasing U.S. securities.[35]

Thus, the federal government can more or less freely print large amounts of money to cover its deficits or for other purposes; for instance, to redistribute income and wealth between creditors and debtors as a means of reducing unemployment. Subject to what the public will tolerate in terms of domestic inflation and the depreciation of the value of the U.S. dollar vis-à-vis foreign currencies, virtually no limit exists with respect to what the U.S. government can do with the nation's money supply.

CONCLUSION

The U.S. government's monopoly position with respect to the issuance of money means we must use a product, specifically, currency, even if it is unsatisfactory. Its monopoly prevents the discovery of better methods of satisfying a need. Periodic inflation and general economic instability may result, in large measure, from the government's monopoly over money, which also assisted in general growth of federal governmental power. Looking back over the twentieth century, the federal government expanded largely assisted by the possibility of covering deficits by issuing money. Government power over money facilitated ever-mounting centralization.

The Nobel laureate Friedrich A. Hayek sought to introduce competition into the production of money.[36] Competition would discipline producers to supply the best producers at the lowest cost. An alternative currency would help in effectively preserving the integrity of local economy and promoting ecological sustainability.

three

The Current Context and Objectives of Local Currency Issuance

This chapter develops the values implicit in and the rationale for a system of local currency issuance, and emphasizes the importance of scale and the decentralization of economic and political power. Building on the need to encourage a greater degree of participation and local self-reliance designed to promote a noninflationary economy characterized by ecological sustainability, human development, and fuller employment, the chapter concludes by discussing how a local currency approach will help us achieve these goals.

THE CURRENT CONTEXT

We depend on a "good" (i.e., growing) economy to get us an interesting job, commensurate with our educational attainments, after graduation from high school, college, or graduate school. We continue to worship economic growth as a means of providing high-paying jobs throughout our work lives. A series of jobs ensures our financial survival, provides for our immediate consumption of goods and services, and, if we are lucky, enables us to build a college education fund for our children as well as a retirement fund for our old age. We calculate our standard of living in material terms. Our lives are oriented to our material possessions, our house, and our cars.[1] We long for more possessions; we expect that "things" will bring us prestige and respect from our families and friends.

In the 1980s, many seemed satisfied with the cornucopia of consumer goods and services. They found it difficult to imagine any limits to economic growth and consumption. In America's shopping malls, people, young and old, were enslaved by material progress. They literally shopped 'til they dropped. We came to associate consumption with happiness.

A malaise now characterizes the 1990s. The roots of our present unease are at least threefold: (1) the economic realities of the 1990s; (2) a growing awareness of our ecological dilemma; and (3) a heightened perception of the impermanence of the material aspects of life.

The Economic Realities of the 1990s

Our quest for a new political economy stems, in part, from the realities of the economic stagnation of the 1990s, following upon the economic boom years of the 1980s. The harsh economic realities serve as a wake-up call to those caught up in the overly "high" levels of consumption evidenced in the 1980s. Easy money no longer flows to many professionals and business executives. Businesses engage in relentless downsizing. Middle managers and white-collar workers are being displaced and not as many attorneys, engineers, and architects, among other professionals, are needed. Finding "good" entry-level jobs is far more difficult for recent high school and college graduates.[2] Also, crushing personal debt burdens, home mortgage, car payments, and credit card debts, as well as physical and mental hazards (for example, stress and lack of enough time to meet the multitude of demands we face), surround our current quest for material success.[3]

Looking to the twenty-first century, the United States faces the prospect that individuals will be far less tied to the production and distribution of goods and services. The collapse of work as we have known it over the past two hundred years will flow from three factors.

First, assuming more people express a preference for less consumption and evidence a greater degree of environmental sensitivity (discussed later in this chapter), a dramatic drop in consumption of goods and services will likely occur. The future needs of society may be met with only a small fraction of the workforce. Estimates indicate that perhaps as little as 7 to 10 percent of the American economy is concerned with the production and distribution of "basic" goods and services.[4]

Second, the competitive pressures from cheaper imported goods and the shift of production to foreign (lower wage) sites will take their toll on U.S. jobs. South China may set the wage rate for the rest of the world. The increased economic integration into global networks will likely be a recipe for net job losses in the United States.

Third, automation and labor-saving technology will increase productivity and at the same time reduce the demand for labor. The revolution in technology, spurred by computers and microelectronics, makes possible the widespread displacement of humans by machines.[5]

The combination of these three factors will make full employment (or anything resembling full employment) an impossibility. The new economy will not generate sufficient new jobs, let alone "good" jobs paying high wages and offering generous fringe benefits, for an expanding workforce. The service sector will not grow fast enough to provide sufficient jobs; in any event, many service jobs will be low-paying, part-time, nonfulfilling, dead-end positions.

Workers of all ages holding jobs will find themselves unemployed or underemployed. Displaced workers will be unable to fill new jobs, even if created, because they lack the requisite skills, which keep changing. Class after class of high school and college graduates, as well as those with postgraduate degrees, may be unable to secure positions, let alone jobs commensurate with their training.[6] Ultimately, the link between earning income on a salaried job will be cut for many Americans and the jobless will be reduced to eking out a living in the informal economy characterized by barter transactions and off-the-books business arrangements. The impossibility of ever again achieving full employment (or anything resembling full employment) will become perhaps the greatest taboo and the most perplexing public policy dilemma of the twenty-first century. It is so threatening because no one knows what to do about it.

The roots of our job dilemma are based in a production-focused society. In the past it seemed to make sense to think of economic production as the de facto goal of society; to think of an ever-increasing fraction of overall human activity being treated as commodities in the mainstream, formal economy; to assume that the individual's primary relationship to society is through a job; to have social thinking dominated by the concept of scarcity, competition, and money exchange. However, this will not be the case in the future when one of our main problems is our capacity to overproduce.

Those of us fortunate enough to have a job increasingly perceive the magnitude of the societal alienation and powerlessness which manifest themselves in many ways. We see the people who hate their dead-end jobs and their meaningless work, as well as those who resent the authority imposed in their work and over their lives generally. We search for and find it difficult to locate a calling to do something meaningful and significant.

Many seek a "right livelihood" which will enable them, fully using their capacities, to make a genuine contribution not only to their personal development but also to the well-being of humanity. As E. F. Schumacher observed, the Buddhist concept of a "right livelihood" has universal relevance because it places spiritual health as a goal along with material well-being.[7] Schumacher maintained: "It is not a question of choosing between 'modern growth' and 'traditional stagnation.' It is a question of finding the right path of development, the middle way between materialist heedlessness and traditional immobility, in short, of finding 'Right Livelihood.' "[8]

Our Ecological Dilemma

We are increasingly reevaluating the impact of our consumption-oriented lifestyle on the ecosystem. The quest for economic growth leads to resource depletion, ecosystem damage, and congestion. We devote additional resources to spurring consumption by creating dissatisfaction with our existing possessions. Rapid obsolescence and replacement with new goods has characterized the twentieth century's throwaway economy. Our wasteful pattern of consumption, which is unrelated to maintaining life or well-being, ties back to economic growth as synonymous with the good life. A society based on manipulative consumption has much broader social and ecological consequences.

Our century-long pursuit of economic growth now faces and will increasingly encounter the limits nature imposes. The planet is nearing its capacity to handle the impact of our economic growth policies and our channeling of the earth's resources into wasteful production resulting in social and ecological degradation.

Six factors set the ecological limits to a political economy based on economic growth.[9] First, the world is a gigantic machine for burning fossil fuels. Modern economies live on nonrenewable resources, such as petroleum and natural gas. Growth has been based on cheap oil, which is becoming ever more scarce.

Second, tropical forests are disappearing at an alarming rate. Whatever the cause, the loss of tropical forests results in massive soil erosion, the conversion of forest into low-grade farm land, and the spoilage of local water supplies.

Third, acid rain, which originates in sulfur and nitrogen oxides that emanate from smokestacks and vehicle exhaust pipes, destroys forests and lakes and thus harms aquatic life. Acid rain also damages a nation's artistic and architectural heritage.

Fourth, we face the depletion of the ozone layer in the upper atmosphere, which shields people from ultraviolet radiation. The catalyst for this change was the release into the atmosphere of chlorofluorocarbons. As a result, incidences of skin cancers will rise and the ocean's food chain will also be disrupted.

Fifth, desertification results from the destruction of vegetation by woodcutting, burning, and overgrazing; by erosion induced by water; and by salinization of irrigated fields. Over two hundred million people, mostly in developing nations, are directly and deleteriously affected by desertification.

Sixth, the world faces its greatest environmental threat from the much discussed "greenhouse effect," a phenomenon caused when increased amounts of carbon dioxide, in combination with the release of other gases, trap the radiant heat emitted from the earth's surface. The net result of the greenhouse effect is an increase in global temperatures that may cause serious environmental damage as soon as the early years of the twenty-first century. The alterations of climatic patterns caused by rising temperatures will likely throw agricultural systems out of balance. Yet, while the probability of global warming is high, its exact consequences and timeline remain uncertain.

These environmental threats built up so slowly in the past that our minds could not perceive the danger to human and planetary existence, but now we can, because of their aggregate effects. Increasingly in the 1990s, we are concerned with and evidence a greater degree of stewardship for the earth and all its inhabitants—human and nonhuman. We are taking steps to recycle more materials. In future decades, we face the need to switch from fossil fuels and to move to the solar age. Agricultural practices, especially the use of life-destroying chemicals which are economically self-defeating in the long run, must also be revamped.

These changes may culminate in an individual ethic and a political economy based on the notion of a sustainable society which serves the ends of human development in an ecologically sound manner. Again, we should strive to find a balance, a middle way which emphasizes the formulation and implementation of policies keyed to ecological and social viability. We should formulate an ecologically sound—popularly known as a sustainable—way of living with and relating to the earth and all other living creatures in the context of using resources to meet human needs and promote human development. Each generation should strive to meet its needs without compromising the ability of future generations to meet theirs. Human development should take place in a framework which avoids irreparable harm to the environment. In addition to nurturing the environment, sustainable development should be based on renewable energy resources and energy conservation. We should formulate a strategy based on and cognizant of the impact of the political economy on the ecosystems on which humans depend for their livelihood and for their existence.

The Impermanence of the "Material" Aspects of Life

We also see about us a heightened focus on the impermanence of the material aspects of life. This impermanence ranges from our possessions to our physical bodies. Despite the technological advances of modern medicine, some day, as much as we try to deny it, we will all die. For all the empirical studies which search to find cause and effect not only in our bodies but also in our lives, meaningfulness in this material world and beyond remains a mystery.

As we search for meaning in life, one conclusion starkly stands out. Consumerism has not provided Americans with a sense of fulfillment. Opinion surveys repeatedly show that the proportion of Americans reporting that they are "very happy" with their lives has remained at about one-third of U.S. population since 1957, even though personal consumption has doubled.[10] We realize our identity transcends our level of consumption. Simply put, we cannot purchase happiness through conspicuous consumption and material wealth.

The emerging political economy will, therefore, emphasize the nature and quality of growth (particularly personal development, as opposed to material growth) and the need to operate within the limits of the planet. Moving from the premise of ecological sustainability, the political economy of the twenty-first century may rest not only on a less consumption-oriented lifestyle of individuals and families but also on more self-sufficient patterns of local production and consumption based on decentralized economic and political institutions.

THE QUEST FOR DECENTRALIZATION

Alienation and loneliness characterize late-twentieth-century America. More human-sized, less complex places of work and governance may help overcome our unease. Making economic and political institutions smaller and more comprehensible may facilitate their revitalization. Increasingly, we may seek to establish a political economy system based on the importance of "human scale."

This section begins with an examination of the concept of scale for economic institutions and then considers the political dimensions of the notion of scale. The scale of our existing economic and political institutions limits effective participation and the benefits derived therefrom. This section next discusses the role of local currency in the decentralization of economic and political institutions. A local currency provides a key element in achieving the goals of sustainable development and empowering people.

Scale in Economic Institutions

We are all too familiar with stifling economic bureaucracies organized in excessively large units characterized by rule-bound behaviors. Large-scale business organizations have resulted in two fundamental deleterious human consequences: first, the destruction of the content and dignity of most forms of work; and second, a continuous stimulation and reliance on greed, envy, avarice, as well as their authoritarian character.[11] As Schumacher stated, economic structures employing hundreds or thousands "cannot possibly preserve order without authoritarianism, no matter how great the wish for democracy might be."[12]

Not only from a human perspective but also on traditional economic efficiency grounds, large institutions, which put a premium on expertise, certitude, and control, suffer from a number of deficiencies. Large hierarchical systems block negative feedback which tells higher-ups in the organization the things they have forgotten or missed. People at the bottom of organizations traditionally have been the least empowered in the control system, but they are the closest to the key sources of information. Also, in an era of rapid change, large, bureaucratic organizations are at a disadvantage compared with smaller, more flexible groups of people.

What will propel the evolution of economic organizations? Seeking to fulfill the notion of a right livelihood—work which makes a contribution to ourselves and to others, and to human well-being—people desire a greater degree of meaningfulness in their lives. In addition to searching for work that facilitates human development and work that is good for an employee, people will seek out and strive to be part of an organization which produces goods and services that promote a more meaningful, ecologically sound world.

People also want to assume a greater degree of control over their work and, more generally, their lives. As a result, they will strive to develop and be part of smaller-scale workplaces of approachable size, graspable scope, and manageable complexity. Human satisfaction, autonomy, and self-development are enhanced by more comprehensible, less complex, and smaller-scale economic institutions. In these smaller institutions, workers, as citizens of the enterprise, meet face-to-face and make decisions face-to-face.

Participation is important in economic units because it: (1) facilitates personal growth and development and serves to make each of us fully human; (2) maintains and facilitates equality of respect, dignity, and status among participants; and (3) protects everyone's interests equally. It also gives more employees a stake in their work, the experience of responsibility, and provides training in collective decision making.[13] In short, work will increasingly be organized into human-sized, comprehensible groups in which ownership is not divorced from personal involvement in the institution. Smaller business organizations are more closely connected with meeting human needs. Social, as well as individual, benefits flow from smaller work units.

These smaller economic units will bring technology to the service of workers and the environment. Decentralized, ecologically sensitive technology may flourish based on frugal energy use. Decentralized economic organizations may rely more on small-scale energy technologies such as solar power, not energy systems such as nuclear power, which require large and complex bureaucracies to manage them. Decentralized energy from renewable sources will promote greater energy self-sufficiency, thereby reducing energy dependency and enabling businesses to meet their energy needs in a more ecologically sound manner. These smaller business organizations may also evidence a greater sensitivity to conserving resources and protecting the environment. The smaller, energy efficient economic units may be nonpolluting and facilitate the recycling of wastes.

A trend toward economic decentralization is already apparent. In the boom years of the 1980s, employees and executives jumped off the corporate ladder and into self-employment and consulting arrangements. They also formed small firms. During this period, small businesses provided most of the jobs added in the U.S. economy as well as most of the innovation.[14]

In the corporate downsizing and restructuring wave during the current period of economic stagnation, those pushed out of corporations have become independent contractors, have reinvigorated family businesses, or formed new companies.[15] Symbiotic relationships flourish. Huge firms are becoming more dependent on a vast subculture of small, high-powered, flexible suppliers, many family run, which can make quick decisions, take daring entrepreneurial risks, and evidence high motivation.[16]

The coming decades will witness a continued blossoming of small-scale, more localized economic activity. We will likely see the growth of an economy of rather small firms, owned and operated by the employees—a kind of cooperative, collective capitalism.[17] Business cooperatives will use the market mechanism to gather information about preferences and allocate resources and income in accordance with these preferences. Goods and services will be produced very simply on a small scale with non–capital intensive (capital saving) technology. Smaller-scale economic units, using capital-saving technologies, would make worker ownership more practical by reducing capital needs which traditionally have retarded the development of business cooperatives.[18] A cooperative working environment will also facilitate a greater degree of worker participation in the management of an enterprise, which in turn will evidence more responsiveness to meeting human needs.

Because members of smaller-scale economic units feel they have a greater stake in the venture, they are also more motivated to make the business succeed. Less employee monitoring will be necessary as employee concern for the health of the business increases. Workers are less likely to slack off on the job; they will not tolerate such behaviors from others. With less required monitoring, the need for middle managers decreases.

These collectively-owned (or perhaps community-owned) organizations may focus on meeting basic human requirements—food, shelter, clothing, education, and preventive health care—in an ecologically sound, resource-conserving manner. Cooperatives may also permit the development of various types of services, such as child care, care of the aged, and transportation, more effectively, with more flexibility, and at lower cost.

Finally, more personalized exchange may characterize a growing informal economy. The bartering of goods and services will continue to surge. The home will flourish as a key production unit. Individuals, characterized as "prosumers" by futurist Alvin Toffler, may produce and consume their own goods and services, thereby lessening their dependence on the traditional market economy.[19] In addition to the coming decentralization of economic institutions, the notion of scale has a political dimension.

Scale in Political Institutions

The devolution of economic power will have profound ramifications and lead to more autonomy, diversity, and the decentralization of political and social institutions; more specifically, to placing more decisions as close to individuals as possible. The emerging political economy may consist of a multiplicity of diverse political units with a more significant role played by smaller-scale institutions, thereby facilitating local decision making. As the futurist Alvin Toffler reminds us:

In any system, democratic or not, there needs to be some congruence between the way a people make wealth and the way they govern themselves. If the political and economic systems are wildly dissimilar, one will eventually destroy the other. And if it is true that a system for wealth creation is superseding smokestack production, then we should expect a historic struggle to remake our political institutions, bringing them into congruence with the requirements of a revolutionary post-mass-production economy.[20]

We see a transformation from the concentration of economic power at nation-state level, based on mass-production technology and organizations. New technologies, for example, computers, make local production competitive again. The combination of a changing technological base together with the emerging fight against bureaucratic, centralized economic institutions will likely give rise to a movement away from an ever-larger scale of government and toward a greater decentralization of political power and political institutions. Citizens may opt for local communities, a sort of grass-roots, direct democracy, to decide more issues of significance.

In considering participatory political institutions, the question of scale once again assumes paramount importance. As with economic institutions, participation in the political process connotes people taking more control over their lives, taking charge and organizing for themselves. Direct democracy—participation—is based on the premise that no one has the right to make political decisions affecting an individual without that person taking part in the decision-making process. Involvement in decision making also serves as a means of promoting human development. The return to human scale in the structuring of political institutions will enable each person to see the need for an active role in society where each person's actions have meaning and impact. Smaller political units are more comprehensible and less complex. More face-to-face contact in the political process facilitates not only social cohesion but also a more developed sense of community. Smaller-scale institutions also reduce social alienation through identification with the well-being of the community.

Participation involves a shift from national representative democracies and centralized bureaucratic structures to facilitating direct democracy in smaller political units. As could well be imagined, limits exist on an effective, democratic participation in decision making as a result of the number of persons involved.[21] The greater the number of citizens in a political unit, the greater the number of decisions that will have to be delegated to officials or made by means of representative democracy, for example, a legislative body. Conversely, in smaller political units, people are more politically active, can understand the issues and personalities far more clearly, participate more in all aspects of government, and regard themselves as having more effective control over decisions impacting on their lives.

Where, then, should political authority lie and what do I have in mind when I use the terms "small scale" and "local community"? In other words, what will be the size of these basic, decentralized political units? For the foreseeable future, we have to make the most of where we are— big cities and their surrounding suburbs. Accepting the geographical status quo, the modern megalopolis or even a medium-sized city, say of 500,000 people, is too large to permit meaningful political participation through institutions of direct democracy. Decentralization may result in a devolution of political power to and greater decision making by more autonomous, self-governing neighborhoods as the political decision-making center.[22]

At the neighborhood level, political and social (nonprofit, volunteer) organizations could take over many activities previously handled by more centralized, public sector bureaucracies, such as education, health, and crime prevention. More and higher levels of self-organizing activities may result in a rebirth of the neighborhood, an urban village which offers the flavor and cohesiveness of a small town together with the sophistication of a larger city.

Political and social structures may emerge which are appropriate to local conditions. Public services may be better supplied at the local level, where problems are understood best, the solutions are most accessible, refinements and adjustments are most easily made, and monitoring the most convenient. Consistent with the decentralization of economic power, local government, at the neighborhood level, may assume responsibility for more economic matters, particularly for facilitating the development of more self-reliant, ecologically sustainable economic activity. New indexes of success, beyond monetary measures, may emerge and may differ among various geographical areas. In short, many problems may be seen as more readily dealt with, in a diverse manner, at the local level.

Over the next century, localities and regions throughout the United States will continue to grow more diverse in many respects and take on their own cultural, technological, and political character. As the disparities widen, so may the demand for regional or local autonomy. This may be difficult for us to imagine in the United States, but the twenty-first and twenty-second centuries, with their attendant pressures to decentralize and demassify the political process, may resemble the political struggles in the early years of the Republic over whether we would be a confederation or a federal system as well as the mid-nineteenth-century divisions that led to the Civil War.

Looking back over the wreckage of the past 150 years, the benefits of the devolution of political power to smaller units may become apparent. More powerful, smaller political units offer several key advantages. While recognizing that smaller units can unite in mutual defense or seek a larger nation-state as a protector, the heightened power advantages possessed by nation-states has increased the duration and severity of warfare. Smaller nations, while certainly not passive, may tend to engage in less fighting and with less violent, certainly fewer universal, consequences. Furthermore, large nation-states have been unable, despite vigorous efforts, to provide the hoped-for economic stability and employment possibilities.[23]

THE CONTOURS OF A SELF-SUFFICIENT, COMMUNITY-BASED POLITICAL ECONOMY

As more people opt for (or are forced out of) lifestyles apart from the conventional patterns of employment and consumption, many will rethink (or be forced to reassess) the traditional notions of living and working. In addition to the emerging economic institutions, notably, business cooperatives and prosumers, and a community-based political economy characterized by a significant degree of local and regional self-sufficiency, may flourish. In such a system, basic goods and services would be produced by small-scale economic units clustered in smaller communities.

Self-reliance provides communities and regions with the ability to satisfy all their needs within their own means; it removes, or at least lessens, energy and resource vulnerability. Greater dependence on renewable energy sources, such as solar energy, should also enhance ecological sustainability.

A reconfiguration of our patterns of living and working, marked by a trend to self-reliant communities, may be triggered, in large part, by the inability of many to secure gainful employment. A social transformation of this magnitude may, however, involve much more than a general unease with the prevailing economic realities.

In modern industrial societies, excessively "large" cities are destructive of human relations and generate a dehumanized anonymity, loneliness, and isolation. Although certainly existing in smaller cities, suburbs, and rural areas, deviance, criminality, social stress, alienation, selfishness, alcoholism, mental illness, and drug abuse characterize "huge" cities. Furthermore, a vast number of urban residents is not needed for a center of creativity and innovation and to support a range of cultural amenities.

According to Kirkpatrick Sale, a leading proponent of decentralization, small cities (in the range of 50,000–100,000) typically outperform larger ones in a number of social variables, including crime, health, mental illness, recreation, education, and higher participation in cultural matters.[24] A "human scale" city, which combines all economic services and productive capabilities, might, therefore, have an optimal size of some 50,000 people.[25]

Building on the promise that our material needs are much simpler than many realize, we may witness a new political economy consisting of small-scale, self-sufficient, decentralized urban and rural communities which will integrate work, life, and the environment. These communities will have as their principal economic function the production of their basic needs for food, clothing, shelter, education, and health. Some of the characteristics of these communities include a cooperative division of labor with a heavy emphasis on face-to-face personal relationships, a more egalitarian sharing of material goods, and widespread participation in the economic, political, and social decisions that affect the community.[26]

The notion that smaller communities will emerge as a key institution in the future political economy rests on the premise that local communities can assert a large measure of control over their economic lives.

Enhanced local economic and political self-reliance is based on smaller-scale communities using local resources to meet local needs. In particular, communities and regions may strive for agricultural self-sufficiency and ecological sustainability. Achieving these goals rests, in large measure, on the revitalization of the family farm. Labor-intensive, less mechanized, organically based family farms are currently competitive in growing agricultural produce.[27] In the future, family farms would produce not only for home consumption but also for the market. Family farms will supply the needs of people who live in nearby cities and towns. Family farms and rural communities could raise a variety of foods for nearly all consumers. Almost all regions of the United States can produce most of the food they need close to population centers.[28] Crops could be grown in greenhouses, thereby enabling a community to meet its basic food needs and reducing the dependency of the community on outsiders for its survival.

A greater degree of agricultural self-sufficiency in smaller communities and regions will also help lessen our dependency on imported petroleum. Three factors account for increased energy self-reliance, within a community-based agricultural system: (1) reducing the use of chemicals and machinery in the production process; (2) lessening the role played by processing and packaging; and (3) reducing the transportation of agricultural produce.

The strategy of agricultural self-sufficiency rests, however, on a change in consumption habits. Food will be more seasonal; some decline in appearance will occur stemming from the reduced use of pesticides. Accepting the notions of agricultural self-sufficiency and ecological sustainability, various estimates of ideal size abound. Robert Dahl, a political scientist, places a limit of 1,000 people for the maximum size of a New England-style, direct democracy town meeting which gains authority from the assembled people.[29]

Kirkpatrick Sale estimates an economically optimum size of a smaller-scale community, with agricultural self-sufficiency, at 4,000 to 5,000 people.[30] A community of the size of 10,000 people should be able, estimates indicate, to staff plants in various basic industries such as textiles, apparel, lumber and wood products, furniture and fixtures, paper, soap and cleaners, stone, clay and glass products, primary metal industries, fabricated metal products, machinery (nonelectrical), electrical and electronic equipment, as well as motorcycles, bicycles, and parts. A community of this size could also supply its population with nearly all necessary manufactured goods while providing considerable economic diversity.[31]

At an upper level, democratic participation is enhanced in cities or viable neighborhoods limited to 50,000 to 100,000 inhabitants, particularly if we focus on the ability of residents to influence decisions regarding city services. A city or neighborhood of such size generally invites participation and creates the feeling that people can have some control over their lives.[32] Decision makers will be able to cut deeply into the daily lives of inhabitants. Thus, a satisfactory level of participation, with its previously discussed attendant benefits, is likely to be achieved. For Dahl, the appropriate size of a city which will facilitate participation at a satisfactory level on matters important to local residents, "looks to me to be a city between about fifty thousand and several hundred thousand inhabitants."[33]

From a more decentralist-oriented prospective, an optimal political society may consist of some 7,000 to 12,000 people.[34] Such a size could offer regular associations between people, easy access to public officers, mutual aid among neighbors, open and trusting social relations; while preserving values of the community including intimacy, trust, honesty, mutuality, cooperation, democracy, and congeniality.[35]

THE ROLE OF LOCAL CURRENCY IN THE EMERGING POLITICAL ECONOMY

The development of neighborhoods and smaller communities as centers of the emerging political economy may turn on the creation and use of a local currency. A local currency system would strengthen both urban and rural communities and promote decentralization and local self-reliance by linking consumers with producers in a mutual effort to build a local economy. It would also foster a shared pride and commitment to the culture and habitat of a region or a city.

This section analyzes the following benefits of a local currency system: (1) overcoming the ecological dilemma; (2) revitalizing local economies; (3) providing a feedback mechanism; (4) promoting employment opportunities; and (5) facilitating a noninflationary monetary system.

Overcoming the Ecological Dilemma

The prevailing money and banking systems are linked to our environmental dilemma.[36] The centralization of money and banking severely distorts the environmental fabric, resulting in ecological degradation.

Today, we are increasingly dependent on impersonal political and economic entities. We rely on remote sources of supply for the basic necessities of life. As part of the trend away from self-reliance, a national currency often leaves local banks and gravitates to financial centers to finance giant projects.[37] A centralized system siphons off local wealth and value into a central and increasingly global, financial vortex. Money deposited in local banks in small towns, rural areas, and inner cities quickly moves to larger, urban financial centers to finance "less risky" loans to large corporations and governmental ventures. Small banks move deposits in the direction of less risk and higher interest rates.

Money-center banks favor loans for large projects. The cost of processing a loan for a large project is generally similar to the costs of processing a loan for a small one.[38] Growth-driven economies create a demand for large projects and reinforce the dependency on fossil fuels as an energy source. A tendency exists for the financial system to fund large, environmentally destructive infrastructure projects, such as airports, roads, high-rise buildings, and nuclear- and coal-fuelled power plants. Large projects often omit their full costs. These costs are, however, internalized on people and the environments in other places and in the future.

National currencies discount the future by externalizing economic and environmental bills to future generations. A national currency approach discourages diversified, local production and distribution while channeling capital to productive facilities into fewer areas that are highly dependent on environmentally degrading, mass-distribution systems. In contrast, a local currency system will revitalize local economies. These smaller political economy units will promote a greater degree of self-reliance, increase agricultural self-reliance, and more generally, promote ecological sustainability.

Revitalizing Local Economies

To help feed the voracious appetite of America's economic center, money-center banks, as noted, collect funds from all regions in the United States and lend these funds to those investing in more profitable, booming regions. A national currency results in the overdevelopment of certain regions and communities. Conversely, the migration of money deprives rural and inner city markets of their buying power. Rural and inner city areas become dependencies of the central financial system as well as large corporations and governments. Money slowly flows back into rural areas and inner cities in the form of externally controlled capital. As a result of the reimportation of capital, "poorer" regions and communities lose control over their economy, their political decision making, and their environment.

In contrast with the prevailing national currency approach, a local currency system will help local economies. An alternative currency (scrip) will liberate communities and regions from the economic costs and political influence of external credit institutions, thereby enhancing self-reliance and facilitating a greater emphasis on the quality of life. Scrip will tend to stay in a local area. As scrip gets further from the region of issuance, it encounters uncertainty about its origins, and the confidence in it lessens. Scrip will remain within the local economy and stimulate community self-reliance and development.

A local currency encourages individuals and businesses to patronize each other rather than buying from outside the community. People will spend an alternative currency locally, for local goods and services and at local merchants and producers, thereby stimulating the local economy. A local currency will promote a greater degree of self-reliance by helping to stimulate more local production of items not currently produced locally. Businesses will use local producers and suppliers, saving transportation costs and reducing the adverse environmental consequences of transportation.

A need exists to provide small businesses with a means to obtain credit without competing in the credit markets with larger, more established businesses[39] and to counteract the overcentralization of wealth in large metropolitan areas. A local currency system would help meet the credit needs of small businesses. Local currency would enhance the amount of economic interchange within a community. More wealth generated in a region or a city would remain there. The retention of more funds in a community would likely facilitate the financing of small-scale economic activities.

A system of local currencies will help create credit on a decentralized basis for small, locally owned and controlled businesses and cooperatives. These ventures will enhance small communities, local towns, and inner cities. A sound regional or local economy rests on many interrelated small businesses.

The creation of numerous small businesses that produce goods and furnish services in the region of their consumption would facilitate a more diversified job base that would, in turn, foster greater flexibility in times of economic crises and promote a more viable regional economy. Small, diversified businesses help promote a more stable economic climate. If an area is more dependent on a large employer, when it folds or relocates, the region faces a severe problem. Smaller, more flexible firms can more easily adapt to changing economic conditions. The loss of one small firm will not capsize a region's economic base.

A local currency will also assist inner cities and rural regions to overcome their stunted economic status relative to more prosperous central cities and suburbs. Over the past 125 years, the centralized monetary system in the United States has victimized rural areas by preventing the creation of adequate funds for local development or distributing funds among regions in disproportionate amounts. In the twentieth century, federal government has met the poverty gap by subsidizing the peripheral regions and inner cities using social welfare subsidies, special economic grants, and agricultural subsidies (e.g., agricultural price supports). Only recently have we realized that traditional policy tools render the subsidized economies ever more dependent. We are also more cognizant of the plight of inner cities characterized by increasing drug use and crime, a breakdown in families and the public school system, and rat-infested housing.

A system of transfer payments also saps the earnings of more prosperous, more dynamic cities and regions. It reduces the ability of cities and regions to serve as customers for another's innovations and diverts city and regional imports to dependent economies that cannot replace imported goods and services.[40] The need for subsidies grows even more voracious in the late twentieth century, but the wherewithal for supplying them is declining. However, so many people, so many businesses, and so many governments depend on transfer payments for their very existence.

Rather than looking to a stream of ever-increasing transfer payments, presently dependent cities and regions need to focus on the development of more import-replacing/export-generating goods and services. Entrepreneurs, small businesses, and cooperatives can help produce a renaissance of inner cities and rural areas. Urban and rural communities can be revitalized by rebuilding economic systems from the ground up. Local currencies, as well as small businesses, can become the engines of community economic transformation. As noted, small businesses can provide seedbed for innovation and job creation. The widespread adoption of an alternative currency approach may minimize the need for governmental redistribution of income and wealth through taxes and transfer payments, such as welfare, thereby reducing the size and cost of government at all levels.

It must be noted, however, that entrepreneurship by itself is not likely to fully displace the decades-old, pervasive welfare culture in America's inner cities. Entrepreneurial development programs can attack social problems, but the challenge is far broader than self-employment and access to credit.

Human reconstruction rests on three principles. First, policies should be based on old-fashioned, but often neglected values, such as responsibility for one's self and one's community, pride, hope for the future, and a work ethic. Second, society must discard or modify institutions and legal rules and regulations that restrict individual initiative. Third, self-help and the development of communities from within rests on involving people in altering the scale of institutions in the emerging political economy. Cities and regions should, therefore, respond with creativity and innovation—the inputs of human insight.

Providing a Feedback Mechanism

Policy makers have focused considerable attention in the twentieth century on promoting economic stability—avoiding serious depressions or runaway inflation. But, their quest for nationally appropriate solutions is flawed. A national government makes decisions centrally, often at the expense of regions and communities.

Jane Jacobs presents the case for local currencies which would float against a national currency.[41] Currencies act as economic feedback controls. National currencies often provide faulty and destructive feedback to regional and urban economies leading to economic and environmental flaws. We increasingly observe the problem of permanently stunted regions and cities and stagnation evidenced by such cities and regions. According to Jacobs, a central system of money creation cannot create the correct amount of credit or money for local regions. A centralized system creates a general level of funds which may be excessive for a region experiencing a boom economy but inadequate for a region undergoing economic stagnation or a depression. In reality, nation-states are economic grab bags, with a variety of different economies. Each region or city has a distinctive character that makes it different from other regions or other cities. Each region or city has its own natural and human resources; each region or city has its own productive capacity.

Local currencies would serve as a feedback mechanism because they would trigger appropriate corrections in response to specific stimuli.[42] Other factors are, of course, important in the economic vitality of a city or a region but currency fluctuations represent a potent form of feedback control. U.S. cities and regions currently suffer from a lack of discipline imposed by currency fluctuations or opportunities presented by currency fluctuations. As Jacobs notes:

Ideally, at a time when a city's exports are doing well, it needs to receive as wide a range and as great a volume of earned imports as it can, especially from other cities, because those funds of earned imports are the grist the city must have for its vital process of import-replacing. Conversely, at a time when its exports are in decline, imports should ideally become expensive because to escape decline from diminishing export work a city desperately needs to replace wide ranges of its imports with local production. It also needs maximum stimulation for tentative new types of export work it may soon be capable of casting up. . . . With falling exports a city needs a declining currency working like an automatic tariff and an automatic export subsidy—but only for as long as they are necessary. Once its exports are doing well, it needs a rising currency to earn the maximum variety and quantity of imports it can.[43]

Thus, a local currency system will increase the ability of a region or a community to regulate its economy. The use of a locally issued and controlled currency will help insulate local economies from the distorting effects of national and global economic trends. It will provide a buffer allowing a community or a region to set its own standards and maintain the desired quality of living.

Promoting Employment Opportunities

As noted earlier in this chapter, communities and regions currently (and will in the future) encounter an insufficiency of "good" jobs. Unemployment and underemployment represent an endemic, structural problem. Official unemployment statistics mask the extent of joblessness. Discouraged workers—persons who have given up looking for a job in the formal economy because they cannot find work—are no longer considered part of the labor force and are not counted as unemployed.

Mainstream economists assume that increased government spending (or substantial tax reductions) will encourage people to spend more. Increased spending will then stimulate the economy. However, untrammeled economic growth runs smack into the planet's limits.

A local currency can reduce unemployment and underemployment in a region, a city, or a community by promoting local job creation. People will work and monetize their labor for an alternative currency they deem trustworthy, especially where there are not enough U.S. dollars circulating in a local economy. An alternative currency would encourage a greater percentage of local income to circulate locally so as to generate more viable economic activity and local employment. It could assist in tapping a labor force that society deems useless and burdensome—the young who cruise the streets, welfare recipients who yearn to be productive, families who vegetate in front of a television set. It offers opportunities for people to be useful, thereby restoring self-esteem. Thus, a local currency system would expand the employment of local people on a permanent, long-term basis by helping local individuals establish their own small businesses and by creating local markets for locally produced goods and services. Employment would be promoted without the need for government intervention.

Facilitating a Noninflationary Monetary System

Many long for a currency having a noninflationary, constant purchasing power. A key goal of a monetary system should focus on enabling people and organizations to make plans and contracts with a high degree of confidence that the currency they use will not change its value over time.

Today, fiat money (irredeemable in any commodity) leaves us nowhere to turn while the U.S. dollar's purchasing power is diluted. We see an inflationary trend which represents an increase in the general level of prices expressed in the terms of U.S. dollars. With nearly a century of experience behind us, we see that central government–sponsored currency generates inflation and economic instability. The value of the U.S.

dollar has depreciated by about 93 percent from 1913 to 1993, so that one dollar in 1993 is currently worth about seven cents.[44]

Inflation represents a market mechanism for devaluing the U.S. dollar in terms of goods and services. Sellers of goods and services protect themselves by raising prices. Lenders increase interest rates, raising the cost and risk of doing business, thereby inhibiting the start-up or expansion of new business activities. Businesses that survive are less profitable.

The integrity of the U.S. currency depends on whatever modicum of integrity the federal government possesses. We cannot assume that monetary authorities, specifically, the Federal Reserve Board, will be able and can be trusted to act in the public interest on a long-term basis. A need thus exists for competition between alternative money-creating institutions which will provide a sound, noninflationary currency. Competition from alternative currencies provides a safeguard against chronic inflation of the U.S. dollar. With competition, consumers will seek out a currency which best maintains its value over time. A currency such as the U.S. dollar (based on its track record over this century), which loses value, will be passed over in favor of a more stable currency.

CONCLUSION

A local currency which matches the needs of the region or community's economy system will not only keep down or perhaps virtually eliminate inflation, it will also help promote a greater degree of local self-help reliance and reduce unemployment and underemployment. Decentralization also prevents large-scale, systemic failure. The failure of one part of a decentralized system would not bring down the entire structure. The healthy parts would take over.

four

Barter: Evolution into a Modern Economic Tool

INTRODUCTION

Bartering has had a long history that saw its decline with the advent of paper currency. The process of finding an individual who was willing to make a direct exchange for the goods and services that another offered was inefficient at best. However, today, with the creation of modern systems, indirect exchanges can be made. A person no longer needs to find someone who is willing to make a direct exchange of goods or services of equivalent value. With modern systems, a person only needs to find someone who is willing to exchange goods or services for barter units or a local currency. These exchanges can boost not only the local economy but also the income of the participants.

The first modern system, known as LETS (Local Employment and Trading System), was developed by Michael Linton in Vancouver Island, British Columbia, Canada in 1983.[1] This system suffers from some major limitations and accordingly has realized only limited success in this country, where about ten LETS systems are in existence. In contrast, Canada, with one-tenth the population of the United States, has 10 LETS programs, Australia 200, New Zealand 90, and Great Britain 170.[2]

However, LETS did lay the groundwork for a program developed in 1991 by Paul Glover, known as Ithaca HOURS, which represents the next step in the evolutionary process of bartering. The Ithaca HOURS program eliminates some of the problems inherent in the LETS system and has achieved considerable success since its inception. This chapter describes both of these programs and provides suggestions for starting one in your community.

LETS PROGRAM

Description

A Local Employment and Trading System (LETS) is a computer-based membership organization in which transactions generate credits that can only be spent within the group. A local LETS system acts as a clearinghouse and information service. Members sign up, usually paying an initiation fee, and describe the goods or services they are offering or seeking. All of the offers and requests are published in a monthly or bimonthly print list distributed to members.

Each LETS member has a computer account starting at zero which is credited (increased) when the member sells a good or service and is debited (decreased) when the member buys something. The buyer and seller individually negotiate a price but no paper currency changes hands. For example, when a member finds someone who is selling the goods or services he or she is seeking, the two members can strike a deal in computer credits, or green dollars as they are sometimes called. The members of a LETS program need not find an individual or an entity who is willing to make a direct exchange. The members also do not need to have cash or an appropriate amount of computer credits on hand to make the deal. A member's account is debited in order to effectuate a transaction.

When the two members make a deal, it is reported by mail or more likely by telephone to a local LETS central office where the account of the user is debited and the account of the provider is credited for the agreed amount. The provider can use the credits to acquire other goods or services. Interest is not payable on a debit balance. No repayment schedule exists. However, a member with a debit balance has a commitment to deliver value to the community in the near future by selling goods or services to bring his or her account balance back to zero.

In short, LETS supports trading among members and maintains accounts for members in a unit of value related to the national currency— the U.S. dollar. The units can be exchanged for goods or services with other members; they are neither an item to be traded nor do they circulate as a hand-to-hand currency. The system rests on the mutual credit and trust of the members. The material backing consists of goods or services which a provider exchanges for credits. The moral backing is the user-buyer's promise to back it with an equivalent value when he or she becomes a provider-seller.

The biggest advantage of a LETS system, which does not use a physical currency, is that no limit exists with respect to the transactions that can occur. When traditional purchase and sale transactions are conducted through the use of a physical currency, the amount of currency in possession and circulation necessarily limit these exchanges. In a LETS system, the parties can enter into a transaction, at least in theory, without regard to the credits in the buyer's account. Unfortunately, while this is the biggest benefit of a LETS system, it is also the cause of the greatest concern about the long-term viability of any LETS program.

The greatest problem of a LETS system turns on the risk of members buying goods and services and accumulating "excessive" debit accounts. Because the credits are unlimited and because it is unnecessary for a member to have credits on hand to purchase an item, a member can accumulate a debit account that he or she will never repay. A massive amount of negative balances could cause a local system to collapse. As noted, the LETS system is based on the mutual trust that each member will repay any debit incurred. In the event that a member does not repay a debit, the other members must absorb the obligation. Widespread abuse could cause a complete breakdown of a system. If members lose faith in one another to repay their debits, the system will likely fail.

The most troubling aspect of the debit repayment problem is that it becomes more likely to occur as the membership in a local LETS program expands. The problem may not be apparent initially because the members are like-minded, idealistic, and small in number. As additional people participate in a program, it is more likely that potential abusers and defaulters will join. As the program grows, it becomes less personal. Members may feel less of a moral commitment to sell goods and services to other members in order to repay their debit balances. In addition, there will always be those who seek to take advantage of the system. As more people join, it becomes more likely that dishonest or noncreditworthy people will participate in a LETS program. The members and founders are then left with the difficult decision of keeping the system small and personal to reduce the risk posed by defaulters. While this decision may protect the current members, it will cause the system to be of only limited benefit to the community. If the members and founders choose to let a LETS program expand to its greatest possible membership, the risk of a breakdown in trust increases, which may cause the demise of the system. To combat this problem, the organizers of a LETS system should consider implementing one or more of the following six suggestions to reduce the risk of members breaching the mutual trust underpinning the program.

Planning to Reduce the Risk of Default

The simplest way to reduce the risk of default centers on limiting the debit balance any member can incur and carry. This approach reduces the amount of debits that the system need absorb in the event of a member's default. It will also lessen the risk of a person buying more than he or she could ever repay by selling goods and services to other members. In addition, capping any member's debit balances will reduce the incentive of a dishonest person to take advantage of the system.

Stating the principle of limiting debit balances is, however, much simpler than its application. The sponsors of a LETS provision must face a difficult question, namely, how large a debit balance should a member be allowed to carry? Some systems may opt for a fixed ceiling per member, say $500 or $1000. Others may limit the amount of credit to be authorized to the number of units an individual or a business can reasonably be expected to redeem in the course of trade in each month. One LETS organizer recommends that each member should be permitted to accumulate a debit balance it could be expected to redeem in trade in a two- or three-month period.[3] This is based on the assumption that a local currency should recirculate each 100 days or about 1 percent per day.

However, limiting the amount of debits a member can incur reduces the key benefit of a noncurrency system such as LETS, namely, of affording members a virtually unlimited means to enter into transactions. Still, the benefits of this safeguard probably far outweigh any disadvantages, and also, as members develop a credit history, each member's debit balance can be adjusted upwards.

Second, in addition to limiting the amount of a member's possible debit position, the central office for a local LETS program can perform a credit check on prospective members. While this technique may provide some measure of security, the expense may exceed its benefits. Also, a person may be creditworthy when he or she is legally required to pay his or her debts, but may not be when he or she is only subject to a moral obligation. While a credit check mechanism may provide some security, its usefulness is limited.

Third, a local office may periodically publish each member's account balance. Although raising privacy concerns, disclosure of debit account balances provides a form of self-regulation. Peer group pressure, particularly in smaller communities, will generally persuade members to trade responsibly. Also, members with "excessive" debit balances may encounter resistance on the part of other members in entering into future transactions.

A fourth option is to use a written membership agreement which provides that each individual must settle his or her accounts before terminating membership. While this technique may provide some measure of security, its benefits are very limited. Take the situation of a person who incurs a debit position far greater than any potential sales of goods and services he or she could effectuate. The membership agreement is not legally enforceable because it stipulates that a member is only morally obligated to restore his or her account balance to a zero position prior to termination. Thus, a member can walk away leaving the other members with the burden of assuming his or her debit position. The best enforcement measure a LETS program has is expulsion. While signing a written agreement may make some members more cautious, an agreement standing on a mutual commitment hardly seems a deterrent to someone seeking to abuse the system.

Fifth, the membership agreement could also provide for periodic settlement of outstanding accounts. This may help to alleviate some possible problems. The membership agreement could require members who incur a large debit position to settle their accounts before purchasing additional goods or services. This approach will probably provide a good check on the mutual trust implicit in the system and will help to catch problem members early.

A sixth option focuses on allowing a member to purchase goods or services only when he or she actually has a credit position. This option, however, eliminates the key advantage of a mutual credit system, namely, the ability of members who lack U.S. dollars to purchase goods and services. The organizers of a LETS program must carefully assess whether this approach is preferable to the risk of defaulters collapsing a local LETS system.

Implementing a LETS System

Organizational Details

In addition to coming up with an approach to deal with the excessive, accumulated debit balances of members, the initial organizational and start-up processes constitute the most difficult part of implementing a LETS system.[4] The sponsors need to organize a core group who will begin trading among themselves. Even before trading begins, the organizers should establish an organization structure for the local LETS system. Typically, they would create a community-based, nonprofit organization (or cooperative owned by its members) which would be run for the benefit of a community, with rights and authority vested in a board of directors with clearly defined, limited powers.

The sponsors must next handle the following nitty-gritty details:

1. Select a unique name for the system and its credit–debit unit.
2. Establish a means for members to make known their desires and offerings of goods and services. This can take the form, for example, of a newsletter containing classified ads listing requests for and offers of goods and services.
3. Set up a central office where a recordkeeper enters members' transactions as reported by members and keeps a membership list. The recordkeeper will periodically update members' account balances and issue periodic statements

for each member's account. The recordkeeper will periodically generate and distribute a summary report showing each member's transactions and his or her beginning and ending account balance. The recordkeeper should also produce a newsletter and/or an updated print list of offerings of and requests for goods and services. The list could take the form of an updated directory for the local network.

4. Obtain a computer with recordkeeping software and one or more telephone lines for members to call in their transactions. Full- or part-time personnel are required to staff the office. The personnel consist of volunteers or individuals who are paid for their services with system credits.

LANDSMAN Community Services will provide support to responsible groups and individuals wishing to establish their own independent, self-sustaining LETS system. An individual or group wishing to register a LETS system may do so by undertaking, among other things: to use the LETS system member agreements originated by LANDSMAN; to operate the LETS system as a nonprofit facility; to pay to LANDSMAN Community Service Ltd. a specified, one-time registration fee. Potential sponsors who feel that LANDSMAN can be helpful in implementing a LETS system can call (604) 338-0213/0214 or write to 1600 Embleton Crescent, Courtnay, B.C., Canada, V9N 6N8.

Recruiting New Members

Having surmounted a multitude of organizational details, the sponsors must focus on recruiting new members. To offer a wide range of goods and services and to generate greater volume of activity, LETS membership should be open not only to individuals but also to businesses, nonprofit groups, and cooperatives.

When recruiting members into the program, the organizers should explain that joining the system will give them an opportunity to use their previously untapped skills and contribute to promoting a sense of community. In addition, new members should understand the mutual trust implicit in the system. Prospective members should realize that when they purchase goods or services they are making a commitment to the community to sell items to offset their debit balance. Having a membership agreement on hand that explains the rights and obligations of members will help recruit new participants and deal with their concerns.

The local administrator must provide application forms to prospective members. He or she should oversee the processing of membership applications and verify information on which debit limits, if used, are based. The local system should also schedule regular membership meetings. These meetings enable members to handle business matters and to get to know one another, thereby promoting mutual trust, which serves as the basis for the program.

Last, but not least, the organizers of a local LETS system must provide a means to generate revenues to meet a program's start-up and operating expenses. A local system can cover its costs by charging an initiation fee and an annual membership fee, as well as debiting each account to cover services provided by the system. The initiation fee, payable when a member signs up for the program, and the annual membership fee enable a system to meet a considerable portion of its operating expenses. However, these fees should not be perceived of as too high, which could present a barrier to recruiting and retaining members.

In addition to the initiation and annual membership fees, the program should supplement its revenues by charging a fixed fee for each service provided by the system. These services include recording transactions, advertising offers and requests, preparing and mailing account statements, and providing a membership directory. The fees and charges for services should be payable in system credits and to some extent in U.S. dollars to cover cash payments for postage, supplies, and photocopying.

In a LETS system, every transaction must be reported to a local central office which keeps a record of each member's account balances. It is much simpler for people to transfer currency, issue a check, or charge a transaction on a debit or credit card than to mail or call in every transaction they make. To overcome this obstacle, as well as the debit balance dilemma, attention in the United States has focused on creating a local currency system based on the model of Ithaca HOURS.

ITHACA HOURS

Description

Ithaca HOURS, founded by Paul Glover in late 1991, represents a flexible system of bartering.[5] The system achieves the greater degree of flexibility by using a paper currency called an Ithaca HOUR, which on one side states: "In Ithaca We Trust." The alternative currency supplements the conventional monetary system and draws on underemployed resources, such as human labor, as needed by the community.

Unlike a bartering system that requires a direct swap of goods or services between two people, an Ithaca HOUR paper currency, similar to a LETS electronic transfer, can be exchanged by one person desiring the goods or services provided by another. The seller can then turn around and use the Ithaca HOURS he or she earns to buy goods or services from others. There is no need for two individuals to find a direct match for the goods or services they desire.

In contrast to the recordkeeping complexities of a LETS system, Ithaca HOURS streamlines recordkeeping. There is no requirement that transactions be entered into a central computer. Individuals and businesses, in the United States at least, may also prefer a hand-to-hand paper currency, such as an Ithaca HOUR, rather than the LETS system of electronic units of exchange.

One Ithaca HOUR currently represents the equivalent of $10, which is the average hourly wage, excluding fringe benefits, for workers in Tompkins County in upstate New York.[6] By basing the system on the county's average hourly wage, the program moves from the premise that one person's time is worth just as much as another's. In other words, each hour of labor has the same dignity. The system represents a leveling force, raising the minimum wage level and permitting people, especially low-wage earners, to buy goods and services previously beyond their reach.

However, the system provides for flexibility recognizing that unique skills require the payment of more than one HOUR for one hour of services. For instance, a dentist may collect several HOURS for each work hour because the dentist, receptionist, and assistant work together, using equipment and materials that must be paid for in U.S. dollars. Also, Ithaca HOURS may be accepted in combination with U.S. dollars in payment for goods or services. All of this flexibility has spawned great interest in community participation in the program.

To participate in an Ithaca HOURS program, an individual or business must be willing to offer goods or services in exchange for Ithaca HOURS. The participant pays a one-dollar registration fee and receives four Ithaca HOURS in return.[7] The goods or services that participants offer or request are published as classified ads in a bimonthly newspaper, *Ithaca Money*. Persons participating in the program use the publication to find other individuals or entities offering the goods or services they seek.

Ithaca Money contains a wide range of goods and services, including food items, construction work, professional services, health care, and handicrafts. The variety of goods and services available in exchange for an Ithaca HOUR gives value to the alternative currency. Each Ithaca HOUR is backed by real skills and real people. As more individuals and businesses accept an Ithaca HOUR, its value increases further. Members can even spend Ithaca HOURS with others who have not signed up as participants, provided they will accept them.

In addition to the four Ithaca HOURS a participant receives when registering in the program, an individual or a business owner can increase his or her supply of HOURS in several other ways. First, a participant can sell goods or services to others in exchange for Ithaca HOURS they hold. Second, a member earns two additional Ithaca HOURS every eight months just for continued participation in the program. To receive the extra Ithaca HOURS, a participant sends in a coupon stating that his or her phone number is current. This helps to increase the supply of the local currency, provides an incentive to remain in the program, and keeps member listings current.

Third, Ithaca HOURS are disbursed by the organizers at public meetings called barter potlucks.[8] Barter potlucks are regular community dinners, referred to as the "Municipal Reserve Board," where participants gather to conduct business and manage the system, particularly how much currency to print and issue, which denominations to print, and how many HOURS to pay to new members and for membership renewals. Individuals who renew their membership at a barter potluck receive an additional Ithaca HOUR.

More significantly, attendees of the barter potlucks make Ithaca HOUR grants which are limited to under 10 percent of the aggregate amount of currency outstanding. All participants attending a barter potluck meeting can vote on whether to give Ithaca HOURS to a local individual, entity, or community organization. If the participants feel a cause is worthy they can vote to give a grant or interest-free loan to an applicant. The grant or loan usually is for twenty Ithaca HOURS. The recipient can then hire individuals who provide goods and services in exchange for the HOURS.

Benefits of the Program

Ithaca HOURS has experienced great success in the local community. When the program began in November 1991, 80 people signed up and 384 HOURS were issued.[9] As of early 1994, over 800 individuals and 200 businesses participated in the system.[10] About 4,800 HOURS have been issued, which is equivalent to $48,000, thereby increasing local transactions by several hundred thousand dollars.[11] Overall, the program has brought increased jobs and prosperity to the Ithaca, New York community. Similar programs have started or are planned in Boulder, Colorado; Kansas City, Missouri; Atlanta, Georgia; Santa Fe, New Mexico; and Portland, Oregon.[12]

The program provides a number of benefits for individuals, businesses, and a community. An Ithaca HOURS system helps to expand a local economy by empowering underemployed and unemployed persons, the housebound, seniors, and part-time employees. Persons with excess time can participate in the program to obtain value for their special skills that would otherwise go uncompensated because of a shortage of U.S. dollars in a community. A person who performs services in exchange for the alternative currency earns HOURS which can be exchanged for goods and services provided by other individuals or entities in the locality.

Employment opportunities also increase the sense of community by having participants learn more about and work with their neighbors.

Also, consumers are encouraged to shop locally and employ each other because the currency can only be used in the particular area, namely, within a twenty-mile radius of Ithaca, New York.[13] Limiting currency use keeps the money in a locality, reinforces trading among people who live relatively close together, promotes the hiring of and trust among participants, and helps improve the overall wealth of a specific community and its residents.

The system may also attract new clientele to an established business and help anyone who wants to develop a part-time or full-time business doing what they like to do. By accepting HOURS, an existing or a new business taps a market of people who previously lacked spending power. HOURS earned by participants result in extra income to the recipients. The holders of HOURS seek out member businesses where they can spend their alternative currency. Spending HOURS at participating businesses results in increased sales for these firms. These businesses can then use the HOURS to receive value in exchange for the local currency, thereby saving U.S. dollars. In sum, the alternative scrip or currency promotes locally owned small firms. A business benefits by attracting new clientele who pay with the alternative currency. Consumers benefit by gaining the ability to spend the alternative currency. The community benefits because the local currency stimulates the local economy. It places a value on skills that might not otherwise receive compensation and teaches people the worth of their skills. Participants also earn additional income in the form of HOURS which they can use to buy local goods and services. Because consumers are encouraged to shop locally and try new products and services, the alternative currency keeps wealth within the local economy.

The system may also help shield a local economy from national economic difficulties. Implementation of an Ithaca HOURS-type program helps a local economy become more self-sufficient, thereby protecting a community from nationwide inflationary pressures, economic downturns, or periods of economic stagnation.

Disadvantages of the Program

The major limitation of an Ithaca HOURS system centers on the possibility that an entity or an individual may accumulate more HOURS than it, he, or she can spend. To meet this problem, an individual or a business should only accept a limited amount of HOURS in exchange for goods and services. A business participant might begin by only accepting HOURS geared to a maximum per purchase or as a percentage of an item's price. By determining beforehand how many HOURS an individual or a business can spend, self-regulation sets limits on acceptance of the alternative currency, thereby avoiding the accumulation problem. For instance, Ithaca HOURS actively recruits other businesses and people with special skills where an individual or a firm could spend the accumulated HOURS. Ithaca HOURS also creates, on request, customized shopping lists for those with regular HOURS income. This has converted many people from cautious acceptors to active pursuers of HOURS.

Also, the system could establish a trading center (as Ithaca HOURS has done), with its own physical space, where businesses and individuals could trade HOURS for goods on display or services. A trading center can help to alleviate the problems that may arise from an excess accumulation of HOURS. In addition, the trading center will facilitate a local import-replacement program based on creating ecologically sustainable jobs.

The system must also deal with the problem of the potential overissuance of currency and the accompanying specter of inflation. Inflationary pressures can be avoided by limiting the issuance of the alternative currency thereby keeping the demand high and the supply low. Because the alternative currency is presently tied to the U.S. dollar, any inflation at the national level will result in a depreciation in the value of an Ithaca HOUR. By developing a system of HOUR prices, which may take the form of a catalog of available goods and services, the group facilitates allowing the HOUR to float independently of the value of the U.S. dollar.[14] As discussed in Chapter 6, the problem can also be alleviated by implementing a local currency system not pegged to the U.S. dollar.

Implementation

With hard work and dedication, activists interested in improving their community's economy can implement an Ithaca HOURS-type program following these seven steps: (1) create an organization; (2) design the currency; (3) recruit individual and business participants; (4) publish a barter newspaper; (5) print the alternative currency; (6) distribute the barter newspaper and the currencies; and (7) publicize the program.[15]

Create an Organization

The first step in starting the program focuses on creating an organization. This can mean one individual taking action or a group of residents working together. Whatever size and form the organization takes, for example, a nonprofit or cooperative entity, its first objective must center on developing a marketing plan that will allow the program to grow at the lowest possible cost. Overhead costs can be minimized by operating out of someone's home. These start-up costs can be recovered by requesting a small initial contribution, say $1 or $2, from each participant who receives voting rights in the organization's governing body and an ongoing listing in a community newspaper published by the sponsoring organization.

Design the Currency

Second, the founders must next design the currency. A good design for the currency is very important. A good currency design will help boost credibility and participation in the program. The alternative scrip should resemble the U.S. dollar, but contain local themes and landmarks. As discussed in Chapter 7, the currency must be sized and designed to avoid confusion with the U.S. dollar and the reach of federal anticounterfeiting laws. It is probably best to size the alternative currency so that it is smaller than the U.S. dollar. This will make it easier for participants to carry it in their wallets.

The organizers should print the currencies in various denominations, for example, 2 HOURS, 1 HOUR, 1/2 HOUR, and 1/4 HOUR. The geographical area within which the currency will be accepted in payment for transactions must also be fixed. As noted, Ithaca HOURS are accepted within a twenty-mile radius around Ithaca, New York.

Recruit Participants

Third, once the organization has designed the alternative currency, the issuer can use the currency as a marketing tool to recruit participants into the program. The founders of the organization can go to stores, union halls, farmer's markets, malls, unemployment offices, and places of worship to find prospective members. They should explain to the potential participants that many people in the community are either unemployed or underemployed. Instead of waiting for public sector action from outside the community, the local residents can make a difference by joining the program. The organizers should focus on explaining the advantages of a local currency as a means of increasing an individual's spending power and the accompanying benefits to the local economy, and should help identify goods and services that each prospective participant may need or want. They should also help to identify goods and services an individual can offer for sale.

Realizing the benefits of participation in the program and agreeing to participate, each new member should, if possible, make a one- or two-dollar contribution to cover start-up and operating costs. In exchange for the contribution, a participant will receive a certain amount of the local currency, say four HOURS, with which he or she can begin trading. Once the members of the organization have signed up enough individuals (perhaps, several dozen) and printed a list of members, the program can then be marketed to local businesses.

Success of the program rests, in large measure, on a sufficient degree of local business participation. Any business seeking to expand or having periods of time where it is running below full capacity can benefit from participation. As noted earlier, the program will generate a number of individuals needing places to spend newly acquired funds denominated in the alternative currency. The business owner can take advantage of the individual members' increased spending power and, in turn, raise his or her own spending power. Showing a business owner the list of members and the goods or services they are willing to provide will make the benefits of participation more concrete. The business owner will see the items on the list of goods and services offered that he or she can use personally or for the business.

The organizers should explain to business owners that this program will help to improve the local economy. Because the alternative currency can only be used locally, it keeps wealth in the community, thereby increasing the purchasing power of the residents.

Once a business owner agrees to join the program, the organizers should help the business owner decide on what is his or her maximum ability to accept the local currency, thus avoiding the problem of excessive currency accumulation. Different types of businesses have different abilities to accept a local currency, depending on their current and projected expenditures. It is very important to set up a plan focusing in detail on how much of the local currency any business can accept in exchange for the goods or services it provides. While the business owner may be very enthusiastic about accepting the new currency, if he or she accepts more than he or she can spend then the business owner may become discouraged. It is best for the business owner to start slowly, recognizing that he or she controls the currency acceptance policy and may subsequently change it.

Publish a Barter Newspaper

Fourth, once an organization has established a sufficient base of individual and business participants, the next step is to publish a barter newspaper. When planning the barter newspaper, strategy becomes very important. Using the barter newspaper as a publicity technique, the organizers should strive to promote the acceptance of the alternative currency while realistically reporting any difficulties that arise. Difficulties should be honestly described in a constructive, positive manner, helping to establish the credibility of the barter newspaper while assisting in resolving any problems. Of course, publishing success stories encourages a greater participation in the program and a wider acceptance of the local currency. The founders must also establish a publication schedule for the barter newspaper.

The organization should consider selling advertisements in the barter newspaper. For example, *Ithaca Money* distributes 5,000 copies of its paper free and currently charges $400 for a full-page display ad, $200 for a half page, $100 for a quarter page, $55 for an eighth page, $30 for a sixteenth page, and $20 for a business card. Full or part payment for the advertisement can be made with the alternative currency. Because readers keep their issues handy until the next publication date, it should be emphasized to advertisers (and potential advertisers) that the ads will stay around for awhile instead of being thrown away a short time after an initial reading.

Additionally, the newspaper can charge a fee, say $1 or $2 per issue, for each item included in a list of goods and services offered or requested. The fee represents a small price to pay for the exposure. The organizers should not encounter problems encouraging people to list items for such a reasonable fee.

Piggybacking on an existing pennysaver-type or other weekly publication provides another avenue to reach members and potential participants. Throughout the United States, pennysavers possess three key requisites: publishing experience; an advertising base; and distribution channels. The barter list can be distributed as a pennysaver insert, thereby providing a win-win situation. The program saves money while achieving its outreach goal. The pennysaver may increase its circulation.

Print the Alternative Currency

Fifth, at the same time as the program gears up to publish its first newspaper (or pennysaver insert), plans must be made to print the alternative currency. The currency should be durable and flexible. Make certain it survives a test in a washing machine. To discourage counterfeiting, Ithaca HOURS are trimmed to an odd size and serial numbers added, stamped deep so they can be felt by hand. Serial numbers convert printed paper into a local currency. A three- to five-digit serial number reinforces the idea that the currency is not printed excessively. It may be wise to start serial numbers in a middle range. Starting with 0001 suggests that the first recipients are brave pioneers in an experiment, rather than part of an ongoing process. The organization should record the name and phone number of each participant to whom it issues the alternative currency as well as the serial numbers.

Also, the organization's books must be open and accurate, so that as the system grows, all notes can be accounted for. The strength of local currency turns on fair and honest disbursement. Misprinted notes and duplicate serial numbers should be destroyed, then listed as destroyed, with serial numbers ripped off and retained as receipts.

Distribute the Barter Newspaper and Alternative Currency

Sixth, the program must distribute the barter newspaper and the alternative currency. The organizers should mail the initial agreed-upon amount of alternative currency and the first issue of the barter newspaper to those on the membership list. Enough currency should be provided to allow small but notable purchases. It is important to give each denomination so every participant knows what the alternative currency looks like. The organizers should also arrange to distribute the barter newspaper for free pickup at stores, places of worship, laundromats, farmer's markets, community centers, and events. Likeliest potential participants in the program define the places of distribution. Deliver signs to participating retailers indicating the acceptance of the local currency.

Publicize the Program

Seventh, the organizers must, in general, orchestrate an extensive publicity campaign. They should contact local newspapers as well as radio and television stations. They should personally visit print and electronic media outlets and distribute a press release, samples of the local currency and the barter newsletter, and ask to be interviewed. Also, whenever newsworthy events occur, inform the press. These events can include milestones in the number of participants who have signed up and the amount of alternative currency that has been issued.

Once the program is under way, the organizers should continue to sign up more individual participants. However, the key to success will likely turn on signing up popular businesses and keeping them satisfied. If a popular firm no longer accepts the currency, it could significantly weaken the program.

While the program promotes the skills of individuals and cottage industries, the amount of currency circulating is limited by the capability of prominent local businesses, such as restaurants, child and adult care providers, grocers, movie theaters, video rentals, and home repair services, to accept it. The more prominent businesses that participate in and remain satisfied with the program, the quicker the system will grow. Therefore, it is imperative that the sponsors help the prominent businesses spend the local currency, either by giving them ideas using existing barterers, recruiting new participants, or providing personalized shopping lists for easy reference.

Also, it is very important to balance the goods and services on the list. It may be that the supply of some services, for instance, computer tutors, will exceed demand. Limit these services so that all participants remain satisfied. The organizers should also try to recruit members who will provide basic items, such as food and home repairs, to facilitate the widespread use of the alternative currency.

If you have any questions about starting an Ithaca HOURS-type program in your community, contact Paul Glover at (607) 273-8025 or write to P.O. Box 6578, Ithaca, NY 14851. He provides a *Hometown Money Starter Kit* and a book, *Hometown Money: How to Enrich Your Community with Local Currency*, each for $25.

CONCLUSION

Starting a bartering system in any community can improve a local economy. Modern bartering programs offer the potential to utilize a community's latent resources. Using these resources will increase the spending power of all participants. With hard work and dedication, interested individuals can start a program that will begin to solve the economic problems in localities across the nation.

five

Discount Scrip: Creating a Local Currency Pegged to the U.S. Dollar

INTRODUCTION

We usually think of bargain purchase or discount coupons as a method for an individual business to attract new customers. Today, with the innovations sponsored by two nonprofit organizations, Self-Help Association for a Regional Economy (SHARE) and the E. F. Schumacher Society, discount coupons have taken on a whole new form, thereby creating a local currency, albeit pegged to the U.S. dollar. Imagine a business in need of cash selling discount coupons redeemable in the future for the store's merchandise. This new method of financing presents an excellent opportunity for businesses around the nation to build upon and tap into the goodwill of their customers to obtain needed cash on favorable terms.[1]

Innovative techniques for boosting local businesses did not end with individual firms issuing discount scrip. In the Berk-Shares program, local businesses joined forces with staff of the Schumacher Society to encourage residents to support their community and shop locally. A discount coupon called a Berk-Share, a local currency pegged to the U.S. dollar, facilitates the promotion of the local economy. With a successful track record, the Berk-Shares program has entered its third year of operation. A Berk-Shares-type program can be used in any community to stimulate the local economy and promote local businesses. While a Berk-Shares promotion only occurs for a specified number of weeks during the year, plans are underway to implement, in conjunction with a local chamber of commerce, an expanded, year-round program.

This chapter describes each of these innovations, their benefits and limitations, and also gives suggestions on implementing these programs in communities throughout the United States.

BARGAIN PURCHASE NOTES ISSUED BY ONE OR SEVERAL BUSINESSES

Several firms in Great Barrington, Massachusetts, have taken the lead in using bargain purchase/discount notes to raise capital on favorable terms. These note issues originated in the second half of 1989.

In the fall of 1989, when his lease expired and his landlord sought to double his rent, Frank Tortoriello, the proprietor of a delicatessen, faced the dilemma of coming up with cash to move his business to a new location or closing up shop. When banks rejected his loan application, he turned to a microenterprise loan program sponsored by a local non-profit organization, SHARE (Self-Help Association for a Regional Economy). Susan Witt, administrator of SHARE and executive director of the E. F. Schumacher Society, suggested to Frank that he issue his own currency, and the idea for "Deli Dollars" was born.[2]

Instead of borrowing money from a bank, Frank sold discount notes to customers redeemable after six months for sandwiches and other deli delights. He issued the burgundy-on-cream-colored $10 notes for $8— giving purchasers a $2 discount. The six-month redemption moratorium enabled Frank to relocate his restaurant and generate a sufficient cash flow to repay his notes in kind. To ensure that all the Deli Dollars did not come in immediately after the expiration of the six-month period, SHARE worked with Frank to date the notes over a ten-month period, thereby staggering the redemption.

The Deli Dollars concept provided Frank with a number of immediate, specific benefits. His customers were so eager to help that he raised the $5,000 he needed in only one month.[3] Even some bankers who rejected the loan request invested their own money in Deli Dollars. Thus, the arrangement gave Tortoriello the cash he needed to relocate his business, let him redeem the notes at a rate his business could absorb, spread the risk of the "loan" across a wide group, and gave his customers an excellent (25 percent) rate of return.[4]

Frank currently enjoys his new, larger location. In addition to using scrip to help support his business through the relocation process, Frank subsequently sold an additional $2,500 in Deli Dollars to raise funds to build a deck on the restaurant. He plans to offer more Deli Dollars to finance future expansion plans. The idea proved so successful that other businesses in the Great Barrington area turned to similar bargain purchase techniques.

Later in 1989, two farmers who operate produce stands in the Great Barrington area, Taft Farms and the Corn Crib, learned of Frank Tortoriello's success with Deli Dollars. With the help of SHARE, they issued a discount scrip called Berkshire Farm Preserve Notes in the winter of 1989–1990.[5] The green-colored notes are adorned with a head of cabbage instead of the head of a president and the motto, "In Farms We Trust" instead of "In God We Trust." The farmers sell the notes for $9 each in the winter, when cash is short. The notes are redeemable for $10 in produce during the peak spring and summer months. By using this bargain purchase mechanism, both farmers are able to tide their operations over the winter months when they face high fuel oil bills to keep their greenhouses going. The farmers repay their customers in produce in May to October. In essence, the customers pay in advance for the following summer's vegetables and fruit.

One key point differentiates Berkshire Farm Preserve Notes from Deli Dollars.[6] Deli Dollars are issued by a sole proprietor. The notes were issued by the deli and return to the deli for redemption. SHARE, a non-profit, community-based group helped with the promotion of Deli Dollars, placing the concept in a larger context of consumer responsiblity to help local businesses. SHARE provided public sponsorship for a private issue of discount coupons. In contrast, the Berkshire Farm Preserve Notes are issued by SHARE in limited numbers to the two farmers who are obligated to return the same number of redeemed notes back to SHARE. The two farm stands sell the common scrip, issued by SHARE, which is redeemable at either market. Because the notes can be spent at either of the two farm stands, SHARE assumes responsibility for any bookkeeping problems associated with the redemption program. As noted, each farm stand must annually return at the end of the season (November 15th to be exact) the same number of notes it receives from SHARE. In the event of any imbalance between notes a farm stand issues and what it redeems, SHARE serves as a clearinghouse to equalize the redemptions. Thus, if a farm stand has an excess of notes because it redeemed more than it sold, SHARE would purchase the excess at $9 per note. Conversely, SHARE requires the farm stand that redeems less than it issued to contribute $9 per note to SHARE. This sum would be returned to the other farmer, thereby equalizing the expenditures.

In practice, rather than settling an imbalance at the end of each season with an exchange of checks, the farmers agree, with SHARE as an intermediary, on an exchange of produce. In 1990, for example, the two farmers settled a $72 imbalance for a winter's worth of potatoes.[7]

The Berkshire Farm Preserve Note program has proven quite successful and has continued on an ongoing basis since the winter of 1989–1990.

In the first two winters, for example, the two farm stands raised more than $17,000.[8] However, the benefits of a discount coupon, local currency, although beginning with raising cash by means of short-term loans, far transcend this objective. Using a bargain purchase scrip allows a business to obtain short-term financing when a bank or other financial institution may be unwilling to do so. Many times a bank will only be interested in making larger, more profitable loans. An alternative currency allows a business to tap into the goodwill of its customers to obtain short-term loans. The business owner can then repay the loans by redeeming the notes for goods or services instead of cash. The notes, thus, enable entrepreneurs to obtain more control over the financing of their operations, eliminate costly bank loans as a supply of credit, and enhance the relationship between producer-distributors and consumers.

A firm derives other business-specific benefits from issuing a bargain purchase scrip. The notes represent a form of advertising that may generate considerable publicity and enable a business to build and broaden its customer base. For example, the Berkshire Farm Preserve Notes generate consumer interest in the two markets. Also, customers who purchase the farm preserve notes receive targeted mailings advertising specials on fruits and vegetables.[9] The notes, thus, represent a clever marketing tool.

As long as a business stays afloat and successfully implements the redemption program, both the business and the consumers win. In sum, a bargain purchase–type local currency serves as a local economic booster providing a return to the participating business on a very modest investment by any individual customer.

Customers and the community also derive benefits from the issuance of bargain purchase scrip. In addition to getting a discount on future purchases of goods or services, customers derive a psychological satisfaction in assisting local firms. Customers liked being part of helping Frank move his restaurant and keeping the deli in town through their own efforts. The Berkshire Farm Preserve Notes gave purchasers a way to take responsibility for the supply of farm products and for maintaining a dwindling number of family farms. Local consumers voted with their cash for fresh, locally grown produce.

The notes circulate in the locality, thereby serving as an alternative currency and providing benefits for the community. Originally, Deli Dollars were spendable only at Frank's deli. As these notes gained recognition as a trusted instrument, they became acceptable at many area concerns. Deli Dollars began to turn up all over town. Other local merchants accepted them in payment for merchandise they sold to their customers. Contractors found the notes were a great Christmas present for their crew members. Deli Dollars appeared on church collection plates and were, in turn, given to those in need.

The local Women, Infants and Children (WIC) program made use of the Berkshire Farm Preserve Notes in an innovative way. In the winter of 1992, recognizing that many families were having difficulty meeting bills and paying for food, the Children's Health Program that administers the WIC program in the Southern Berkshires established a fund called "Project Milk." The donated monies were used to purchase Berkshire Farm Preserve Notes which were then given to needy families. The Children's Health Program had the assurance that the monies would be spent for produce at the farm stands, thereby helping local farmers and families with children at the same time. The recipients had the dignity of being able to choose what they wanted to buy at the farm stands and of not being distinguishable from other Berkshire Farm Preserve Note customers. The Farm Note distribution proved to be a fully local alternative to Food Stamps.[10]

In the Southern Berkshire town of Monterey, the locally owned Monterey General Store is in its fifth year of successful issue of "Monterey General Store Notes." The sale and use of the notes reinforce a strong community pride and self-help ethic. Store manager Maynard Forbes notices that because of the Notes, residents are doing a larger percentage of their food shopping in Monterey. Monterey General Store Notes are now a local institution, reflecting the independent spirit of this small hill town.[11]

A discount-type, local currency is not, however, without its limitations. Successful use of a bargain purchase scrip requires a business to have the trust and confidence of its customers. Scrip works if consumers are comfortable with a business. This means an established business. Discount scrip issues usually do not work for start-ups that lack a solid customer base.

The problem of scale and the accompanying issue of neighborly trust also play a significant role in the viability of a local currency based on discount coupons.[12] While small-town residents may be willing to help local businesses, people living in suburbs and in larger cities are probably less likely to offer the same support. A business owner in these less hospitable areas may encounter difficulty finding customers willing to buy discount coupons redeemable in kind for future goods or services. People in urban areas and their suburbs, who shop in malls or through mail order catalogs, may have little or no incentive to support local firms.

Because the notes sell for relatively small amounts, a business owner or community group may still be able to generate support for their purchase, even in larger communities. The established business owner only risks the rather nominal printing costs; so it may be worth the gamble to attempt to implement the program in any community. In addition, the urban business firm could strive to appeal to neighborhood—not citywide—pride and contacts and a degree of willingness, however attenuated, to help a friend in a time of need. Nevertheless, business owners and community groups must face a stark reality—a discount scrip works best in areas, notably small towns, where there are strong community ties and people look favorably on local firms and using local resources to achieve a degree of self-sufficiency.

Another disadvantage is noteworthy. Customers within a given community may only be willing to invest, in the aggregate, a limited amount of funds. The business owner who needs capital, thus, can obtain only a portion of the required financing through the sale of discount notes. Other sources must supply the remainder of the needed funds. If no other sources are available and the business cannot obtain the requisite cash through the sale of the bargain purchase notes, the firm faces the possibility that it may close its doors. The sale of discount notes provides an opportunity for a business to revive itself in the absence of other, viable alternatives.

Implementing a discount coupon–type, local currency program for any business is quite simple and inexpensive. The business owner need only design the currency and then print the desired amount. This type of financing requires almost no overhead except the minimal costs of designing and printing the notes and the attendant bookkeeping expenses. The scrip should specify the date after which it is redeemable or the dates between which the notes may be redeemed. Spaces to punch out or mark off the amount of the purchases should be provided on the front or back of the scrip. The reverse of the scrip should contain an issue number, for what and where the scrip is redeemable, and the name of the issuer.

Promotion plays an important role in the successful implementation of a bargain purchase coupon program. The role of a nonprofit community group, such as SHARE, cannot be overemphasized. A nonprofit can qualify for free press releases to advertise the discount coupons and can help create a general climate for consumer support of buying locally. It is important for the nonprofit group to review the financial condition of the business to determine that there is a solid chance that the investment in the discount coupons will be repaid in the future, before publicly recommending the purchase of coupons. At the same time, the merchants involved with scrip in the Berkshire examples displayed a spirit of cooperation with other merchants by encouraging the issue of other discount coupons. This noncompetitive tone reinforced the community aspect of the initiative. Business owners and community groups should therefore market the alternative currency as discount coupons that benefit the business owner, customers, and the community alike.

Using an attractive design for the coupons is essential to soliciting more customers. Consumers liked having the Deli Dollars and the Berkshire Farm Preserve Notes in their pockets. They are good-looking conversation pieces and are appropriate for gifts.

A business should keep track of the distribution of its coupon by recording the serial numbers. Offer the currency in a time when cash is short and make them redeemable over a period of time in which a firm can absorb the outflow of goods or services. Stagger the redemption dates, so the cash flow of a business will not be crimped by the rush of patrons seeking redemptions.

BERK-SHARES

In today's retail market dominated by omnipresent large national chains, malls, and warehouse discount stores, a community needs to work together to promote its local economy. The Berk-Shares program provides such an opportunity and serves as the next step to a truly local currency that will keep money generated in a region circulating in that area.

Building on the successes enjoyed by Deli Dollars and Berkshire Farm Preserve Notes in the late 1980s and early 1990s, the Main Street Action Association, a merchants organization funded through a state economic development grant for the purpose of revitalizing the downtown district in Great Barrington, in conjunction with staff from the E. F. Schumacher Society, organized the first Berk-Shares program, which began in August 1992.[13] The Southern Berkshire Chamber of Commerce has joined in sponsorship for the program, now in its third season.

In a Berk–Shares type program, local businesses band together and give away one Berk-Share, a discount coupon valued at $1, for every $10 spent in a participating store. Many customers seek out the participating stores to accumulate as many Berk-Shares as possible during a limited giveaway period, typically five to seven weeks.

At the end of the giveaway period, a festive redemption period takes place. The redemption period can span one long weekend, one week, or a ten-day period encompassing two weekends. A longer redemption period increases transactions in discount coupons and accommodates those who might be out of town for one weekend. Holders of Berk-Shares can use them in any participating store, regardless of where customers originally acquired them. In this way, the Berk-Shares are closer to a transferrable local scrip. The businesses separately set their redemption policy and, as the program has evolved, the sponsors require the merchants to accept Berk-Shares for a specified minimum redemption discount, currently 25 percent, of an item's purchase price. Thus, in a store offering a 25 percent redemption term, a $100 item can be purchased for $75 in U.S. dollars and 25 Berk-Shares. However, the discount offered by any participating firm may be higher than the 25 percent minimum.

The major benefit of a Berk-Shares program is that it stimulates local businesses. Participating firms send the public message about the importance of supporting local enterprises. By promoting local businesses, consumers are encouraged to shop locally instead of at large, national chain stores or at malls. Buying locally keeps wealth within the region, it keeps and creates jobs, and supports an economy of small, diversified, locally owned firms.

Specifically, the Berk-Shares program achieved a considerable measure of success even in its initial season of operation. In 1992, over 75,000 Berk-Shares were issued, representing $750,000 in Berk-Shares trade, and over 28,000 were redeemed.[14] This represents a remarkable return for the first year of a discount program.

The 1992 redemption pattern illustrated the strong interconnectedness of businesses on Great Barrington's Main Street. Clothing stores, hardware and gift stores, and flower shops had the best returns. The few participating professional service firms did only a small amount of trade in Berk-Shares. Small restaurants did not have a large return, probably because each purchase was rather modest in amount.[15]

A business owner's major incentive for participating in the Berk-Shares program centers on obtaining a low-cost means of promotion which results in increased profits during the period the program is in existence. Businesses are given a new, inexpensive way to draw customers and provide shoppers with a somewhat unique way to save money on their purchases. For any one business, printing and distributing discount coupons on its own is likely to be much more expensive than sharing the cost with other firms. The only cost to each business is the participation fee, presently at $65, and the reduced revenue from the sale of discounted goods or services. Firms hope that these costs will be made up by the increased sales the discount coupons generate. As long as a business realizes an increase in profits, it benefits from the program.

Also, customers benefit from the program by gaining the opportunity to purchase items they would not normally buy. The Berk-Shares, in essence, increase a consumer's disposable income, thereby serving as an incentive for the public to participate in the program. In short, the Berk-Shares program furthers the existing cooperation between merchants and consumers, thereby promoting the survival of the community. Consumers vote with their purchases to support small businesses.

Successful implementation of a Berk-Shares program turns on five points: (1) marketing the program to the local business owners; (2) working out the details; (3) informing the public; (4) printing the currency; and (5) keeping records.

First, the sponsoring organization must focus on marketing the program to local firms. Probably the most difficult part of implementing a Berk-Shares program in a community centers on obtaining the cooperation of local merchants. Because businesses are accustomed to competing against each other instead of working together to improve the economy for everyone, some businesses may initially be reluctant to participate. However, once proprietors realize that this program represents a low-cost way to increase profits and improve the local economy, the organizers have probably accomplished their most difficult task.

When marketing the program to a business owner, the sponsor should explain that he or she can increase profits by participating in the program for only a small annual fee of, say, under $100. This fee is much cheaper and much more effective than any promotion the business could do on its own. The annual fee represents a small amount to pay for the business and community opportunities as well as the goodwill gained from participation.

Next, the organizers must deal with a myriad of details. The agreement among the participating merchants must be carefully structured and clearly stated. The agreement should specify the giveaway period as well as the redemption period. Limited-life discount coupons force redemptions to take place within a finite time period. Business owners should also agree on and adhere to a minimum discount policy. Subject to providing minimum percentage discount, each participating business itself must then decide what percentage of the sales price to accept in the form of discount coupons. This percentage will, of course, be based on each firm's costs and its estimated profit margin. Merchants should specify their redemption terms when they sign up to participate in the program. Beyond the redemption terms, the sponsor should, however, require businesses to permit the use of discount coupons across the board for all of the firm's goods or services. The sponsor may also want to place a limit on the number of coupons a consumer may acquire in a single transaction, for example, 100 coupons for $1,000 worth of merchandise.

Third, it is very important for the sponsor to publicize the program. Consumer awareness is vital to the success of the program. Revenues received from the participation fees paid by merchants should go mostly toward publicizing the program. The sponsors should strive to inform the public that the program serves as a new way for them to realize savings on their purchases, while improving the local economy. Many consumers will likely participate enthusiastically.

In addition to group advertising, the organization should develop a handout listing each of the participating merchants, with the individual redemption terms for each store. Consumer handouts should be given out with each sale as needed. Also, the participating businesses should be given an easily visible promotional sign and display posters indicating their membership in the program. The merchants should be advised to place the posters where they can readily be seen by customers.

Fourth, the sponsor needs to print the coupons. Good design is very important to the success of the program. The organizers should print $1, $5, and $10 denominations to facilitate transactions. Space should be provided for a hole punch on the $5 and $10 denominations, so consumers will not have to spend the entire coupon at one location. The sponsor should try to obtain past monthly sales estimates from the participating businesses to get an idea of how many coupons need to be printed.

The merchants must sign and/or stamp all coupons prior to distribution. The sponsor should advise merchants that unsigned or unstamped coupons should not be redeemed and that a customer presenting such coupons should be advised to return to the firm where he or she received such coupons and obtain the requisite signature and/or stamp. The participating merchants' employees should be advised not to hand out the coupons frivolously. Each merchant is responsible for the legitimate distribution of coupons for purchases actually made or services rendered.

Finally, the sponsor must keep records of the number of coupons issued to each participating store. Also, the store owners should be encouraged to record the number of coupons they issue as well as the coupons redeemed in their store. Good recordkeeping will help in analyzing the success of the program.

Merchants should be advised to keep track of coupons as redeemed by putting them in an envelope provided. The sponsor should arrange for the envelopes to be picked up at the end of the promotional period when the coupons are redeemed. The merchant should cancel each note as redeemed, for example, by putting an "X" across the front. The sponsoring organization should separately bundle and set aside the unused coupons, and should track the total number of coupons actually handed out so it can analyze what percentage are returned for redemption.

As potential sponsors in other communities consider implementing a Berk-Shares program, a major limitation of the program, which stems from the reason why consumers participate in the first place, is noteworthy. Consumers participate more enthusiastically when stores selling higher priced items are involved in the program. Many customers buy their lower priced necessities from the participating stores during the giveaway period, earn their discount coupons, and then redeem them for more expensive, nonnecessary items.

The stores selling necessities may realize increased sales from customers seeking to make their purchases of lower priced goods or services from participating merchants. However, it is unlikely that customers will buy more necessities than are needed. The discount coupons, perceived as a means of increasing consumers' disposable income, will likely be redeemed for luxury items. Because the consumers know that they will purchase their luxury items for a discount during the redemption period, they are unlikely to purchase these items during the period in which merchants give away the discount coupons.

Thus, the participating businesses selling mostly luxury items may not realize any increase in business, and conversely may experience a decrease, until the redemption period. However, during the redemption period they will sell their goods or services at a substantial discount and may not generate any increased profits. Even though it is vital that businesses selling luxury items participate in the program, these firms may derive only limited gains, if any. Therefore, they may cease participating in the program, thereby reducing the overall incentive for consumers to buy their lower priced necessities from the remaining stores.

However, if a business owner can obtain value for the redeemed discount coupons then he or she will be much happier to accept them in exchange for merchandise. To build increased satisfaction on the part of local enterprises, organizers of the program should allow merchants to set their own special redemption period at the end of the general redemption period. The extended redemption period would maintain all the current benefits while reducing the program's inherent limitations, particularly for purveyors of higher priced items. The discount coupons would act much more as a local currency and would increase the likelihood of expanding the local economy. Furthermore, implementing this change in the program would likely create a snowball effect. The merchants would more eagerly accept the bargain purchase program, so that they would develop and implement more liberal discount policies. The more liberal redemption policies would provide further incentives for consumer participation. The program will become more valuable to businesses and consumers, so many more will participate. The program will expand further and the local economy will become even more self-sufficient.

EXPANDED BERK-SHARES PROGRAM

With the Berk-Shares program enjoying three successful seasons, the Schumacher Society wishes to implement, in conjunction with the Main Street Action Association and the Southern Berkshire Chamber of Commerce, an Expanded Berk-Shares Program which would provide for a year-round, 10 percent discount note.[16] A merchant-based, cooperative program would provide benefits to participating firms and banks in that they would supplement the U.S. dollars circulating in the community with a local medium of exchange, thereby permitting the public to transact a greater volume of trade. Because anyone could spend the discount notes, everyone in the community would benefit. As participating businesses thrive, other firms will accept the coupons, resulting in more discount notes in circulation, providing the community with greater control over its economic life.

As envisioned, the public could acquire a $10 bargain purchase note at a participating bank for $9. Participating merchants would redeem each note, throughout the year, for $10 worth of goods or services. The business owner would recirculate the turned-in note by spending it on purchases from any other member or anyone willing to accept it in payment, or sell the note back to a participating bank at a 10 percent discount. The willingness of one or more local banks to facilitate transactions in the discount notes would give the expanded program a strong, viable base and provide instant credibility.

Implementation of an Expanded Berk-Shares program would build on the success of the existing Berk-Shares project. Specific tasks include: (1) consummating arrangements (such as contractual agreements) with local banks and merchants, and setting up the necessary procedures for the issuer as well as the participating banks and merchants; (2) printing the discount notes; (3) compiling and printing a directory of participating businesses; (4) printing signs and decals for store windows; and (5) arranging publicity including meetings with local business groups (such as Rotary or a chamber of commerce) and the media. The issuer must generally be prepared to answer all requests for information about the program. Involving local business groups, such as a chamber of commerce or Rotary, will give the program further credibility.

The expenses of the year-round bargain purchase program could be met from four sources. First, as with the current Berk-Shares program, each participating business would pay a specified annual fee. Second, the interest earned on the bank deposit account between the time the Berk-Shares are purchased by a consumer and redemption by a merchant would cover a part of the financial institution's expenses. Third, the banks and store owners would arrange to share handling expenses incurred in connection with the notes.

Fourth, the program would encounter the extraordinary first-year start-up expenses, particularly those incurred by the initial demonstration project. These expenses include: (1) dealing with the media and educating the public; (2) preparing materials (handouts) to answer questions from the media and the public; and (3) spending time with bank directors and merchants. Foundation support may be needed to provide the necessary funds for staff members of sponsoring organizations as well as brochures.

As other communities adopt this local currency model, first-year start-up expenses and time commitment will substantially diminish. For example, other sponsors will be able to call chamber of commerce officers and bank executives connected with the original Expanded Berk-Shares project and "pick their brains."

Once the pilot program gets off the ground, after, say, one year of operation, the project should be firmly based in the business and banking community, thereby ensuring a broad and sustainable commitment to local economic development. The program will provide a model for other urban and rural communities seeking to ensure that wealth generated in a region recirculates in that area.

CONCLUSION

Innovative discount coupon programs provide businesses and communities with new methods for improving local economies. Instead of using bargain purchase scrip simply as a technique for attracting new customers, businesses and communities can use this type of instrument to support their local economy and locally owned firms. In practice, these programs have been very successful. Consideration should be given to implementing these programs in communities throughout the United States. Such projects educate consumers about the importance of buying locally and enable them to strengthen their local economy in an easy, practical manner. If you are interested in starting a discount coupon program, contact the E. F. Schumacher Society, Box 76, RD 3, Great Barrington, MA 01230, or phone the Society at 413-528-1737. These bargain purchase scrip programs set the stage for the next step—a local currency not pegged to the U.S. dollar.

six

Local Currency Not Pegged to the U.S. Dollar

The development of a local currency based on barter transactions or one pegged to the U.S. dollar represent significant steps forward. However, the importance of creating a local currency which does not use the U.S. dollar to measure the value of goods and services cannot be stressed enough. Only when this is accomplished will it be possible to achieve the major objectives set out in Chapter 3, namely: (1) strengthening urban and rural communities by promoting decentralization and local self-reliance based on linking producers with consumers; (2) reducing unemployment and underemployment in a region or city by promoting local job creation in an ecologically sound manner; and (3) promoting economic stability by providing a noninflationary currency with a constant purchasing power, in contrast to the U.S. dollar which has continually diminished in value because of the irresponsible issuance of paper money resulting in general price inflation. Thus, decoupling the value of a local currency from the value of the U.S. dollar means that as the U.S. dollar continues to be debased, the value of a local currency should rise.

After describing the Constant local currency project of the 1970s, this chapter considers the basics of creating a viable local currency including: (1) the reserve for its issue; (2) who will be the issuer; and (3) the relationship of the issuer to the existing banks. Also discussed are several possible objections to a local currency not geared to the U.S. dollar.

THE CONSTANT PROJECT

For a number of years, Ralph Borsodi, an economic consultant and a pioneer in self-sufficient living experiments, had sought to create a currency based on a basket of a specified number of commodities with the proportion of each commodity in the basket equal to the rate at which each commodity is produced and consumed in the world. Such a system would be little affected by excesses or shortages in any one commodity but would keep fairly in line with aggregate economy activity. Borsodi asserted that if his program realized its potential, inflation would cease to exist.[1]

Borsodi expected that the alternative monetary system, if widely adopted, could stabilize prices by making the price of the commodities basket (a rough price index) stable at the basket's face value. Stability would be achieved by the private interest of competing organizations issuing the money. Each issuer of a local currency would be committed to maintain a money supply designed to keep a specified price index at a particular value. The system would not rely on the wisdom or benevolence of public sector management.

In 1973, Borsodi implemented his local currency project. He issued a currency, called the Constant, in the town of Exeter, New Hampshire.[2] The currency, issued in denominations of 10, 50, and 100 Constants, was designed to remain constant in value over time.

In theory, the value of the Constant was to be based on the market value of a basket of thirty commodities[3] including agricultural commodities, metals, and energy sources with the value of each reflecting the relative global production and consumption of each commodity. The commodities making up the basket were chosen to make their aggregate value correlate as closely as possible with the general price level. As a standard of value, Borsodi used a basket consisting of large numbers of tangible commodities: (1) that were internationally used and consumed, internationally wanted, traded, and valued; (2) which in the aggregate were designed to be constant in value; (3) which could be used to redeem money; and (4) which would always be amply supplied and thus available for redemption. A change in the nonmonetary demand or production technology might alter the value of one commodity in the basket; it would only impact slightly on the value of the whole bundle.[4]

The Constant circulated as hand-to-hand money for eighteen months from June 1972 to January 1974, proving that people would use a currency other than the U.S. dollar. Estimates indicate that about 180 people owned Constants and actively participated in the experiment.[5] Merchants accepted the Constant in payment for goods and services; customers received change in Constants or U.S. dollars. The Exeter police even accepted Constants in payment of parking violations.[6]

Two local banks permitted customers to open checking accounts denominated in Constants. In the Constant experiment, Independent Arbitrage International (IAI), a nonprofit corporation, ran a joint checking account for all participants with an average monthly balance of $100,000. The two participating banks treated the IAI account as one account with many signatures. People made U.S. dollar deposits into the IAI account, which was kept in Constants, through which IAI did all the bookkeeping. Withdrawals were made directly at the two local banks against the IAI account. The IAI also redeemed Constants for U.S. dollars according to dollar-conversion tables which were widely available in Exeter. Merchants who received more Constants in trade than they could use for their own buying needs went to two participating banks (or to the IAI office) and exchanged them for U.S. dollars at the prevailing dollar-Constant exchange rate.[7]

In the Exeter project, because the Constants were not in fact backed by an actual basket of commodities, holders lacked the ability to obtain physical delivery of the specified commodities in exchange for surrendering a paper certificate. Because Borsodi was not able to acquire enough funds to fully implement the project, IAI never purchased the basket of commodities to back the currency. Instead, IAI invested the holders' funds in short-term U.S. Treasury securities. As the Constants were redeemed, the participants realized a small profit because the Constants rose 17 percent in value in relation to the U.S. dollar during the eighteen-month period of the experiment.[8]

The Constant project was self-funded. Borsodi and several associates "invested" about $100,000 as a reserve for the project. To redeem Constants in U.S. dollars, Borsodi expected that the interest income on U.S. Treasury securities held by IAI would cover not only the increases in the value of the Constant but also the project's bookkeeping and other costs. However, in addition to the interest generated by the investments in U.S. Treasury obligations, Borsodi and his associates also dipped into their own funds to cover the increased costs of redeeming the Constants, which resulted from their appreciation in value vis-à-vis the U.S. dollar.[9]

Although the experiment demonstrated the feasibility and acceptability of an inflation-proof currency,[10] Borsodi realized more funds were needed for full-scale implementation of the project. He estimated that a viable long-term project would have required an investment in 1973 of $250,000 U.S. dollars (about $750,000 today). Borsodi hoped to cover the cost of a large-scale, future venture by hiring an arbitrageur who would generate profits by engaging in arbitrage activities, that is, commodity speculation focusing on taking offsetting positions in one commodity or between/among similar commodities, or in buying a commodity (or futures contract) in one national market and selling in another national market.[11] If the projected arbitrage activities proved successful, minute price differentials would have resulted in substantial profits as a result of the large trading transaction in large quantities. In short, arbitrage would have afforded the opportunity to earn substantial profits to cover the expenses of an expanded, commodity-backed local currency experiment.

Borsodi was unable to implement his grand vision. In 1974, he discontinued the Constant project after it was underway for eighteen months because of his advanced age and because he felt it achieved the desired results. In addition, a major difficulty arose which blocked Borsodi from expanding the use of Constants, namely, the public lacked a sufficient understanding of the program. While this problem could have been overcome in due time, given sufficient resources and staff, the Exeter experiment ended before the project generated widespread, local public acceptance.

During the eighteen-month Constant experiment, the purchasing value of the paper certificate remained constant relative to the price of the basket of commodities and increased relative to the U.S. dollar. All those who participated were satisfied with the project, happily receiving a profit when they redeemed Constants for U.S. dollars at the end of the experiment. In sum, the short-lived Constant program confirmed Borsodi's belief that an inflation-proof currency could actually exist.

CREATING A VIABLE LOCAL CURRENCY IN COMMUNITIES THROUGHOUT THE UNITED STATES

The implementation of a viable local currency project rests on securing the broad-based participation of a number of local businesses and individuals who would agree to accept the alternative scrip in payment for goods and services. To promote membership and participation, the organizers should begin by listing participating businesses and the individuals in a directory of member businesses and individuals and in advertisements naming member businesses and individuals.

In addition to obtaining widespread community interest in a local currency project and focusing on a myriad of administrative details, discussed later in this chapter, at the outset, the organizers face three key issues: (1) how should the local currency be backed; (2) who will be the issuer; and (3) what will be the relationship of the project to the banking system.

Backing the Local Currency

Backing a local currency with a reserve/redemption system provides a number of benefits. A reserve/redemption system creates and maintains confidence in the scrip. Such a system convinces people in a community as to the value of a currency. A reserve/redemption mechanism also provides protection against fraud and any tendency to devalue the currency by overissuance. Also, if the commodity circulates widely outside the community, providing a relatively stable basis for exchange, it permits U.S. dollar-holder redemption where external trade is involved.

Thus, a need exists to establish a backing mechanism—a measurement of value—for the alternative currency that would be as universal as possible and subject to few swings in value upward or downward. The alternative scrip should remain as constant in value as possible to establish a sense of security and permanency. The organizers must, therefore, determine into what commodity or basket of commodities will the paper money be convertible.

A local currency could be backed in one of three ways: (1) a single universal commodity, such as gold; (2) a single commodity which has special importance for the local economy, such as a cord of wood, which is widely traded in local commerce; or (3) composite commodity standard based on a market basket of commodities designed to be stable and apolitical.

Gold-Backed Currency

Gold traditionally had a number of advantages as a currency reserve. First, gold has a high value-to-weight ratio and thus is relatively portable. Second, it is easily subdivided and recombined. Finally, gold is relatively easy to measure and to evaluate as genuine. However, a number of problems exist with using gold as a commodity reserve for a modern local currency. The purchasing power of gold depends on the interaction between supply of and demand for a relatively unimportant industrial substance being supplied and demanded primarily for monetary purposes. World production of gold bears little or no relationship to world production of all commodities. The value of gold has, over the past fifteen years, varied erratically; its purchasing power has been subject to violent and sudden fluctuations. Gold also fluctuates widely in value relative to other commodities.

If the idea of a local currency system takes off, there may not be enough gold to serve as a reserve for the amount of money needed to be issued for normal requirements of the modern business world. In other words, a shortage of gold may exist on a worldwide basis.

Currency Backed By a Single, Locally Based Commodity

An issuer may wish to create a local currency based on a community's principal good or service, thereby proving, in part, credit necessary to finance such production. In contemplating a single reserve commodity for a community financial system, the designated commodity must, of course, be produced by the community. Otherwise, the stability of a local financial system depends on trading activities with other commodities which are not produced by the community, not the relative abundance of the selected commodity in the community.

Historically, different communities used various commodities either as money or to back currencies at different times and often more than one type of commodity was used in the community at the same time. Also, a commodity used as money often was consumable (e.g., tobacco). Using a consumable commodity provided a way to control the volume of money created and thus control inflation. Use of produce, such as grain, has modern-day appeal because the quantity of money created will reflect the volume of economic activity in the community. Grain is also in common use and represents a community need. However, the production of agricultural produce can vary widely and thus suffer wide changes in value. The value of a single consumable commodity, such as grain, often is influenced by transitory conditions, such as weather, and its market can be more easily manipulated by large traders and governments. One possibility, grain, suffers from two further disadvantages. It is perishable, making storage difficult. Grain also has a low value on a per-pound basis.

Another contemporary possibility turns on using forest resources, specifically cordwood, as a reserve commodity.[12] Forests increase in quantity over time as they grow. Unlike grain, the rate of growth of forests remains consistent regardless of weather, because of the deep root system and ability to withstand hot or cold weather. Fire and wind, although posing a natural danger to trees, constitute only a small percentage of loss; certainly less than the rate of growth of forests. The most prevalent modern danger centers on human beings who destroy forests in search for timber and energy. The use of forests as a reserve commodity provides a number of advantages. Such a reserve would increase the value of standing trees, help heighten the awareness of the value of trees, and facilitate ecologically sound, sustainable long-term forest management.

From an ecological perspective, wood constitutes a renewable resource which can be put to a number of uses. For instance, wood is used in buildings, it can be converted into many kinds of plastics, it serves as a food source in the case of nut and fruit trees, and wood also constitutes a renewable energy source. Wood wastes from forests, specifically from dead, diseased, overmature, overcrowded trees, can efficiently be converted into energy, in a nonpolluting manner. Wood does not contain sulphur, the primary source of pollution from coal. With the right technology, such as a pyrolytic converter, wood can produce heat, gas, and electricity at a cost competitive with other forms of energy.

More specifically, using forests as a currency reserve focuses on cordwood obtained by culling excess timber in a forest. Cordwood represents a locally produced commodity in a number of areas in the United States, such as western Massachusetts. Landowners pay to have their over-grown woodlots thinned. Access to cordwood is available to anyone who owns or rents a chain saw and who is willing to work hard. The timber so obtained is bundled up into a four-foot by four-foot by eight-foot package described as a cord. Thus the term "cordwood," which is used to denote a package of 128 cubic feet of green mixed hardwoods, cut to sixteen inches, split to five inches, which when stacked equals three stacks of sixteen-inch wood, eight feet long by four feet wide.

To satisfy any demand for redemption in kind on the part of the holders of the local paper currency, the issuer could actually buy and hold the requisite cordwood. More likely, however, the issuer would enter into option contracts with local cordwood dealers, under which dealers would agree to deliver and the issuer would agree to purchase a standard cord of split, green hardwood for a fixed dollar price, from specified woodlots owned by or under contract to the dealers. If the issuer lacks sufficient U.S. dollars to redeem the local currency presented, the issuer would exercise its option contracts and purchase the cordwood. The option contract would provide that within a specified number of days after the issuer's demand, the dealer would deliver required cords of wood from a specified geographical area and the issuer would make full payment to the dealer at time of delivery, in U.S. dollars or alternative scrip, at the option of the dealer. Any arrangement between the issuer and a dealer must provide a fallback/default mechanism if a dealer is unable or unwilling to perform, for example, because the price of cordwood spirals upward. If the dealer is unable to perform on issuer's demand, the dealer could then pay the issuer, for example, 20 percent (or some other mutually agreed-upon percentage) of the purchase price of the cordwood for which the option is granted.

Despite the seeming elegance of using cordwood as a reserve commodity, the proposal suffers from a number of disadvantages. It might promote speculation in forest land and propel the increased indiscriminate cutting of timber. Beyond these suppositions, three practical hurdles exist: (1) there is no uniformity in the supply of cordwood; (2) there is a lack of dependable supplies of cordwood; and (3) there is no futures market for cordwood. Also, the price of cordwood parallels in large measure the fluctuations in the price of petroleum. Because of the impact of the Organization of Petroleum Countries (OPEC) cartel, the petroleum does not freely trade on the spot or futures market.

Consideration may be given to using some form of energy, preferably renewable energy, as a unit of measurement and as the reserve commodity.[13] Renewable energy sources can be converted into electricity and measured in kilowatt hours. The paper money can then be backed by power produced by a renewable energy source—a unit of electrical power output, namely, a kilowatt hour.

The owner of an electrical power generator, for instance, a community-based business which produces energy from locally available sources, could serve as the issuer of a local currency. The alternative scrip could take the form of a voucher or note to supply a specified number of kilowatt hours of electricity at a specified future time.

The owner of the generator could issue the notes and use the U.S. dollars received in exchange for the notes to pay for the purchase and installation of electrical generators using renewable energy sources. The aggregate output of the generators would limit the value of notes which could be issued and redemption provided for within a given time period. The community organization would issue notes in an amount equal to the projected output of electricity, thereby guarding against an excessive issuance and the accompanying currency devaluation. The holder of an energy note would further be protected against future increases in electricity rates.

The issuer would offer notes for sale at the going rate for electricity. For instance, if the local utility rate is 10 U.S. cents per kilowatt hour, a one note, initially pegged at one U.S. dollar, would buy 10 kilowatt hours of electricity for future delivery. The energy-backed notes could be sold in denominations of 10, 50, and 100 units.

An energy-based alternative currency provides a number of ecological and human advantages. Energy would be produced locally from renewable sources. Also, a renewable energy system is democratic within a community because each individual could own a small, renewable electrical energy source to supply personal needs as well as others' needs.

Anti-inflation economic benefits also exist. The volume of energy paper money to be created directly relates to the installed capacity of electrical generators which is, in turn, related to the total economic activity in the community. Correlating the amount of local currency with a community's economic activity should provide a safeguard against an inflationary spiral resulting from an oversupply of paper money.

The electricity generated by a community-owned, renewable energy source could be fed into the existing grids of utility companies, thereby yielding cash for the community-based organization. Federal legislation, the Public Utility Regulating Policies Act of 1978, requires utilities to buy power at a "just and reasonable" price from individuals or groups who own generators producing electric power from various sources, including renewable energy sources.[14] The power seller must be a "qualifying small power production facility," specifically, a solar, wind, waste, or geothermal facility which has a minimal (less than 80 percent megawatts) production capacity.[15]

The purchaser utility could pay for the generated power by check denominated in U.S. dollars or the local currency. The utility could also agree to accept the alternative scrip issued by the community-based energy organization in payment for the utility bills of its customers, kilo-watt hour for kilowatt hour. The issuing community organization could also serve as the note redeemer based on its earnings from its ownership of a renewable energy source which generates electricity.

An energy-based currency, for example, backed by electricity gener-ated from renewable energy sources, suffers from several disadvantages. Just as with cordwood, OPEC fixes petroleum prices which in turn gen-erally impact on energy prices, including electricity. Current federal en-ergy policies also subsidize the production of centralized energy sources. The future removal of such subsidies (or the provision of subsidies for renewable energy production or energy conservation) would make small power generators more competitive with large, centralized generators using nonrenewable energy sources. In other words, a shift in federal policies would facilitate using renewable sources, such as electricity, as a currency reserve.

Currency Backed by a Basket of Commodities

Finally, consideration must be given to Borsodi's concept of a basket of commodities as a reserve mechanism. The issuer could back a local currency, in whole or in part, with a basket of commodities whose his-toric price increases have mirrored (or exceeded) the rate of inflation in the United States. To ensure that no commodity would have a disruptive influence resulting from extreme price changes, the basket would contain a number of different commodities. A commodity basket would be more stable than any one component of the basket. Stability is enhanced by choosing a mix of commodities and their respective weighting to ensure stable purchasing power of the basket over time.

The issuer must first decide on a list of commodities to include in the basket defining the value of the currency. The issuer should select com-modities for which well-developed international markets exist. Instead of Borsodi's thirty commodities, perhaps only three to twelve different commodities need be used.

Next, the issuer must prepare the basket by determining the specific weights for each component commodity. The issuer should back test the basket by computer simulation with actual prices from the past thirty years to include several price shocks such as the oil and gold boom of the 1970s. In short, the issuer should select a basket which has a stable purchasing value (a constant value) in the international market over time.

The storage of commodities is expensive and impractical for a large collection of items. No need exists to hold physical commodities because of the proliferation of organized commodity futures exchanges where cash and futures prices of many different commodities are daily deter-mined in an open auction by the forces of supply and demand. Thus, a nonpublic sector issuer of a commodity basket–based currency need not store the physical commodities, but need only hold futures contracts on the commodities. A futures contract is a contract in which a buyer agrees to accept delivery at a specified price of a specified quantity of the commodity at a designated future time.

Each commodity publicly traded on a commodities exchange increasingly has one world price.[16] As a result of instantaneous, worldwide satellite communication, market participants know the prices of all traded commodities at the same time. Major price differences no longer exist between different locales, except those based on transportation costs. The emergence of one world price helps the issuer of a commodity-based currency by eliminating arbitrage opportunities.

Despite the benefits afforded by a basket of commodities, several questions remain. First, what if a general collapse occurs in the commodity markets? Second, what is the relevance of a basket of commodities to a smaller community (region or city) seeking a stable, independent monetary system? In other words, the issuer should strive to design a basket of commodities that will reflect the growth in productivity of a local economy over time. Third, will the organizer of a local currency system possess the power to change commodities in the basket and their relative amounts? To guard against this possibility, the system should provide for a reference unit of value which is not subject to discretion, except in time of local emergency, as to what commodities are used and in what proportions.

The emergence of interest-generating, constant-value money market funds enables the issuer of an alternative scrip to back its currency, in whole or in part, by the acquisition of money market assets in the form of a variety of funds based in different nations. Thus, in addition to (or as an alternative to) the commodity basket, a local currency could also be backed by the issuer investing in non–U.S. money market funds based in a number of economically and politically stable countries, and denominated in German marks, Japanese yen, or Swiss francs. Investing in non–U.S. hard currency money market funds enables an issuer to back its currency, in whole or in part, with money market assets that provide protection against the depreciation in the value of the U.S. dollar.[17]

Conclusion

Having surveyed possible currency reserve mechanisms in this section, one point stands out. To provide confidence in the value of a locally issued alternative currency not pegged to the U.S. dollar, some type of redemption mechanism seems essential. Which reserve system, gold, a local-based commodity, or basket of commodities, would predominate is uncertain. Not unexpectedly, "gold bugs" would guess that gold, with its long history and continued serviceability as well as its tangibility as a redemption medium, would have a competitive advantage.

Two points are, however, reasonably certain. First, competition among issuers would reveal which redemption system better secures the trust of the public. Second, the issuer should back its currency with assets which represent value in the production and distribution chain (i.e., assets on the way to market) or assets which can easily be liquidated in small amounts. An issuer should not use real estate or capital equipment as a reserve for its currency.

Who Will Issue the Currency?

The question of who will issue the currency is not often discussed. However, the nature of the organization issuing and regulating the local currency must be considered as well as a number of implementation details and the need to publicize the project.

Organizational and Membership Structure

In considering who will issue the currency, proponents of an alternative currency system would assert that the profit motive provides issuers with an incentive to create a mechanism to achieve operational efficiency guided by a more or less effective goal—profitability. However, a nonprofit or cooperative organization offers significant advantages.

Using a nonprofit or cooperative structure will help the public understand that the issuing organization will not unduly benefit any individuals or group of persons. In other words, a nonprofit or cooperative structure reinforces the social and ecological function of a local currency system. Thus, in many areas of the United States, alternative currency systems would be organized at the local level and controlled by the entire community. The issuing organization, furthermore, should be free of any government regulation or control, except for existing inspection and disclosure rules and regulations applicable to all nonprofit or cooperative organizations and those institutions engaged in the issuance of currency, to prevent decision making based on political grounds or motives.

Carrying out the themes of community control and personal empowerment, the issuing organization should be democratic in structure with membership and voting rights open not only to business persons (producers, merchants, and service persons) and nonprofit organizations but also to all residents of the region or community. The members will elect the board of directors who will oversee the currency issuance. The members will further establish the organization's goals and the basic ground rules for the currency issuance.

Organizational Details

Beyond deciding on form of the organization and its membership criteria, setting up a nonprofit or cooperative organization involves the following six administrative details:

1. Form a protem group;
2. Enlist potential members through discussions at public meetings and by means of letters;
3. Form the organization and promulgate a set of bylaws;[18]
4. The members will elect a board of directors who will monitor the operation of the organization and the currency issuance;
5. The board will then hire an administrator, on a volunteer or paid basis, to supervise: the printing of the currency; advertising and public relations; making contractual arrangements; handling bookkeeping; and engaging in troubleshooting;
6. Periodically (annually, or more frequently) publish a list of members as well as a newsletter.

In addition to these administrative details, the organizers of a local currency system must focus on the design of the currency. Although hard-and-fast principles do not exist, the currency should conform, in considerable degree, to the size and denominations of Federal Reserve notes. Nevertheless, it should be clearly different in color, printed words, and images. Any reserve/redemption system as well as issuer should clearly be indicated on the currency.

Effective anticounterfeiting measures exist and must be utilized. Governments and issuing central banks currently utilize these techniques to protect their currencies. Anticounterfeiting measures include: close scrutiny of the printing process; use of special inks and papers; and serial numbering of the currency. Also, the possible designation of a limited area in which a local scrip will be accepted discourages the counterfeiting outside the specified region.

The organization must also carefully assess and provide a means to cover normal business start-up and operating expenses. These expenditures include incorporating, printing the currency, publicity, and time to work out the system with local businesses. Techniques available to meet expenses include: (1) assessing membership fees, both initially and periodically thereafter, and (2) implementing a fixed fee for redemption of the currency which will reduce the tendency for holders to opt for redemption and pay for the cost of the currency's commodity-backing. Just as with a local currency system pegged to the U.S. dollar, foundation support may be needed to provide the necessary funds to cover start-up staff and promotional expenses. As other communities adopt a local currency not pegged to the U.S. dollar, first-year start-up expenses as well as the accompanying time commitment on the part of the organizers should substantially diminish.

Publicizing the Local Currency

After surmounting the array of administrative details, the sponsoring organization will start by issuing hand-to-hand currency in order to make it visible, to promote the concept, and to educate the public. The local currency will initially be issued to members and circulate among members. The organization should encourage employees of member businesses and local governmental bodies, as well as the general public to accept the currency. Employees of member businesses should be encouraged to accept part of their wages in the local currency. Governments could permit the use of local currency to pay a portion of any tax bills. The public sector could distribute a portion of welfare, workfare, and other payments (e.g., to its employees) in the alternative scrip.

To avoid the corrosive effects of U.S. dollar inflation in the community, the alternative currency must circulate sufficiently so that a significant portion of all wages could be paid in local currency. Wage earners could then make purchases without exchanging U.S. dollars for the local currency.

As part of the general promotional process, the sponsoring organization should publish and disseminate a newsletter and supply print and radio-TV journalists with press releases designed to educate the public as to what is going on. It is essential that the sponsor educate the public on the usefulness and advantages of the local currency. Without widespread public support, the program will encounter difficulties in succeeding.

After the hand-to-hand currency gains credibility and reasonably wide circulation, the issuing organization should consider implementing alternative scrip-denominated checking and savings accounts, credit and debit cards, and electronic funds transfers as well as currency availability at automatic teller machines. As part of these steps, the issuer must involve one or more banks in local currency transactions. Working with one or more banks whose physical facilities and staff are already in place will reduce overhead costs and enable the alternative scrip to gain widespread acceptance.

Relationship of the Issuer and the Local Currency System to Banks

Once the currency begins to circulate in a community or a region, the issuer should involve one or more banks in the alternative system with the aim of developing a broad local market and trade in the currency.

Bank participation heightens the visibility of the local currency and gives it additional credibility. Also, the risk of counterfeiting decreases as the currency passes under the hand-to-hand watchful eye of bank tellers.

Creating an Issuer–Bank Relationship

Using a bank's existing physical facilities and staff reduces the currency issuer's overhead costs. Initially, the issuer could involve a local bank in the servicing of alternative currency accounts. The bank might begin by handling deposits into and withdrawals from two specially designated local currency accounts.[19]

The issuer–bank relationship could commence with the issuer opening two special accounts at the participating bank (or banks): one would be a money market account which would only accept U.S. dollar deposits by the issuer or the public; and a second, a business checking account which would serve as an account for limited local currency withdrawals, as discussed below. When the fund balance in the checking account drops below a specified level, the bank would be authorized to transfer funds from the money market account to the checking account.

To facilitate bank involvement with the alternative currency system, the issuer would begin by placing part of its local currency notes in a safe deposit box at the bank. The issuer would ask the bank to designate one or more tellers to service the two local scrip accounts. The teller(s) would have authority to withdraw and deposit local currency in the safe deposit box. Each business day the teller would keep a supply of the alternative currency at his/her window. The issuer would assume the initial responsibility for providing the current information on the exchange rate between the local currency and the U.S. dollar. It is highly likely that the media would also carry exchange rate information.

An individual wishing to purchase the local currency would go to the designated teller and deposit Federal Reserve notes into the money market account and receive, in return, the alternative scrip at the prevailing exchange rate. To promote efficiency, the bank could require a U.S. dollar deposit equal to a specific minimum amount of local currency. Anyone could make a deposit into the money market account and receive local currency in return, subject to the bank having an adequate supply of the local scrip to meet the needs of the exchange transaction.

The bank would also offer limited withdrawals in U.S. dollars from the issuer's checking account. Initially, withdrawals could be limited to those member businesses and individuals having written authorization from the issuer to make withdrawals. An authorized merchant would fill out a withdrawal slip. The teller would verify the signature on the withdrawal authorization card and check the identification of the card-holder. Once these items were verified, the teller would make payment, at the current exchange rate, in U.S. dollars withdrawn from the issuer's checking account. If there were insufficient funds in the issuer's checking account to meet a verified request for a withdrawal in U.S. dollars, the teller would so notify the customer. The issuer would assume full responsibility for maintaining sufficient U.S. dollar funds in its checking account at the participating bank.

The issuer and the bank should also consider building flexibility into the program by permitting the issuer periodically, initially perhaps quarterly, to transfer funds into or out of the money market account and/or the checking account without the receipt or transfer of local currency. Even if the bank and the issuer agree on this mechanism, the transfer of funds might only be undertaken by a supermajority (e.g., two-thirds) of the directors or the issuer.

Stepping back from these details, the issuer and the bank should clearly delineate the responsibility of each party in the implementation of an alternative currency system, with the participating bank offering predefined services to the community at competitive rates. Basically, the issuer should bear legal and financial responsibility for the local currency program. The bank would merely service transactions between the issuer and its customers who are also members of the alternative system. Apart from any currency exchange transactions, the designated teller could also be authorized to change denominations of the local scrip on the request of the bank's customers and members of the public.

The bank would be responsible for all normal recordkeeping and for the reporting of all transactions in the issuer's money market account and the checking account. The bank would provide the issuer, initially on a weekly basis, with a copy of deposit and withdrawal slips pertaining to the money market account and the checking accounts. Periodically, initially perhaps quarterly, the bank would verify the amount of local currency on hand and reconcile that amount with the amount of alternative scrip originally received from the issuer.

During the first year of operation, the bank would not be responsible for discrepancies in accounting for local currency on hand. During this period, the issuer would assume responsibility for the amount of local scrip on hand in the bank. The one-year experimental period would provide the bank, its employees, the issuer, the issuer's members, and the public with time to work efficiently with the new system. After the first year, the issuer would require the bank to establish a percentage of possible error in handling the local currency transactions and to assume responsibility for discrepancies above that margin.

Although subject to negotiations between the issuer and the bank, the bank would probably not assume responsibility for at least three items: (1) insufficient funds for withdrawals from the checking account; (2) counterfeit local currency notes exchanged; or (3) keeping a supply of the local currency on hand.

As compensation to the bank for providing the various services in connection with the local currency system, for the first year the issuer would basically assume all risk for the operation of the program. During this period, the bank and its employees would incur no responsibility for any loss or discrepancies in the alternative currency account or available from the safe deposit box. Thereafter, as indicated below, the bank would assume responsibility for discrepancy in handling local currency transactions above a specified margin of error.

As continuing compensation to the bank for the time spent servicing two special accounts, the bank's involvement in the project would, it is hoped, bring increased activity to the bank and be a statement of the bank's commitment to local interests, thereby earning the bank additional regular accounts and customers. The issuer could also agree to seek new customers for the bank who would indicate they were establishing a banking relationship because of the bank's cooperation with the issuer in expanding the implementation of the alternative currency project. In the alternative, after the first year, the bank could assess the issuer with an agreed-upon fee for handling the special accounts and the local currency transactions.

Community Reinvestment Acts Will Serve to Spur Bank Involvement

The obligations of banks under federal and state community reinvestment acts constitute a powerful incentive for bank participation in a local currency system. As part of the Federal Housing and Community Development Act of 1977, in the Community Reinvestment Act (CRA),[20] the U.S. Congress determined that federally regulated financial institutions must demonstrate that their deposit facilities and credit services serve the "convenience and needs of the communities in which they are chartered to do business."[21] Specifically, in connection with an examination of a bank, "the appropriate Federal financial supervisory agency shall— (1) assess the institution's record of meeting the credit needs of its entire community, including low- and moderate-income neighborhoods consistent with the safe and sound operation of such institution; and (2) take such record into account in its evaluation of an application for a deposit facility by such institution."[22] An application for a deposit facility includes a request for a bank charter, deposit insurance, the establishment of a branch, or the merger or acquisition of another insured bank.

Implementation of the CRA is directly entrusted to the various federal regulators of financial institutions. Through the examination process, regulators develop their own guidelines to encourage banks to meet community needs.[23] Generally, all loans must be reported and are scrutinized as part of a determination of compliance with CRA. Examiners generally require that loans of a certain type be available in every community served by the bank, although not every borrower need be eligible. As amended by the Housing and Community Development Act of 1992, the CRA further authorizes regulators to consider the efforts of banks to invest and participate in loans, and otherwise engage in ventures with female and minority-owned financial institutions that benefit a community by meeting a local community's credit needs.[24] Federal examiners rate each bank. Those with unsatisfactory community reinvestment ratings face difficulties in obtaining approval for new activities or acquisitions.

In addition, many states have adopted specific community reinvestment legislation. State laws vary, from those that basically restate federal law, to others that provide for state regulatory evaluation according to assessment factors which depart from the federal pattern.[25] Furthermore, regulators in states outside the bank's jurisdiction of incorporation also consider the community reinvestment record of a bank-holding company before allowing that holding company to engage in an interstate acquisition in their jurisdiction.[26]

Building Further Bank Involvement with a Local Currency System

Hand-to-hand currency is not, however, a primary medium of exchange in the United States. Book entries—checks and electronic funds transfers—have replaced the physical transfer of currency as a means of discharging monetary obligations. Thus, after one or more banks become involved in and achieve a level of comfort with an alternative scrip system, the issuer should obtain bank participation with local currency–denominated checking accounts, savings accounts, automatic teller machine transactions, credit and debt cards, and electronic funds transfers.

As banks permit depositors to issue checks (or electronic funds transfers) denominated in the new currency, a need arises for a private clearinghouse to permit banks to swap checks drawn on other banks, which are denominated in the local scrip, and tendered by customers for deposit or loan repayment, among other transactions. A check exchange arrangement will increase the marketability of an alternative currency system. It will improve negotiability of every participant's checks. A clearinghouse will enhance the "moneyness" of the currency or checks relative to the redeemable, reserve commodity backing the scrip.

More specifically, a private clearinghouse mechanism facilitates the mutual acceptance of checks at face value by participating banks as well as the periodic settlement of the claims each bank collects against the others. In settling these interbank claims, members of a clearinghouse may economize in commodity reserve transshipments by settling balances partly through transfer of highly marketable, interest-bearing assets.

Despite the proliferation of book entry systems—checks and electronic funds transfers and the emergence of private clearinghouses—hand-to-hand currency will survive. Cash provides three advantages: It is convenient to use in small payments; its acceptance entails no risk that the payor's funds may be insufficient; and it leaves behind no possibly incriminating records of payments.[27]

Issuer–Bank Participation in Making Local Currency Loans

Issuer-bank cooperation can also build upon more than a decade of experience with Self-Help Association for a Regional Economy (SHARE) loans.[28] As part of an alternative scrip system, SHARE loans denominated in the local currency could be made to finance "productive" local businesses. The SHARE approach to lending represents a particularly appealing technique to people interested in entering into loans denominated in an alternative currency.

A detailed examination of the SHARE approach to lending is useful. SHARE traditionally targets prospective borrowers who typically do not hold significant assets because they are young or unemployed. Any assets presently owned by a young or unemployed person (e.g., a car) are likely to be mortgaged to a financial institution.

Typically, SHARE loans help promote small business ventures that produce locally consumed goods and services. SHARE coordinates borrowers with those willing to invest in local businesses that are unable to obtain conventional bank financing. SHARE creates a source of funds which are lent by a local bank at favorable (below market) interest rates to businesses or individuals meeting SHARE's criteria but who are unable to obtain or cannot afford conventional bank financing. The low interest rate SHARE offers borrowers provides very significant assistance to small businesses getting started. Any business or individual in the community or region may apply for collateral support from SHARE for loans to be made through the participating bank. If a loan proposal meets SHARE's criteria, SHARE approves the use of its depositors to collateralize the loan.

In providing the collateral support for loans, SHARE operates as a membership organization open to anyone in the region who opens a SHARE account at a local participating bank. The minimum deposit in the SHARE account is $100; it is an interest-bearing ninety-day notice account. Most deposits run between $100 and $500. There are no really large deposits. When opening a SHARE account, a depositor agrees to keep money on deposit for two years and let SHARE use 75 percent of the account's deposit to collateralize loans meeting its social, environmental, and financial criteria. SHARE advises all the depositors in the program that withdrawals of 75 percent of the funds in a passbook account will be restricted in the event a SHARE loan defaults, but that withdrawals from the 75 percent of such funds will be honored in order of receipt when the defaulted loan is repaid. At least 25 percent of any deposit in a SHARE account is available for withdrawal at any time, subject to the bank's rules. However, SHARE discourages frequent withdrawals by requesting that depositors view their accounts as long-term investments in the community.

SHARE is a nonprofit, democratically controlled, community-based organization. Depositors become members of SHARE and are entitled to elect the organization's board of directors, who serve on a volunteer basis. Members also help shape SHARE's loan criteria and are entitled to apply for business loans through SHARE.

Loan proposals are made to SHARE's board, up to a current maximum of $3,000. The board seeks input on a loan proposal from a peer group of local businesspersons in the same field as the applicant, and consumers, who review the loan application. Thus, community members have input into SHARE's loan decisions. After approval by the peer-consumer group, and subject to the final approval of the lending committee of SHARE's board, SHARE's staff goes to the local participating bank with the applicant. Rather than securing a loan with an applicant's assets, as is typically done, SHARE brings sufficient members' passbooks to collateralize the loan. The bank charges the loan applicant interest at the rate of 3 percent above the interest it pays on the passbook deposits.

From a bank's viewpoint it is more efficient to make larger, rather than smaller, loans. The time and paper work involved in making a small loan is approximately the same as with a large loan. Banks thus discourage small loans or, to compensate for the extra expense, charge a higher interest rate for small loans. The SHARE–bank collaboration overcomes the reluctance of banks to make small business loans. The 3 percent premium the bank charges for a SHARE loan represents a fee for the bank's bookkeeping and loan repayment and collection services. The bank does not perform any loan investigatory functions. Because the loans are fully collateralized by passbook deposits, the bank does not assume any lending risks. SHARE depositors assume all of the risks of debtors defaulting on the loans.

SHARE handles the lending aspects of the loan transaction. From SHARE's perspective, the bank's participation avoids imposing on SHARE additional overhead and staff costs. By handling the recording both of funds deposited and borrowed in its normal, routine way, the participating bank's involvement simplifies SHARE's administrative tasks. SHARE funds its operating budget through a one-time membership fee imposed on depositors. SHARE has also sponsored annual, local fund-raising events.

The SHARE–bank collaboration has broader ramifications. Being a successful SHARE borrower creates a future bank credit reference for the borrower who may graduate to a bank's conventional lending window. The bank's participation may also help ensure repayment of the loan because the borrower realizes that his or her credit rating is at stake.

SHARE loans have an unparalleled repayment record. Since 1982, SHARE has made dozens of loans without a default.[29] The 100 percent loan repayment rate stems from the pursuit of three basic community-oriented lending guidelines. First, SHARE strives to facilitate short-term loans, not to exceed two years, which can only be used for producing goods or services for sale. SHARE generally discourages consumer loans. Obviously, the definitions of productive (as opposed to nonproductive) and short-term (as opposed to long-term) are very slippery.

Second, SHARE has sought self-financing ventures which can repay loans relatively quickly. A potential borrower must demonstrate that the probable earnings from goods or services sold to local customers can support interest and principal payments. Thus, a prospective project should be capable of producing more value in a relatively short period than represented by the credit extended. Peer groups, which review proposed loans, play a significant role not only in investigating loans, but also in helping borrowers. The peer groups become aware and supportive of borrowers. In short, in making loans SHARE moves from the premise that if a business serves a community, the community will want it to succeed.

Third, the borrower must be socially and ecologically responsible, for example, by conserving energy, being nonpolluting, striving to use local resources, and increasing local employment. In addition to those who are ecologically friendly, SHARE seeks borrowers who will facilitate the production of basic necessities and promote community self-sufficiency.

In practice, SHARE is more than a loan collateralization program. Members receive newsletters describing businesses that receive collateral support provided by member-depositors. Members take a personal interest in businesses and often steer potential customers to SHARE borrowers. One example illustrates how SHARE's members encourage the development of local markets. A SHARE borrower who produced goat cheese saw her business blossom after SHARE members requested the product at local grocery stores and specialty shops. Thus, community support for businesses receiving SHARE loans increases the success rate of borrowers.

In the context of a local currency system, a community-based, SHARE-type organization could make alternative currency-denominated loans to finance "productive" local businesses, particularly home-based cottage industries. Applicants could be approved by the board of an organization modeled after SHARE. Loans could be made in amounts up to a maximum of $5,000. The loans would take the form of a deposit by the bank into a local currency checking account in the borrower's name. As with a traditional SHARE loan, the participating bank would charge a 3 percent origination fee. The borrower will use the loan to purchase goods and services from local businesses and individuals. As a borrower's enterprise generates revenues, it will repay the SHARE loan, in whole or in part, in the local currency.

POTENTIAL PROBLEMS WITH A LOCAL CURRENCY SYSTEM NOT PEGGED TO THE U.S. DOLLAR

At least three potential problems exist with a local currency system not pegged to the U.S. dollar: (1) whether money is a public good; (2) whether an alternative scrip will be marked by fraud and an overissuance of the currency; and (3) whether there is a natural monopoly in money which will result in the U.S. dollar wiping out any competition. This section discusses each of these objections and seeks to refute the contentions raised by alternative currency opponents.

Is Money a Public Good?

Although there is no generally agreed-upon definition of a public good, the argument runs that if a potential issuer—the producer of a public good—cannot sell the external benefits it would generate, the good (for instance, currency) may be underproduced or not produced at all if left to the free market. For example, the noted economic historian Charles P. Kindleberger refers to the public good provided by money as a unit of account and a standard of measurement.[30]

Arguably, money is a public good because it exhibits, among other characteristics, "nonexcludability" in consumption so that some people act as free riders in that they share in the benefits without cost that others have made sacrifices to acquire. Because of the free availability of money as a unit of account and calculation even to parties who hold little or none of it, a well-behaved, nongovernmental issuer, arguably, could not collect compensation for all the advantages it confers on the general public.[31]

The public good argument can be refuted on both practical and theoretical grounds. On a practical business level, an issuer, particularly a nonprofit, community-based issuer, should at least be able to cover its costs in the issuance and continued operation of a local currency system. Several revenue sources include: (1) imposing an initial and subsequent annual membership fee payable in the local currency or an equivalent amount of U.S. dollars; and (2) a fixed fee, say 5 percent, charged for commodity redemption of the currency, which would reduce the tendency for holders to opt for redemption and pay for the cost of the currency's commodity-backing. Participating banks could generate income from: (1) transaction fees from the purchase and sale of the alternative currency; (2) various services charges; and (3) origination fees (or the interest spread) on loans denominated in the local scrip. Thus, the issuer and the participating banks can cover their costs and the banks earn reasonable profits. Richard W. Rahn, former chief economist of the U.S. Chamber of Commerce, further concludes that issuers can make a profit by providing a currency people consider superior to government money.[32]

On a theoretical level, Lawrence H. White, an economist, offers a number of arguments in support of the conclusion that money is not a public good.[33] According to White, proponents of the public good argument assume that the government can produce a money with the desired characteristics that the non–public sector issuers cannot produce. But, White asserts that there is simply no evidence of this. Furthermore, a government currency monopoly can stay in business producing a money worse than a non–public sector producer likely would.

White next refutes the argument that the government provides a public good by suppressing the variety of moneys prevailing under open competition. According to White, this argument holds against the proliferation of a variety of products or brands in any industry. Too much choice makes life difficult for consumers; therefore, let the government choose for them.

Relying on neoclassical economic position, White reasons that market competition discovers which products and how many brands best serve consumer preferences. The time consumers spend on choosing a limited number of goods or services is not a wasteful aspect of competition that should be supplanted by government edict. In other words, if the market will support a number of brands, entry barriers serve no welfare-enhancing purposes.

White finally states that proponents of the public good argument may assert that paper money produced by the public sector represents a social savings because paper is cheaper to produce than commodity-backed money. But, how do we know whether consumers prefer fiat hand-to-hand currency and whether inconvertibility confers social benefits because it reduces the costs of producing money?

For White, consumers may prefer commodity-backed money to fiat money strongly enough to consider the resource costs worth bearing. Consumers might consent to the replacement of commodity currency by fiat currency if they enjoyed the resource savings. However, who captures the alleged resource savings? White maintains that the implementation of a fiat money system gives the government opportunities, through inflationary finance, to enrich itself at the expense of the populace. The injection of hand-to-hand paper currency by a central bank acting as a lender of last resort redistributes wealth involuntarily. The tacit dilution of the purchasing power of existing currency holdings shifts from bank shareholders to money-holding public the risk burdens associated with banking. Because the central bank, as the lender of last resort, relieves bank shareholders of more of the risks from bad loans, profit-maximizing banks take on loans riskier than those they otherwise would have.

In sum, open competition will test the public good argument. Open competition would erode the monopoly profit the federal government currently enjoys in the production of hand-to-hand paper money as well as check the increasingly pervasive dominance of the public sector in many areas of our daily existence. As one commentator concludes: "The only operational proof that a common money is more efficient than currency competition and that the government is the most efficient provider of the common money would be to permit free currency competition."[34]

Will a Non–Public Sector Issuer Circulate an Excessive Amount of Currency or Engage in Fraudulent Practices?

Opponents of a local currency system may argue that a non–public sector issuer of scrip will circulate an excessive amount of money. In addition to devaluing their money by producing too much of it, the issue of excessive notes by one or a few issuers may threaten the stability of issuers that do not overissue.

Proponents of a system characterized by competing currencies concurrently circulating in a community, such as Nobel laureate Friedrich A. Hayek, would rely on market forces to provide checks and balances on the competing currencies.[35] Currency inflation will be inhibited, as an unsound currency will be used less frequently. According to Hayek, each issuer would have its own currency unit. Different units would freely fluctuate against each other. The value of each unit would depend on the forces of supply and demand. Each currency would have a market (exchange market) of its own and a price (exchange rate) of its own. Thus, the supply of and demand for each currency would be equilibrated relatively painlessly.

In a competitive system, each issuer thus has an incentive to restrain its scrip issue, so the argument runs, in order to keep the purchasing power of its currency unit stable, thus attracting more holders. Success in restraining its issue to the volume demanded at a stable value of its unit would strengthen demand. Virtue would bring its own reward. If people wish to acquire additional holdings of a particular currency, this scrip would rise in value on the intercurrency exchange market and likely increase in purchasing power. Thus, the market would lead an issuer of a popular scrip to increase the amount of its currency in circulation.

Conversely, if people wanted to reduce their holdings of a particular currency, this scrip would decline in exchange value and probably in purchasing power, forcing an issuer, anxious to preserve its reputation, to try to reduce its outstanding issue, for example, by means of a repurchase program using other currencies. Through exchange rates, purchasing power, and quantity changes (especially the latter), Hayek concludes that the equilibrium between the desired actual amounts of particular currencies would be maintained or restored. Thus, for Hayek, each issuer would have the power to assure customers that the value of its currency will be kept stable by regulating the amount of the currency in circulation by, among other activities, selling or buying its currencies against other currencies.[36]

Building on Hayek's argument, White posits three points which limit the possibility of excessive currency issuance. First, the holders may seek a direct redemption for commodities, that is, the issuer will immediately experience a loss of commodity reserves.

Second, the holders may deposit the paper currency with a participating bank. Assuming periodic settlement among participating banks of claims represented by notes in the form of an interbank exchange of notes, the deposit of an unusually large volume of notes in banks will result in an adverse clearing balance at the note exchange. The balance will be settled by transfer of the reserve commodity from the issuer; thus, a more expansive issuer will again suffer a loss of resources.

Third, the holders may keep the currency they hold or spend in a region in circulation and exert upward pressure on prices. This scrip will ultimately be returned to the issuer when redeemed for commodities, or indirectly via deposits in other banks. Thus, an overexpansive issuer will be forced to replenish reserves by pursuing a relatively restrictive issuance policy for a period or selling off its notes to acquire additional stocks of the reserve commodities.[37]

In addition, the print and electronic media would provide a useful function by watching the efforts of issuers and daily quoting how much the currencies deviate from self-set standards as well as the various exchange rates between different alternative scrip and the U.S. dollar.[38] In addition, banks would maintain regular quotes on the rate of exchange of local currencies to and from the U.S. dollar as well as the exchange rate among various alternative currencies.

In short, the possibility of overissuance or fraudulent practices is ever-present; however, these fears are probably overblown in a modern economy with well-developed institutions for generating and transmitting information regarding alternative scrips, various issuers, and their financial condition. Scrip offered by a financially shaky issuer, or one that engaged in the overissuance of its currency, would sell at an inconvenient discount, thereby reducing its demand. The market and informational forces would prompt an issuer to devote attention to its reputation. Customers would shift away from any issuer that devalues a currency by fraud or excessive issuance. In theory, an issuer would strive to induce the use of its currency by maintaining its quality.

Beyond these market forces, a commodity-backed currency and the accompanying redemption feature would make operational the expectation that an issuer would strive to keep its monetary units stable in purchasing power. As noted earlier in this chapter, convertibility of a currency means an issuer would be required to do something on the initiative of the holders of its money. Demonstrating an ability to redeem its currency will facilitate public acceptance of the money.

Naturally, the costs of any potential redemption increase with the amount of an issuer's money outstanding. These heightened costs will refocus the issuer's attention on the most effective redemption mechanism. As Hayek indicates, for an issuer to keep a large and growing amount of its currency in circulation, the willingness of the public to hold it probably is decisive. If a system of competing non–public sector currencies were put into practice, Hayek asserts that, in theory, convertibility into a commodity would be unnecessary. For Hayek, commodity convertibility would not be needed. Hayek reasons that competing issuers will not be able to maintain themselves in business, unless they provide money at least as advantageous to the user as anyone else. The currency would be trusted to be kept scarce by an issuer and would be held by people only so long as the issuer justifies that trust, by confirming its acceptability at an established, constant value, perhaps in terms of a stated collection of foreign currencies. Hayek asserts that such a mechanism would be far cheaper than accumulation and storing reserve commodities.[39] Computer and modern communication techniques further obviate the need for a redeemable, claim check kind of money. True to his free–market orientation, Hayek would let the market decide on the best monetary institution and whether a reserve/redemption mechanism is needed.[40]

The competitive market safeguards face two additional challenges. First, is caveat emptor in the local currency context sufficient for the twenty-first century? For Hayek, experience will teach people how to improve their position by switching to (and among) various kinds of money.[41] However, experience can be a painful (and costly) teacher. Can each money holder decide whether any non–public sector issuer is unstable depending on his or her individual degree of risk aversion? Will competition weed out the crooked and incompetent? Will good money drive out bad money? With continuing demand dependent on the success in keeping the value of its currency constant, many would place their trust in a non–public sector issuer making every effort to achieve the noninflationary goal better than would any government monopolist.

At present, a federal governmental monopoly of currency issuance can defraud the public with considerable impunity by increasing the money supply and thus contributing to inflationary pressures.

Second, in a system of non–public sector issued money, particularly if the scrip is not backed by a commodity reserve, will an issuer be tempted to seek to profit from one-shot, large-scale issuance of currency? An issuer might conclude that it could profit-maximize, at least in the short term, by reneging on its announced intention to keep purchasing power of money constant in terms of a basket of goods. This may reinforce the need for an explicit contractual commitment to commodity redeemability.[42]

Relying on nonprofit/cooperative issuers may also diminish the currency temptation to make a "quick buck." Democratically organized, community-based issuers will likely emphasize their societal responsibilities with respect to regulating currency issuance.

In sum, the currency issuance should be open to competing issuers— profit, nonprofit, or cooperative. Lack of restriction on formation of competing associations provides several benefits including preventing fraud and overissuance by ensuring the observance of proper procedures, and contributing to innovations in exchange processes.

Is There a Natural Monopoly in Money?

Proponents of the natural monopoly position argue that even in a competitive market, government-issued money will win out for four reasons. First, as a theoretical matter, the natural monopoly rationale is based on the premise that exchange becomes less costly as the number of currencies in a society decreases. Society wants to reduce transaction costs through a common medium of exchange. The government traditionally provides that medium of exchange.

Second, the production of money may involve significant economies of scale so that the supply of money represents a natural monopoly. In other words, society is better off as a result of a high degree of standardization of currency issuance. One issuer, theoretically, may be more efficient in supplying the demand for currency than a number of small issuers.

Third, the argument for a governmental monopoly is premised on the notion that the more gullible may be the object of financial swindles. Finally, low-cost notes offer a great attraction to counterfeiters, especially in an environment in which many different notes would circulate simultaneously. To prevent fraud, the public may gravitate to one kind of note.[43]

Expanding on the transactional cost argument, critics of a local currency system may assert that an informational problem will arise involving the efficient use of resources. Time and effort will be expended in thinking about what currency a consumer wishes to give a merchant in the purchase of goods and services, what to receive in change from a merchant, and how long he or she wants to keep a currency. With one or more alternative currencies existing in tandem with the U.S. dollar, nearly every transaction might require the services of a money changer/exchange service.

However, the specter of the multiplicity of currencies pales in light of modern technologies. Computers and credit cards would assist in surmounting technical difficulties and inconveniences. Retailers would use appropriate calculating equipment. Also, if several local currencies circulate in a region, one way to arrange for a degree of standardization is for different issuers of alternative moneys to use the same commodity in the same units as the currency reserve. All of these moneys, absent questions about an issuer's shaky financial condition or fraudulent practices, should trade on a one-to-one basis for comparable denominations.

As an empirical matter, we do not know if money constitutes a natural monopoly. One commentator concludes that the nineteenth-century historical and empirical evidence in the United States shows a tendency, under unrestricted entry, to a plurality of note-issuing banks.[44] As we look to the twenty-first century, the natural monopoly issue represents an empirical question to be answered based on competition of various alternative currencies issued by non–public sector issuers. If money production is in fact a natural monopoly, there would be no need to restrict entry by giving the government a monopoly.[45] The federal government simply will win the competitive struggle.

As a further empirical matter, it is unclear whether confidence building is more costly for a private issuer than for the government. Today, we permit traveler's checks to be competitively supplied. Alternative currencies could come to be considered as trustworthy by the public as traveler's checks. Trustworthiness is based on need for a non–public sector issuer to establish confidence in its money, which may rest on capital cost of creating such confidence.[46] Thus, it seems desirable to let any issuer, particularly the federal government, employ whatever theoretical advantage it possesses in production of money to discourage or outcompete any rival. To achieve the theoretical monopoly position in a competitive system, a public sector issuer would be required to take steps to improve the popularity of its notes.

Beyond the various theoretical and empirical arguments, experts differ on the "bottom line." One commentator concludes, "There is no strong a priori case for the view that competition in currency supply will lead to the emergence of a single bank of issue."[47]

For Hayek, the simultaneous existence in the same community of several dominant moneys produced by different non–public sector issuers is a real possibility. Hayek concludes that non–public sector issuers who produce a medium of exchange with constant purchasing power would be appropriate for different areas or groups and thus "a number of different competitive money producers would survive, with extensive overlap of border areas."[48]

In the battle of Nobel laureates, Milton Friedman is skeptical of Hayek's belief that a number of different competitive money issuers would survive. Based on an analysis of the historical evidence, Friedman concludes that it is not possible to have the simultaneous existence in the same community of various issues of privately issued money convertible into different commodities, except when two metals (such as gold and silver) are circulated simultaneously at flexible exchange rates.[49]

Friedman is especially skeptical given the starting point characterized by a firmly established federal government–issued money. Friedman doubts whether any non-public sector issuer, at least of a fiat (non-commodity-based) money, could likely compete successfully with the U.S. government. According to Friedman, no historical precedent exists for such competition, particularly in view of the federal government's monopoly position. For Friedman, the historical evidence suggests that a nongovernment, commodity-based currency is the only plausible alternative to government-issued fiat money. But, even that outcome is highly unlikely unless a major national currency collapse occurs, for example, through hyperinflation. For Friedman, hand-to-hand currency will at least be certified and generally issued by the national government.[50] He concludes: "the advantage of a single national currency unit buttressed by long tradition, will, I suspect, serve to prevent any other type of private currency unit from seriously challenging the dominant government currency."[51]

However, assessing the prospects for a viable alternative currency, we should not expect a non–public sector-issued scrip to battle the U.S. dollar on a nationwide basis. Rather, we look to a decentralized approach marked by the parallel existence of various local currencies and the U.S. dollar in a multitude of communities throughout the United States.

CONCLUSION

The idea of a local currency not pegged to the U.S. dollar presents exciting possibilities. No longer will the populace be helpless as the federal government overissues its currency, causing inflation. Local economies will have the opportunity to flourish. Of course, creating a new, widely used local currency requires time, hard work, and a degree of resources. But given the possibilities, community groups will find it worthwhile to put forth the effort.

seven

Legal Aspects of Local Currency

A basic need of a society is money, the form of which adapts contextually. History, replete with examples, confirms that the evolution (or devolution) of monetary systems hinges upon the varying needs of society. Local currency systems, prevalent before ratification of the United States Constitution, have existed throughout American history and have reappeared today. Most of the earlier local currency schemes passed away because they were prohibited by law or were no longer necessary given the circumstances. The question remains whether today's local currency systems are consistent with the law. This chapter begins with a discussion of federal and state law relating to local currency before analyzing federal and state banking laws, federal and state securities laws, and federal income tax aspects of local scrip.

FEDERAL LAWS RELATING TO LOCAL CURRENCY

The federal laws relating to a local currency program consist of the constitutional framework, prohibition on private coinage, and anticounterfeiting legislation. This discussion will demonstrate that no federal barriers exists to the issuance of local paper currency. However, local coinage cannot be minted.

United States Constitutional Framework

The U.S. Constitution does not prohibit private issuance of money. The Framers were concerned primarily with restricting the states from influencing monetary policy,[1] and averting "embarrassments of a perpetually fluctuating and variable currency"[2] caused by "[t]he floods of depreciated paper-money, with which most of the States . . . were inundated."[3] Consequently, the framing document forbids the states to "coin Money,"[4] to "emit Bills of Credit,"[5] and to "make any Thing but gold and silver Coin a Tender in Payment of Debts."[6] The U.S. Constitution also grants to the U.S. Congress the powers "[t]o borrow Money on the credit of the United States,"[7] "[t]o coin Money, regulate the Value thereof, and of foreign Coin, and fix the Standard of Weights and Measures,"[8] and "[t]o provide for the Punishment of counterfeiting the Securities and current Coin of the United States."[9]

Consistent with the hostility felt toward paper money at the time of the Constitutional Convention,[10] the Framers defined "Money" of the United States as coin alone.[11] The authority in the U.S. Constitution "[t]o coin Money,"[12] lifted from the Articles of Confederation,[13] represents the lone constitutional grant of power to create "Money" and limits specifically the means of generation to "coin[ing]."[14]

While the U.S. Constitution prohibits the states from issuing paper currency by barring them from "emit[ing] Bills of Credit,"[15] it is silent on whether the federal government may issue such bills. Distrusting paper money, the Constitutional Convention deliberately struck a provision from the initial draft of the U.S. Constitution empowering the federal government to emit bills of credit.[16] In *The Legal Tender Cases*,[17] the U.S. Supreme Court, however, later held and affirmed that Congress has the authority to emit bills of credit and declare them legal tender for some categories of public and private debts.

Thus, the U.S. Congress may supply the nation with adequate coinage under its power to coin money,[18] but nothing in the U.S. Constitution prohibits private parties from issuing gold, silver, or metal-based coins or the federal government in permitting or assisting private coinage. Moreover, the U.S. Constitution is silent on private issuance of paper currency.

Recognition of Private Issue

Through the Coinage Act of 1792,[19] "Establishing a Mint and Regulating the Coins of the United States," and subsequent coinage acts into the middle of the nineteenth century, Congress developed the foundations for a national monetary system. The coinage acts codified many of the principles set forth by Secretary of the Treasury Alexander Hamilton's *Report on the Subject of a Mint*,[20] which focused primarily on establishing the unit of the system and bimetallism—where the ideal unit is defined in terms of both gold and silver on the basis of fixed gold-silver ratio.[21] Like the U.S. Constitution, the coinage acts did not speak to private coinage or currency.

Parallel currencies—two unrelated currencies circulating within the same territory—continued to exist. Money issued privately proceeded to enter circulation, especially under emergency circumstances.[22] Under the societary theory of money—acceptance of money that is current and in circulation in a community at the time it is received or simply to protect bona fide payments made with private issue—the courts upheld the validity of payments made in otherwise illegal currency. For instance, in *Thorington v. Smith*,[23] private parties residing in the same city within Confederate territory during the Civil War entered into a contract where part of the debt was to be paid in Confederate notes. The U.S. Supreme Court held that the contract was enforceable in a court of the United States, despite the fact that the Confederate government had no authority to issue such notes, because at the time of the transaction, Confederate notes had become "almost exclusively the currency of the insurgent States" and they "were used as money in nearly all the business transaction of many millions of people."[24] Consistent with the societary theory of money, private coins, current in California in the 1850s, were not recognized as money in Massachusetts where they were not current.[25]

With the maturation of the national monetary system and the concomitant growth of private currency, Congress passed legislation barring or restricting private issue. Recognizing that Congress intended primarily to prevent competition with the national currency, the U.S. Supreme Court, in *United States v. Van Auken*[26] and *Hollister v. Mercantile Institution*,[27] validated private notes issued in 1874 and 1876, respectively, and payable in merchandise at a business, under the principle that such notes would not circulate beyond a limited neighborhood. In *Van Auken*, where the defendant was charged with violating a statute seeking to provide a monopoly to an experimental national "postage currency," the Court stated:

Small notes payable in any specific articles, if issued, could have only a neighborhood circulation, and but a limited one there. It could be but little in the way of the stamps or small notes issued for the purposes of circulating change by the United States. Congress could, therefore, have had little or no motive to interfere with respect to the former.[28]

The *Hollister* Court cited *Van Auken* and the same principle.[29]

Federal Law Prohibits Private Coinage

As noted, the U.S. Constitution specifically prohibits the states from coining money. This prohibition extends to every branch, agency, and instrumentality of state government.[30] The private issuance of money did not become a concern of the federal government until 1860. Between 1830 and 1860, prompted by the "Gold Rush," private manufacturers of gold coins flourished.[31] These coins did not imitate the designs of United States coins.[32] Rather, they bore the names and places of the manufacturer.[33] In Georgia, North Carolina, California, Oregon, Utah, and Colorado, the private coins varied in weight and fineness.[34]

By the Act of June 8, 1864,[35] Congress prohibited private coinage, regardless of whether the coins were similar in appearance to coins of the United States. Congress codified this prohibition on the issuance of private coinage in 1873,[36] 1909,[37] and 1948.[38] No substantive changes in subsequent versions were made.[39] The current statute provides:

Whoever, except as authorized by law, makes or utters or passes, or attempts to utter or pass, any coins of gold or silver or other metal, or alloys of metals, intended for use as current money, whether in the resemblance of coins of the United States or of foreign countries, or of original design, shall be fined for more than $3,000 or imprisoned not more than five years, or both.[40]

Modern local paper currency described in Chapters 4, 5, and 6, however, is not prohibited by this statute. First, the statute prohibiting private coinage does not address paper money. In other words, the prohibition on the issuance of private coinage does not bar a modern, local paper currency. However, fractional paper currency with a value of less than one dollar is subject to criminal sanctions.[41]

Second, the statute requires that the illegal coins be "for use as current money." Interpreting the predecessor statute to the present provision, the court, in *United States v. Gellman*,[42] held that tokens with inscriptions: "No Cash Value" and "For Amusement Purposes Only" were not used as money because there was "no promise to pay money or anything of value, either impliedly or by reason of any express inscription on the coin."[43] The *Gellman* Court relied on language from *United States v. Roussopulous*:[44]

It does not purport to be money, or an obligation to pay money, and the obligation expressed is in terms solvable in merchandise. It cannot, therefore, have been intended to circulate as money, or to be received and used in lieu of lawful money.[45]

The term "current money" has also been defined in *State v. Quackenbush*[46] as:

[W]hatever is lawfully and actually current in buying and selling, of the value and as the equivalent of coin (citations omitted). "Current money" means money which passes from hand to hand and from person to person and circulates through the community. (citation omitted). It is synonymous with "lawful money" (citation omitted). Whatever is intended to, and does actually, circulate as money (citation omitted). . . . "Current money," that which is generally used as a medium of exchange.[47]

In *Anchorage Centennial Dev. Co. v. Van Wormer & Rodriguez, Inc.*,[48] the Supreme Court of Alaska, citing *Quackenbush,* held that there was no intention to use the coins in question as "current money" where the coins were to bear the proposed inscription, "Good for One Dollar in Trade at Any Cooperating Business Redeemable at Face Value at the Anchorage Centennial Exposition Site Until December 31, 1967" and actually read, "Redeemable at Face Value at Anchorage the Air Crossroads of the World."[49]

Moreover, the *Gellman* Court concluded that the 1864 Act was "primarily adopted to prevent the coining of money in competition with the United States."[50] In *United States v. Falvey,*[51] the First Circuit reached the same conclusion.

Therefore, a local issuer may issue coins so long as it does not intend for the coins to circulate as money of the United States. For example, a private individual or entity may issue coins or tokens that may be used to redeem merchandise at particular businesses in a community. But the local issuer may not issue coins with the intention that the coins will be used in lieu of lawful money to purchase goods or to pay debts on a wide scale where the coins would be competing with lawful money.

Other Federal Anticounterfeiting Legislation

Other modern federal legislation prohibiting private counterfeiting[52] similarly does not bar local currency schemes as described in Chapters 4, 5, and 6. The modern statutory provision with the catchline "Tokens or paper used as money,"[53] generally, prohibits anyone from making or using anything, including paper currency, that is similar to lawful currency or legal tender issued by the federal government in the United States as lawful currency or legal tender.[54]

The anticounterfeiting provision dealing with paper currency requires that the tokens or paper be "similar in size and shape to any of the lawful coins or other currency of the United States" or to be "receive[d] . . . [as] lawful coins of other currency of the United States."[55] In other words, the tokens or paper in question must be used as lawful or "current money." Even though the term "current money"—the same term used in the statute prohibiting private coinage described above—is not used in the anticounterfeiting statute addressing counterfeit paper currency, the courts have required that the tokens or paper in question be used as "current money" to violate the statute. The same definition of "current money" stated above was used in both *Gellman*, interpreting the predecessor to the modern anticounterfeiting statute dealing with paper currency,[56] and *Van Wormer*, interpreting the anticounterfeiting statute itself.[57]

Similarly, other federal anticounterfeiting statutes fall short of proscribing the local currency systems. In *United States v. Smith*,[58] the Fourth Circuit held that two slips of paper, each the size of a federal reserve note and each bearing a crude, backwards facsimile of one, were not "counterfeit" under a statutory provision which prohibits the uttering of counterfeit obligations or securities. The slips of paper must have been an imitation or "similitude"; otherwise, there is no counterfeit in fact.[59] Moreover, unless the pieces of paper purported to fool an "honest, sensible and unsuspecting person of ordinary observation and care,"[60] there is no counterfeit in law.

In a case involving a provision criminalizing the control, custody, or possession of certain plates, stones, or anything else used to print counterfeit obligations and securities of the United States, the court cited and followed Smith's definition of "counterfeit."[61] Local issuers using tools and other equipment to print their currency would, therefore, not be violating any anticounterfeiting statutes unless their equipment imitated and simulated the plates, stones, or other things used by the Secretary of the Treasury to print obligations or securities of the United States. Finally, the *Federal Jury Practice and Instructions*, used by federal district court judges in civil and criminal cases, also uses the Smith definition:

An item is "counterfeit" if it bears such likeness or a resemblance to a genuine obligation or security issued under the authority of the United States as is calculated to deceive an honest, sensible and unsuspecting person of ordinary observation and care dealing with a person supposed to be honest and upright.[62]

State Issuance of Bills of Credit

While the U.S. Constitution explicitly prohibits the states from emitting bills of credit, and therefore, from directly issuing their own currency, does the prohibition extend to other public bodies (e.g., municipalities or counties) or the private sector? As defined in *Craig v. State of Missouri*,[63] "'bills of credit' signify a paper medium, intended to circulate between individuals, and between the government and individuals, for the ordinary purposes of society."[64] The *Craig* court further stated:

The word "emit" is never employed in describing those contracts by which a state binds itself to pay money at a future day for services actually received, or for money borrowed for present use; nor are instruments executed for such purposes, in common language, denominated "bill of credit." To "emit bill of credit," conveys to the mind the idea of issuing paper intended to circulate through the community for its ordinary purposes, as money, which paper is redeemable at a future day.[65]

In *Briscoe v. Bank of Kentucky*,[66] the court clarified its definition of a "bill of credit":

The definition, then which does include all classes of bills of credit, emitted by the colonies or states, is a paper issued by the sovereign power, containing a pledge of its faith and designed to circulate as money. . . . To constitute a bill of credit, within the Constitution, it must be issued by a state, on the faith of the state, and be designed to circulate as money. It must be a paper which circulates on the credit of the state, and is so received and used in the ordinary business of life.[67]

Within the definition of a bill of credit, the U.S. Supreme Court has permitted states to issue monetary-like instruments that are not intended to circulate as money. In *Poindexter v. Greenhow*,[68] the Court permitted a state to issue coupons receivable for taxes even though the state issued the coupons, the coupons were promises to pay money, and their payment and redemption were based on the credit of the state because "they were not emitted by the State . . . as a substitute for money. And there is nothing on the face of the instruments, nor in their form or nature, nor in the circumstances of their creation or use . . . that these coupons were designed to circulate, in the common transactions of business, as money, nor that in fact they were so used."[69]

Without running afoul of the constitutional prohibition, the U.S. Supreme Court has also ruled that states may also: (1) execute instruments binding themselves to pay money to individuals at a future day for services rendered or money borrowed,[70] and (2) charter banks which issue notes,[71] regardless of whether the state is the sole stockholder of the bank,[72] the officers of the bank were elected by the state legislature,[73] or that the capital of the bank was raised by the sale of state bonds.[74]

The constitutional bar on emitting bills of credit appears to extend to other public bodies as well. The U.S. Supreme Court has held that "trustees or representative officers of a parish, county, or other local jurisdiction" have no authority, implied or otherwise, to issue negotiable securities or coupons, "payable in the future" and "of such a character as to be unimpeachable in the hands of bona fide holders."[75] Moreover, the Court has also held that a municipal corporation, "a subordinate branch of the domestic government of a State" and with no "purposes of private gain" has no power to issue paper clothed with all the attributes of negotiability.[76]

Because bills of credit must be issued by the state or by an individual or committee who has the power to bind the state acting as agents thereof without imparting, as individuals, any credit to the paper,[77] nongovernmental entities, acting alone, are not subject to the constitutional prohibition on states issuing bills of credit. In his famous dissent in the *Briscoe* decision, Justice Story clarified the applicability of the constitutional prohibition:

The Constitution does not prohibit the emission of all bills of credit, but only the emission of bills of credit by the State: and when I say, by a State, I mean by or in behalf of a State, in whatever form issued. It does not prohibit private persons, or private partnerships, or private corporations . . . from issuing bills of credit. No evils, or, at least, no permanent evils, have ever flowed from such a source. . . . The mischief was not there. . . . It was the issue of bills of credit, as a currency; authorized by the State on its own funds, and for its own purposes; which constituted the real evil to be provided against.[78]

Prior Tax on Notes Not Issued by National Banks

Another method Congress utilized to limit the circulation of notes other than those of federally chartered national banks was to impose a tax on their circulation. As noted in Chapter 2, the U.S. Congress authorized the federal government to issue "notes for circulation"—popularly known as "greenbacks"—through the National Banking Act of 1863.[79]

In 1863, Congress also passed a statute which required all banks, associations, corporations, and individuals issuing notes or bills for circulation as currency to pay a duty of 1 percent each half year on the average amount of their circulation over a certain sum, and a tax of 5 percent on all notes of bills issued in sums representing any fractional part of a dollar.[80] This use of the federal government's power to tax was followed in 1864 by Congress imposing a tax upon the average amount of circulation issued by any bank, association, corporation, company, or person "including as circulation all certified checks, and all notes and other obligations calculated or intended to circulate, or to be used as money."[81]

In 1865, however, Congress implemented another tax designed to crush the decentralized issuance of paper currency and to further a federal government monopoly with respect to paper money. Congress imposed the "death tax" of 10 percent on every state bank or banking association. The tax was imposed on the amount of notes issued by these institutions.[82] This duty was extended to include persons in 1866.[83] Stating that Congress is authorized to provide "a sound and uniform currency for the country," and to "secure the benefit of it to the people by appropriate legislation," the U.S. Supreme Court in *Veazie Bank v. Fenno*[84] upheld the 1865 and 1866 acts. In the following year, the 10 percent tax included notes issued by any town, city, or municipal corporation.[85] In 1875, Congress combined the 1865, 1866, and 1867 acts, effectively extending the 1867 act to all persons, firms, associations, and corporations.[86]

The "death tax" effectively outlawed notes except those issued by national banks. Banks under state charters were induced to convert into national banks and the circulation of state bank notes disappeared entirely. Foreign banks[87] and notes issued by municipalities[88] also fell prey.

Congress's aim to eliminate state banks altogether almost succeeded. On October 5, 1863, there were only 66 national banks in operation while 1,466 state banks existed.[89] By October 1, 1866, after the tax on state bank circulation became effective (on July 1, 1866), the number of national banks increased to 1,634 while the number of state banks dwindled to 297.[90] State banks survived and later actually became more numerous by becoming banks of deposit rather than banks of issue, aided by the change to checking deposits instead of bank notes as money.

In *Hollister v. Mercantile Institute*,[91] the U.S. Supreme Court defined what "notes" would be subject to the punitive tax scheme:

["Notes" include] only such notes as are in law negotiable, so as to carry title in their circulation from hand to hand, are the subjects of taxation under the statute. It was, no doubt, the purpose of Congress, in imposing this tax, to provide against competition with the established national currency for circulation as money, but as it was not likely that obligations payable in anything else than money would pass beyond a limited neighborhood, no attention was given to such issues as affecting the volume of the currency, or its circulating value.[92]

The Court went on to hold that a note stating, "Pay David O. Calder or bearer five dollars in merchandise at retail" was not a note under the 1875 act.[93] Thus, unsigned "clearing-house certificates" issued by state banks were held not to be "notes" under the 1875 tax because the 10 percent tax applied only to promissory notes and not to other negotiable or quasi-negotiable paper, and the bearer could not sue the issuer and recover money damages with the paper alone.[94] Neither were all negotiable promissory notes taxable under the punitive tax.[95] The issuer must intend that its notes be used as currency in competition with national currency.[96]

Under the Tax Reform Act of 1976,[97] the 10 percent "death tax" was repealed as obsolete.[98] According to the Comptroller of the Currency, any issuance of notes under the punitive 10 percent tax "is also illegal under other provisions of Federal law."[99] Regardless of the enigmatical reference to other provisions, the local currency described in Chapters 4, 5, and 6, would not be considered "notes" under the previous statute.

The Gold Clause, Its Repeal, and Reinstatement

Generally, a gold clause is a promise to pay a debt in gold. Promises to pay debts in gold coin are called "gold-coin clauses" while promises to pay the value of gold coin are "gold-value clauses." In 1879, the United States resumed payments of specie (i.e., gold coin) in redemption of its paper currency.[100] In the Gold Standard Act of 1900, Congress eliminated the remnants of the role of silver as a monetary standard.[101] With the collapse of the gold standard, Congress, in 1933, banned gold clauses from public and private contracts.[102] The Gold Reserve Act of 1934 went further, withdrawing all gold from circulation.[103] As President Franklin D. Roosevelt stated, the Act "abolished gold coin as a component of our monetary system."[104]

The constitutionality of the ban was questioned by the U.S. Supreme Court in the *Gold Clause Cases*.[105] The Court upheld the abrogation of gold clauses involving private obligations[106] and obligations involving the federal government.[107] Congress's power, the Court reasoned, came not only from the coinage power, but also from:

the aggregate of the powers granted to the Congress, embracing the powers to lay and collect taxes, to borrow money, to regulate commerce with foreign nations and among the several States, to coin money, regulate the value thereof, and of foreign coin, and fix the standards of weights and measures, and the added express power "to make all laws which shall be necessary and proper for carrying into execution" the other enumerated powers.[108]

In 1977, the abrogation of gold clauses was repealed.[109] American citizens may now buy and sell gold freely,[110] and courts can enforce gold clauses.[111] Thus, today contracts can provide for the payment in U.S. dollars, scrip pegged to the U.S. dollar, or an alternative currency.

STATE LAWS RELATING TO LOCAL CURRENCY

State codes may affect the circulation and use of alternative currencies. At least thirteen states either prohibit paying employees in scrip or require employers to pay their workers in U.S. currency.[112] Two states, Florida and Massachusetts, have their own anticounterfeiting statutes. The Florida statute, for example, prohibits the issuance or circulation of scrip "as a substitute in any respect for currency recognized by law."[113]

Most troublesome are the Virginia and Arkansas statutes. The Virginia statute prohibits any "individual or entity unless authorized by law" from (a) issuing, "with intent that the same be circulated as currency, any note, bill, scrip, or other paper or thing," or (b) otherwise dealing, trading or carrying on "business as a bank of circulation."[114] Seemingly, the Virginia statute would permit the issuance of discount notes redeemable for goods or services as well as an Ithaca HOURS barter-type exchange mechanism. These arrangements arguably are not issued with the intent to circulate as "currency." A barter-type exchange mechanism may face a bar in Arkansas which restricts instruments to be used as a medium of trade in lieu of money. The Virginia statute would, on its face, bar a local currency not pegged to the U.S. dollar because such scrip would be issued with the requisite intent, namely, to circulate as currency. This conclusion also follows in Arkansas, which prohibits the creation or circulation of instruments to be used as money.

Despite the sweep of these two state statutes, planning opportunities exist. The Arkansas statute only applies to persons, not entities. The Virginia statute defines an entity to include "any association, corporation, partnership, firm, company."[115] Thus, the term "association" would encompass a cooperative association. Seemingly, a charitable organization would not, however, fall under any of the more specific definitions of the general term "entity." Therefore, the bar of the Virginia statute would not apply to any type of local currency issued by a nonprofit corporation.

Only Vermont specifically authorizes the formation of a corporation for the sole purpose of issuing scrip.[116] In addition, Vermont prohibits the counterfeiting of such scrip.[117]

FEDERAL AND STATE BANKING LAW RELATING TO LOCAL CURRENCY WHICH TRADES INDEPENDENTLY OF THE U.S. DOLLAR

Dual Banking System

The American banking system operates under a dual system where commercial banks and other depository institutions (savings and loans, savings banks, and credit unions) may be chartered and regulated by either state or federal administrations. The structure of regulation is complex. Generally, the dual banking system functions as two interrelated schemes in which federal laws are applicable, to a varying breadth, to state-chartered banks; and state laws, to varying degrees, are applicable to federally chartered banks.[118]

With respect to commercial banks, there are four classes of banks and the regulation, as well as the competitive position, of any bank hinges upon the class to which it belongs. First, there are "national" banks which are chartered under federal law by the Comptroller of the Currency. "National" banks are required to become members of the Federal Reserve System[119] and are insured by the Federal Deposit Insurance Corporation (FDIC).[120] National banks operate under the regulations of the Comptroller of the Currency, the Federal Reserve Act (FRA),[121] the National Banking Act,[122] and the Federal Deposit Insurance Act (FDIA).[123] Second, there are "state member banks," which are chartered under state law, voluntarily join the Federal Reserve System,[124] and are also insured by the FDIC.[125] State member banks also operate under regulations of the Federal Reserve Act and other federal laws. Third, if a bank, chartered under state law, declines to join the Federal Reserve System but voluntarily obtains federal deposit insurance, it is a "nonmember insured state bank" and subject to the FDIA and other federal laws. Finally, "nonmember noninsured state banks" are state chartered banks which elect neither to join the Federal Reserve System nor to obtain federal deposit insurance.[126]

The principle federal banking regulators are the Board of Governors of the Federal Reserve System, the Comptroller of the Currency, and the FDIC. The Board of Governors has the primary responsibility of regulating banks which are members of the Federal Reserve System. The Comptroller of the Currency is responsible primarily for the administration of the national banking laws and the examination of the national banks. The FDIC, like the Comptroller of the Currency, administers the law and examines those banks which are federally insured. Additionally, the FDIC oversees insured savings institutions.[127]

Each state bank is subject to the laws of its own state—laws which differ in countless respects. State banks in adjoining states may be subject to additional restrictions. Every state has banking departments and state banking supervisors or commissioners who regulate state banks. In a majority of the states, the state banking supervisors or commissioners also charter banks. Banking boards or commissions charter the banks in the remaining jurisdictions.[128]

Transferring Local Currency

To transfer funds within the dual banking system, individuals utilize checks and electronic wire communications. Checks, generally, are orders on a bank (the drawee or payor) by a depositor (the drawer) to pay a certain sum of money to a third party (the payee). The term "check" is defined more specifically by, for example, the Uniform Commercial Code (UCC) and Federal Reserve regulations. In addition to the transfer of paper instruments between banks, electronic wire services participate in the transferring of funds. To facilitate the transfer, a payments system has evolved whereby the government (the Federal Reserve) and the private sector (automated clearinghouses) adjust the balances of banks and other depository institutions many times over the day, reducing the need for bank-to-bank dealings.

Assuming that an alternative currency flourishes and local banks agree to accept deposits not denominated in U.S. dollars, individuals accepting the local scrip would require a system that would transfer the new hand-to-hand currency from one bank to another. Although there are restrictions to transferring such local scrip within the Federal Reserve System, the alternative currency may be transferred through private efforts outside the Federal Reserve System.

*Limitations on the Transfer of Funds in the Federal Reserve
System*

Within the Federal Reserve System, no national bank may issue any
notes which circulate as money other than those authorized by the federal banking statutes.[129] Additionally, a national bank may neither put
in circulation the notes of any bank which does not receive those notes
at par nor put in circulation any notes of any bank which is not redeem-
ing its circulating currency in lawful money of the United States.[130] The
restrictions on circulating notes of other banks include any state bank as
well as member banks.[131]

The "notes" that these provisions refer to are Federal Reserve notes[132]
or national bank notes which must be in certain denominations in certain
proportions,[133] engraved by the Comptroller of the Currency's plates and
dies,[134] have the charter numbers of the national bank to be printed on
them,[135] and printed on distinctive paper.[136] In short, hand-to-hand currency not denominated in U.S. dollars cannot circulate within the Federal
Reserve System. However, these provisions do not bar banks, even national banks, from dealing in the alternative scrip and joining a scrip and
clearinghouse system to transfer the currency among participating banks.

With respect to collecting checks, Regulation CC establishes rules designed to speed the collection and return of unpaid checks.[137] The Board
of Governors of the Federal Reserve System issued Regulation CC to
implement the Expedited Funds Availability Act[138] which creates time
limits within which depository institutions are required to make available for withdrawal the proceeds of checks deposited for collection.[139]
Subpart C of Regulation CC sets forth the rules to ensure the expeditious
return of checks, the responsibilities of paying and returning banks, authorization of direct returns, notification of nonpayment of large-dollar
returns by the paying bank, check endorsement standards and other related charges to the check collection system.[140] The term "bank" as used
in the regulation includes "any person engaged in the business of banking, including . . . a state or unit of general local government to the extent
that the state or unit of general local government acts as a paying
bank."[141] A "paying bank" includes the bank by which the check is payable and to which the check is sent for payment or collection.[142] Therefore, the Board of Governors has broad authority to apply its check
collection rules to all checks, regardless of whether they were collected
through the Federal Reserve System. Moreover, a "check" does not include an item payable in anything other than United States money.[143]
However, this definition of the term "check" is limited to Subpart C of
Regulation CC which deals with the collection of checks.[144]

Federal Reserve Banks may receive, or solely for the purpose of
exchange and collection, the checks of member and nonmember banks

alike, so long as the checks are payable upon presentation within that the Federal Reserve Bank's district.[145] This banking provision is accompanied and interpreted by Regulation J.[146] Regulation J defines "check" as a draft, as defined in the Uniform Commercial Code (UCC).[147] "Draft" is defined by the UCC as "order"[148] which the UCC defines as "a written instruction to pay money signed by the person giving the instruction."[149] The UCC describes "money" as "a medium of exchange authorized or adopted by a domestic or foreign government."[150] Thus, under the UCC, a check may be payable in specific foreign money. The UCC provides:

Unless the instrument otherwise provides, an instrument that states the amount payable in foreign money may be paid in the foreign money or in an equivalent amount in dollars calculated by using the current bank-offered spot rate at the place of payment for the purchase of dollars on the day on which the instrument is paid.[151]

Thus, the twelve Federal Reserve Banks which comprise the Federal Reserve System, as well as the clearinghouse mechanism provided by the Federal Reserve System, cannot receive for exchange and collection checks denominated in a unit of exchange which is neither the U.S. dollar nor a foreign currency, as defined. However, private clearinghouses may exist and provide for the transfer of checks not denominated in U.S. dollars.

Clearinghouses

A clearinghouse is an institution where representatives of various banks which are members in the clearinghouse meet to exchange checks drawn on each other and to make or receive payment of balances and so clear the transactions of the day for each member bank. Private, automated clearinghouses, such as the New York Automated Clearing House (NYACH) and the Clearing House Interbank Payment System (CHIPS), have flourished. Until 1983, the NYACH was the only privately owned and operated unit in the national clearinghouse network and in 1990, had a total volume of $127.7 billion.[152] CHIPS was formed in 1970 to replace paper checks with electronic signals for the exchange and settlement of international dollar transactions between the United States and foreign banks.[153] CHIPS now handles over 95 percent of all dollar payments that move between countries throughout the world.[154] In light of the absence of federal and state limitations on private clearinghouses, banks participating in the alternative currency program could create a regional or local clearinghouse to exchange checks not denominated in U.S. dollars. Initially, two or three banks could establish an informal clearinghouse between or among the participating financial institutions.

State Banks Acting as Agents for Local Issuers

In addition to transferring local scrip through private clearinghouses and banks acting beyond the Federal Reserve System, state banks in several states, such as Massachusetts, have the power to act as financial agents for the issuers and users of alternative currency. In Massachusetts, state banks have the power "[t]o act as financial or other agent for a person, association, trust, corporation, municipal corporation or government, and in their behalf to negotiate loans and the sale, purchase or other disposition or acquisition of securities or other property."[155] In a letter to the administrator to the SHARE program, the Office of the Commissioner of Banks confirmed that Massachusetts state banks have the power to act as financial agents in SHARE's "Local Stable Currency Experiment."[156] Twenty other states have statutes[157] similar to Massachusetts. In these jurisdictions, state banks can participate in alternative scrip programs, including entering into exchange transactions involving a local currency, accepting checking and other deposits in the scrip, implementing automatic teller transactions and electronic funds transfers in the scrip, issuing credit and debt cards, and making loans repayable in the local currency.

FEDERAL AND STATE REGULATION OF SECURITIES

The laws of securities regulation, both federal and state, constitute a complex and comprehensive scheme to protect both the offerees and purchasers of securities. These laws govern only what are deemed "securities." Once an instrument is determined to be a "security," the registration and disclosure requirements of the Federal Securities Act of 1933[158] and various state securities laws, commonly known as "blue sky" laws, typically restrict their offer and sale, unless they fall into an exemption.

Disclosure Requirements and the Registration Process

The basic purpose of the Securities Act of 1933 is to assure that the investor has adequate information upon which to base his or her investment decision with respect to publicly offered securities. To achieve this objective, the 1933 Act prohibits the sale or offer of a security to the public unless it is registered or falls within a statutory exemption.[159] Anyone who purchases illegally an unregistered security from the issuer (or a financial intermediary) may rescind the transaction and get his or her money back at any time within one year after the sale.[160]

An issuer registers a security by filing a "registration statement" with the Securities and Exchange Commission (SEC). The SEC rules specify what information the registration statement must contain. Included in the registration statement is the "prospectus" which is provided to every purchaser.

Registration is a costly procedure, both temporally and financially.[161] The registration process is divided into three time periods.[162] The prefiling period is the time prior to completing and filing the registration statement. The time between filing the registration statement and when it becomes effective is known as the waiting period. During the waiting period, offers are permitted using a simplified, preliminary prospectus (a so-called "red herring" because of the legend announcing its preliminary character printed on the cover in red) but sales are prohibited. In the posteffective period, the 1933 Act generally requires that the prospectus be delivered to the purchaser prior to or at the same time as the security.[163] In reality, the purchaser thus receives a "retrospectus," the decision to purchase having been made prior to the receipt of any form of prospectus.

Moreover, the movement of the security from the issuer to the public is very expensive. Because most issuers do not have the necessary expertise in the financial industry to maneuver a public offering, issuers typically employ underwriters and other intermediaries. In addition to underwriting costs, the issuer must pay related expenses including, but not limited to, legal fees, accounting fees, printing fees, an SEC filing fee, state (blue sky) filing fees if applicable, and trustees' fees.[164] The average total underwriting costs as a percentage of proceeds is about 6 percent,[165] and typically, the costs are much higher as the size of issue decreases.[166]

An issuer of a local currency can avoid the registration process and the accompanying disclosure requirements by gaining a statutory exemption, of which there are two types: exempt securities and exempt transactions. Before considering these exemptions, the definition of a security must be considered.

What Is a "Security"?

"Security" is defined in Section 2(1) of the Securities Act of 1933 to include:

any *note, stock,* treasury stock, bond, debenture, *evidence of indebtedness, certificate of interest or participation in any profit-sharing agreement,* collateral-trust certificate, preorganization certificate or subscription, transferable share, *investment contract,* voting-trust certificate, certificate of deposit for a security, fractional undivided interest in oil, gas, or other mineral rights, any put, call, straddle, option, or privilege on any security, certificate of deposit, or group or index of securities (including any interest therein or based on the value thereof), or any put, call straddle, option, or privilege entered into on a national securities exchange relating to foreign currency, or in general, any interest or instrument commonly known as a "security," or any certificate of interest or participation in, temporary or interim certificate for, receipt for, guarantee of, or warrant or right to subscribe to or purchase, any of the foregoing.[167]

The broad statutory definition of the term "security" encompasses many types of instruments. Because there is no universal definition, the issuer of a local currency needs to focus on: notes and evidences of indebtedness, stocks, and investment contracts.

Notes and Evidences of Indebtedness

Contrary to what the statutory definition may lead one to believe, "any note" is not considered a "security." Prior to the U.S. Supreme Court's decision in *Reves v. Ernst & Young*,[168] the lower federal courts were sharply divided on the applicable criteria in determining whether a note was a "security." Four approaches predominated: (1) the commercial/investment test; (2) the family resemblance test; (3) the risk capital test; and (4) the *Howey* test. First, under the commercial/investment standard, courts look to whether the note can be characterized as commercial or investment in nature. If the note is a commercial instrument, then it is not deemed a "security." Conversely, if the note is an investment instrument, then it is a "security."[169] Second, under the family resemblance test, courts presume that a note is a "security" unless the presumption is rebutted by showing a strong family resemblance to a judicially crafted list of nonsecurities.[170] Third, under the risk-capital test, courts determine whether risk capital was subject to the efforts of others. If the purchaser invested risk capital, then the note would be a "security."[171] Finally, under the *Howey* criteria, courts ask whether the note involves an investment of money in a common enterprise with the expectation of profits arising solely from the efforts of others.[172]

In *Reves*, the U.S. Supreme Court sought to establish the definitive approach to be taken in determining the federal securities law status of notes in contrast to the prevailing uncertainty. The *Reves* Court adopted and modified the "family resemblance" test employed by the Second Circuit in *Exchange National Bank v. Touche Ross & Co.*[173] which presumes that a note is a "security" unless it resembles a note on a list of categories of notes that are not considered "securities." That list includes:

[T]he note delivered in consumer financing, the note secured by a mortgage on a home, the short-term note secured by a lien on a small business or some of its assets, the note evidencing a "character" loan to a bank customer, short-term notes secured by an assignment of accounts receivable, or a note which simply formalizes an open-account debt incurred in the ordinary course of business (particularly if, as in the case of the customer of a broker, it is collateralized).[174]

The *Reves* Court's modified "family resemblance" test involves two parts. First, it begins with the Second Circuit's test where "[a] note is presumed to be a 'security,' and that presumption may be rebutted only by showing that the note bears a strong resemblance"[175] to one of the notes on the list of exceptions in terms of four factors: (1) the motivations of a reasonable seller and buyer in entering into the transaction;[176] (2) whether the note is an instrument in which there is "common trading for speculation or investment"; (3) what are the "reasonable expectations" of the public; and (4) whether the transaction is governed by another regulatory scheme which "significantly reduces the risk of the instrument," making the application of federal securities laws unnecessary.[177] But "[i]f an instrument is not sufficiently similar to an item on the list," a second step involves whether another category should be added by considering the same four factors.[178]

Under two of the four *Reves* factors, local scrip (e.g., Deli Dollars) cast in the form of notes should not be a security. When examining the motives of the seller and buyer under *Reves'* first consideration, a note would be a "security" if the seller sought "to raise money for the general use of a business enterprise or to finance substantial investments and the buyer "is interested primarily in the profit the note is expected to generate."[179] "Profit," in the context of notes, is the return on the investment "which undoubtedly includes interest."[180] Arguably, the issuers of discount notes were not seeking to finance a business venture and the note purchasers were not interested primarily in the profit (the interest) the notes were expected to return. The issuers were not motivated by profit and the notes did not purport to yield interest. Rather, community and human empowerment were the leading motivators. Thus, the local currency described in Chapter 5 (e.g., Deli Dollars) does not satisfy the second criterion under *Reves*.

Under the third *Reves* factor, the public could reasonably perceive local scrip as a mere currency, providing a medium of exchange and store of value. Thus, an alternative currency would not be considered a "security" under the reasonable expectations of the public.

More troublesome are the two other *Reves* factors. The existence of a "risk reducing" factor, as the U.S. Supreme Court stated, would make application of the federal securities laws "unnecessary."[181] Like the demand notes in *Reves*, notes such as Deli Dollars are uncollateralized. Thus, such notes do not sufficiently decrease risk to distinguish them from the notes in *Reves*.

A local scrip cast in the form of a note such as Deli Dollars may also satisfy the "common trading for speculation" which is defined narrowly to include as a "security" notes "sold to a broad segment of the population" and not traded on an exchange.[182] Similar to the notes in *Reves* which were offered to more than 23,000 individuals and held by more than 1,600 people, Deli Dollars were and continue to be offered and sold to a broad segment of the public.

The statutory definition of a "security" also encompasses an "evidence of indebtedness."[183] Obviously, the phrase is so broad that a literal reading is impossible. The criteria developed by courts in dealing with notes will likely guide the judiciary in interpreting the phrase "evidence of indebtedness."[184] What can be stated with assurance is that SEC staff declined administrative no-action protection, that is, assurance that the Commission would not take administrative action against the issuer with respect to retail incentive programs rebating 50 percent of the purchase price of certain merchandise in case ten years after purchase.[185]

Investment Contracts

Investments in money-raising schemes may be deemed an "investment contract," a "certificate of interest," or a "profit-sharing agreement" and thus fall in the category of "security" subject to the reach of the 1933 Securities Act, particularly the registration requirement. In *SEC v. W.J. Howey*,[186] the U.S. Supreme Court laid out the basic test: "An investment contract for the purposes of the Securities Act means a contract, transaction or scheme whereby a person [1] invests his money [2] in a common enterprise and [3] is led to expect profits [4] solely from the efforts of the promoter or a third party."[187]

The U.S. Supreme Court has implied that an investment of money must have an affirmative, voluntary nature.[188] For instance, interests in a noncontributory pension plan are not "securities" because the contributions by employers could not be considered an "investment of money."[189] Courts have divided on whether, under the "common enterprise" requirement, investors must share in a single pool of assets ("horizontal commonality") or whether a profit-sharing arrangement between the promoter and each investor ("vertical commonality") is sufficient. The requirement that profits be secured "solely" from the efforts of others has been diluted to one that the profits come "primarily" or "substantially" from the efforts of others.[190]

The *Howey* definition of an investment contract may, thus, raise concerns for certain alternative currencies. A for-profit issuer of local currency, which floats independently of the U.S. dollar (e.g., the Constant), may face scrutiny by the SEC. The Commission may view an investment in such an instrument as a common enterprise in which the purchaser expects profits (a rise in the value of the alternative scrip in relation to the U.S. dollar) primarily from the promoter's efforts. In other words, the SEC might view the scrip issuance as a means of financing the issuer's operation. The issuer, relying on the *Forman* case, discussed next, could counter that the purchaser of an alternative currency does not possess an expectation of substantial profits from the transaction. The main purpose, arguably, was to promote the local economy in a sustainable manner. Using a reasonable expectations test may enable an issuer to remove its scrip from the definition of a "security" under the *Howey* test.

Stocks

As with notes, the words "any ... stock," contained in the statutory definition of a "security," are not always interpreted literally. In *United Housing Foundation v. Forman*,[191] the U.S. Supreme Court held that while most instruments bearing the label of "stock" are likely to be covered by the definition,[192] that fact alone is not sufficient to invoke coverage of the federal securities laws. Instead, the *Forman* Court concluded that it would also determine whether the instrument possessed the traditional indicia of stock, that is, the right to receive dividends, the conferring of voting rights apportioned according to the number of shares owned, and the possibility of appreciating in value.[193] Thus, the Court in *Forman* held that shares of stock in a cooperative housing corporation were not "securities" where "the inducement to purchase was solely to acquire low-cost subsidized living space" and the shares bore none of the characteristics typically associated with stock.[194] Moreover, the purchasers were not misled into believing that federal securities laws applied to their purchase.[195]

Under the "sale of business doctrine," courts once held that the transfer of all outstanding stock in the sale of a business was not a sale of "securities" because the sale was merely a transfer of the ownership and management of the corporation's assets.[196] However, the U.S. Supreme Court rejected the "sale of business" doctrine in *Landreth v. Landreth*,[197] affirming *Forman*, holding that the sale of shares having traditional indicia of stock was a sale of "securities" regardless of the purpose of the transaction or the percentage of shares sold.

Exempt Securities—Short-Term Notes

Even if an instrument meets the definition of a "security," it may be exempt from federal registration requirements. Section 3(a) of the 1933 Securities Act lists several "exempted securities." Generally, an "exempted security" is not subject to the federal registration requirements but may be subject to the federal antifraud and civil liability provisions for the sale of a "security" by misleading statements or omissions.[198]

Section 3(a) (3) exempts "any note ... which has a maturity at the time of issuance of not exceeding nine months."[199] A broad, literal interpretation of this exemption would include any note with a maturity of less than nine months. However, many courts have limited the short-term note exemption to high-grade commercial paper issued by large corporations to finance their current operations.[200]

In *Reves*, the U.S. Supreme Court declined to answer which interpretation would control because the demand notes in question were not short-term notes under either approach. Four of the five justices in the majority, led by Justice Thurgood Marshall, found that the notes in question were not short-term notes even under the literal interpretation.[201] Justice Marshall wrote that a note payable on demand under state law did not make the "maturity" of the demand note less than nine months because the term "maturity" is defined by federal law and Congress could not have intended that the exemptions be applied differently to the same transactions, depending upon which state law happened to apply.[202] Justice John Paul Stevens, writing in concurrence, adopted the commercial paper interpretation and found the notes to be "securities" under the majority test.[203] Four Justices in dissent, led by Justice William H. Rehnquist, declared that the notes in question did have a maturity of nine months or less and embraced the literal approach.[204]

Thus, the local scrip described in Chapter 5 (e.g., Deli Dollars) would probably fall under the exemption for short-term notes. In dictum, the *Reves* Court stated a demand note may be an "exempted security" if "the design of the transaction suggested that both parties contemplated that demand would be made within [the nine-month] period."[205] Properly structured, the maturity of the discount or bargain purchase-type local currency must not exceed nine months. Additionally, unlike *Reves*, there are no laws that vary from state to state that would affect the "maturity" of local scrip.

They *Reves* Court also emphasized that the statutory exclusion for short-term notes must be interpreted in accordance with the exemption's legislative purpose.[206] The persuasive argument that the Court adopted hypothetically was that Congress intended to create a bright-line rule exempting from coverage all notes of less than nine months' duration on the ground that short-term notes are sufficiently safe that the protection afforded investors by the federal securities laws is unnecessary.[207] Given this purpose, a discount or bargain purchase–type note would fall into the exemption provided it has the requisite of short term.

State "Blue Sky" Laws

State securities laws—"blue sky" laws—contain some form of one or more of three basic regulatory devices: (1) registration or licensing of securities prior to any dealing in the securities, which frequently involves procedures and standards for an affirmative administrative review of the merits of a particular issue; (2) antifraud provisions which make it unlawful to make a false or misleading statement or to omit a material fact in connection with the sale of a security; (3) registration or licensing of certain persons engaged in the securities business prior to their trading in securities within a state. Although the details of registration and disclosure requirements of the various state securities laws are beyond the scope of this work, these state statutes define what a "security" is as well as set out various exemptions.

Every U.S. jurisdiction, including Guam[208] and Puerto Rico,[209] defines "security" in terms similar to the federal definition. In their definitions, forty-four states and the District of Columbia explicitly express what is not a "security" in addition to what is.[210] The remaining five states simply list what a "security" is.[211] Additionally, every state, except Ohio and Oregon, exempts short-term notes with maturity of less than nine months.[212]

Exempt Securities—Nonprofit Exemption

Also exempt from the registration and disclosure requirements from the 1933 Act is "[a]ny security issued by a person organized and operated exclusively for religious, educational, benevolent, fraternal, charitable, or reformatory purposes and not for pecuniary profit, and no part of the net earnings of which inures to the benefit of any person, private stockholder, or individual."[213] Similarly, forty-seven jurisdictions, including the District of Columbia, have a comparable non–profit exemption.[214]

A local scrip, such as Deli Dollars, promoted by a for-profit issuer clearly falls outside this nonprofit exemption. However, a local scrip issued by a nonprofit organization, meeting the statutory definition, should qualify for the exemption even if it otherwise meets the definition of a security. The issuer satisfies the first requirement, namely, that it is exclusively organized for religious, educational, or charitable purposes, by receiving a ruling from the Internal Revenue Service that it qualifies as a tax-exempt organization. Because profit motives may make the exemption unavailable,[215] the issuer should also carefully adhere to and operate as a nonprofit organization.

Exempt Transactions—Intrastate Exemption

Section 3(a) (11) of the 1933 Securities Act[216] establishes the "intrastate offering exemption" which, in theory, may prove useful for a profit-seeking issuer of a local scrip that meets the definition of a "security." This exemption from the federal registration burdens is available only for a securities issue offered and sold exclusively to persons resident within one state by an issuer resident and doing business within the state.[217] Thus, if a potential offeree is domiciled outside the state, the exemption is unavailable not only for that offer but also for the entire issue (unless another federal securities law exemption is available), therefore opening the seller-issuer to liability to every person who purchased the security—the local scrip—in the offering. In reality, the intrastate exemption may be of little utility.

Exempt Transactions—Limited Offerings

Section 3(b) of the 1933 Securities Act empowers the SEC to exempt, according to such conditions as it sees fit to establish, the issuance of securities of up to $5 million. Rule 504 of the SEC rules provides an exemption for "small" offerings which may be of interest to a for-profit local scrip issuer offering an instrument meeting the definition of a "security" under the 1933 Securities Act. Any nonpublic issuer can sell up to $1,000,000 in securities during a twelve-month period without having to comply with any federal registration requirements.[218] However, state securities laws remain applicable. In addition, there is no limit under federal securities law on the number of offerees to whom the securities can be sold. Rule 504 also allows for the general solicitation of investors and generally provides for the free transferability of securities under the rule.[219] The antifraud provisions of the federal securities laws still apply.

The multiplicity of state blue sky laws complicate the use of Rule 504 as an exemption from the federal registration requirements pursuant to the 1933 Act. Planners should consider using the Small Corporate Offering Registration Form (SCOR), known as Form U-7, which is available in about thirty-five states. The creation of SCOR makes Rule 504 a more viable exemption. SCOR provides a simplified question and answer disclosure document that serves as a uniform registration form for purposes of state securities registration in those jurisdictions which have adopted the SCOR approach.

FEDERAL INCOME TAX ASPECTS OF LOCAL CURRENCY

Taxation of Barter Exchanges

Income Aspects

As a general matter, the income tax aspects of barter transactions—the exchange of one commodity (or service) for another—are quite simple. The fair market value of the commodity (or service) received represents gross income.[220] The income is realized and recognized in the year the commodity (or service) is received.

At the outset, it is also useful to keep in mind that noncash exchanges may (1) take the form of direct transactions or (2) be handled by barter clubs in which commodities or services may be exchanged for credits which can, in turn, be used to obtain goods or services.

The IRS gives the following example of a two-party bartering transaction that produces taxable income for both parties.[221] A lawyer performed personal legal services for a housepainter who in return painted the attorney's house. In the IRS's example, the lawyer and the painter belonged to a barter club, all of whose members are professional or business persons. The club provided a directory of members who contact each other directly and negotiate for the services to be performed. The IRS concluded that the lawyer and the painter must each include in income the fair market value of the services received from the other.

The IRS has reached similar results in indirect, three-party exchanges accomplished through a barter club. Income tax consequences arose where members of a barter club receive "credit units" as a medium of exchange. For example, a club credits a member's account for goods or services rendered to other members on the basis that one credit unit equals one U.S. dollar of value. Assume the club charges a member a 10 percent commission. The club does not, however, guarantee that a member will be able to use any of his or her credit units. The club does not pay a member cash for any unused credit units. A member can use his or her credit units to purchase goods or services offered by other club members. A member may transfer or sell his or her credit units to another club member.

Under a system involving credit units in a barter club, the members receive taxable income when the credit units are credited to their accounts, up to the U.S. dollar value of the units. Assume that A, B, and C, who use the cash method of accounting, that is, income is realized and recognized for income tax purposes when items are actually or constructively received regardless of when the claims actually arose.[222] The club members agree to provide specific services to any other club member for a specified number of hours while members are entitled to receive services provided by other members. Using a directory provided by the club, members contact each other and request services to be performed. The IRS concluded that the fair market value of the services received by A, B, and C is eligible to be included in their gross incomes in the taxable year in which received, not when the credits are spent. The services received by the taxpayers represent advance compensation for their agreeing to provide future services to other club members.[223]

Information Reporting Requirements

Barter exchanges are also subject to information reporting requirements. A "barter exchange," for purposes of the information reporting requirements, is any organization of members who provide property or services and who jointly either with each other or with the entity contract to trade or barter such property or services directly or through the entity.[224] The term "barter exchange" does not, however, include arrangements that solely provide for the informal exchange of similar services on a noncommercial basis, such as a carpool for commuters to and from work.[225]

Under the Treasury Regulations,[226] a barter exchange must report information with respect to the calendar year in which exchanges of personal property or services are made through the exchange among its members or between its members and the exchange. For this purpose, property or services are exchanged through a barter exchange if: (1) the barter exchange arranges a direct exchange of property or services among its members or exchanges property or services with a member, or (2) if payment for property or services is made by means of a credit on the books of the barter exchange or scrip issued by the barter exchange.[227] These regulations would appear applicable to a LETS approach or an Ithaca HOUR–type system discussed in Chapter 4. However, this rule does not apply to transactions with exempt foreign persons[228] or a barter exchange through which there are fewer than one hundred exchanges during a calendar year. The IRS may require multiple barter exchanges to be combined for the purposes of the information filing requirement if it determines that a material purpose for the formation or continuation of one or more of the barter exchanges was to receive an exemption.[229]

Barter exchanges required to file information returns with respect to exchanges of property or services must file IRS Form 1096 for each calendar year that they are subject to the reporting requirements.[230] IRS Form 1096 is an annual summary that must accompany the transmittal of the IRS information returns to exchange members.

Except for exchanges involving corporate members (which are subject to special rules), for each exchange of property or services that is reportable by a barter exchange, the exchange must file an information return showing: the name, address, and identification number of each member providing property or services in the exchange; the property or services provided; the amount received for such property or services; the date on which the exchange occurred; and any other information required by IRS Form 1096.[231]

For each corporate member providing property or services in an exchange for which an information return is required, the barter exchange reports: the name, address, and identification number of the corporate member; the aggregate amount received by the corporate member during the calendar year for property or services provided by such corporate member for which an information return is required; and any other information required by the information return.[232]

The information return required for both noncorporate and corporate members is IRS Form 1099-B (Statement for Recipients of Proceeds from Broker and Barter Exchange Transactions).[233]

Planners should note the definition of three key terms, "exchange," "amount received," and "fair market value" in connection with the information reporting requirements. An "exchange" occurs with respect to a member of a barter exchange on the date cash, property, services, a credit, or scrip is actually or constructively received by the member as a result of the exchange.[234] The doctrine of constructive receipt deals with when items of income, although not actually received by a taxpayer using the cash method of accounting, should be included in income.

The "amount received" in a barter exchange equals the fair market value of: (1) any credits to the account of the member on the books of the barter exchange; or (2) any issued to the member by the barter exchange. However, the term does not include any amount received in exchange for credits or scrips. The "fair market value" of a credit or scrip equals the value assigned to such credit or scrip by the barter exchange for the purposes of the exchanges unless the IRS requires the use of a different value that the Service determines more accurately reflects fair market value.[235]

If a barter exchange is required to report an exchange pursuant to the information reporting requirements contained in section 6045 of the Internal Revenue Code, it is required to impose backup withholding if: (1) a member of the exchange does not provide a taxpayer identification number (TIN) in the manner referred; or (2) the IRS notified the exchange that the TIN provided by the member is incorrect.[236]

Special Exception from the Information Reporting Requirement

A special exception exists for credits posted to volunteer's accounts in a barter exchange.[237] In the IRS Letter Ruling which gave rise to this exception, the taxpayer in question, a nonprofit organization, supervised a community self-help program. The program, operated by volunteers, maintained a file of individuals with specific skills. The organization linked these skilled individuals with people needing assistance. The assistance provided (e.g., housekeeping, babysitting, house painting) was voluntary. Neither the volunteer service provided nor the service recipient incurred any contractual obligations.

The taxpayer organization kept records of the hours a volunteer spent performing services. When a volunteer performed a service, the taxpayer credited the hours spent to the service provider's account and debited the hours to the service recipient's account. The credits posted to a service provider's account served as a means to motivate the volunteers.

The service providers did not receive a contractual right to receive services when they performed services. The taxpayer organization attempted, however, to link a service provider with other volunteers if a service provider required assistance.

The Service reasoned that the community self-help program in question was not a "barter exchange" under section 6045(c) (3) of the Internal Revenue Code.[238] The Service reasoned that the credits posted to a volunteer service provider's account had no monetary value. The service recipients did not incur a contractual liability on the receipt of services. The service providers did not earn a contractual right to receive services in exchange for performing services. The credits served as a means to motivate volunteers to continue their community service. In other words, the credits provided recognition and a form of bonding. The credits did not serve as a cash substitute.

Deduction Aspects

Commissions paid by a member to a barter exchange are deductible as a business expense if he or she acquires an item for use in his or her trade or business[239] or for investment purposes.[240] Commissions are not deductible if paid to acquire an item for personal purposes.[241]

For tax purposes there are two basic methods of accounting—the cash method and the accrual method. The cash method of tax accounting is used by almost all wage earners and employees. It is also used by taxpayers rendering personal services and other small-scale proprietorships in which inventories are not significant.

The cash method has the merit of simplicity. Under the cash method, the receipt and disbursement of cash, property, or services controls the timing of the realization and recognition of income and deductions. Revenues and expenditures are realized and recognized at the time such items are actually or constructively received or actually paid out, regardless of when the claims or obligations actually arose.[242] The cash method minimizes bookkeeping and accounting duties; indeed for most cash method taxpayers, all "accounting" is done in the family checkbook.

Under the cash method, the disbursement of property or services controls the timing of the deductions. Expenditures, if deductible, are realized and recognized at the time such items are actually paid out, regardless of when the obligations actually arose.[243]

The accrual method of tax accounting was authorized to enable taxpayers to use for their tax books and records the same accounting principles as generally used by the accounting profession. Accountants determine income by (1) "timing" the recognition of revenue and (2) "matching" the related expense items against such revenue. The cash method makes no effort to "time" or to "match" revenue against expenses, because the recognition of revenue or expense only occurs when a receivable or a payable is reduced to cash, property, or services. This simple method is suitable for individuals rendering personal services.

However, a more sophisticated tax accounting method is required to determine more satisfactorily annual income for business taxpayers engaged in the sale of merchandise (such as manufacturers or distributors) who extend credit to customers or who receive credit from suppliers. Almost all businesses of any substantial size use the accrual method of accounting for the recognition of the revenues and expenses. And after 1986, Section 448 of the Internal Revenue Code[244] requires, for income tax purposes, many businesses to be on the accrual method.

In general, under the accrual method, a taxpayer (1) reports income when earned (rather than when actually or constructively received) and (2) takes a deduction when the liability for payment arises, not when an expense item is paid. Thus, accounts receivable (amounts owed to a taxpayer by its customers) and accounts payable (amounts owed by a taxpayer to its suppliers) are generally taken into account when the obligation becomes fixed, even though payment is not received or made until a later period.

In determining when an accrual method taxpayer may deduct expenses, a two-part test must be met. First, the taxpayer must meet an "all events" test, that is, "all events have occurred which determine the fact of liability and the amount of such liability can be determined with reasonable accuracy."[245] Second, economic performance must occur with respect to an item.[246] The net effect of the "economic performance" provision is to postpone a deduction that meets the "all events" test to a time closer to the actual payment of the liability. The requirement of "economic performance" acts as a time constraint on the deductibility of liabilities that satisfy the "all events" test.

Thus, if, in a barter transaction, the liability of a taxpayer requires the taxpayer to provide services, property, or the use of property, and arises out of the use of property by the taxpayer (or out of the provision of services or property to the taxpayer by another person), economic performance occurs to the extent of the lesser of: (1) the extent to which the taxpayer incurs costs in connection with its liability to provide services or property, or (2) the extent to which services or property are provided to the taxpayer.[247]

Even if an item is deductible, the Internal Revenue Code generally prohibits a full and immediate deduction for capital expenditures, that is, an item with a useful life extending substantially beyond the close of the taxable year in which it is acquired.[248] Thus, commissions are treated as a capital expenditure if paid in connection with acquiring a capital item, regardless of a taxpayer's accounting method, even if used in the taxpayer's trade or business. The capitalized amount becomes part of the taxpayer's basis in the asset for which the commission is incurred.

Tax Consequences of Bargain Purchase or Discount Notes

Income Aspects

For income tax purposes, there are two ways of looking at notes such as Deli Dollars: (1) a nontaxable purchase discount transaction; or (2) a taxable discounted note.

A Deli Dollars scrip may serve as a tax-free means to provide purchasers of goods and services with a trade discount. Under long-standing judicial precedent, trade discounts are not included in the seller-taxpayer's gross income.[249] Thus, a seller-taxpayer realizes and recognizes $9 of income when scrip with a face value of $10 is sold to a purchaser. When the purchaser turns in the scrip he or she receives $10 worth of goods or services in a tax-free transaction.

Another way of looking at scrip involves viewing the scrip as a discount note. Thus, the $1 difference between the $9 paid for the scrip and $10 in goods or services for which the scrip is redeemed represents interest. For federal income tax purposes, interest is a payment for the use or forbearance of money made in connection with a valid debt.[250] The IRS treats payments that represent compensation for the use or forbearance of money as interest, regardless of how they are designated by the parties.

Indebtedness exists only if both parties intend to establish an enforceable obligation of repayment—in other words, a debt obligation.[251] The presence or absence of an intent to create a debt is normally tested at the time the "debt" is incurred.

In addition to the "intent" test, to be treated as debt, the obligation must be: (1) enforceable; (2) provable (here the scrip evidences the debt's existence); and (3) unconditional.[252] A further word or two is in order with respect to the enforceability prong of the test for indebtedness. According to the case law, to be classified as debt, the instrument must represent a legally enforceable obligation to make payment in money.[253] Does it make a difference that the payment here takes the form of goods or services? Probably what is more significant is that the scrip was given in exchange for consideration ($9 in U.S. cash). According to one commentator, indebtedness is a "present obligation to repay a money debt, which is not a sham or a disguise for some other relationship."[254]

If the difference between the face amount of the scrip ($10) and the amount paid for it ($9) represents interest, then it is included in the gross income of the scrip holder and is deductible by the business owner. A cash method scrip holder realizes and recognizes the interest in gross income in the year in which he or she redeems the scrip and receives goods and services from the business owner.

Deduction Aspects

Internal Revenue Code Section 163(a) provides a deduction for a taxpayer's adjusted gross income for interest paid or accrued on indebtedness within the taxable year. The terms "paid or accrued" are defined in Section 7701(a) (25) of the Internal Revenue Code.[255] The proper year for the deduction of interest depends mainly on whether the seller-taxpayer uses the cash method or the accrual method for tax accounting purposes. For a cash-method taxpayer–business owner rendering personal services, actual payment is the critical factor.[256] Thus, interest is paid when the scrip holder receives the goods or services from the business owner in exchange for the note.

As discussed earlier, the timing of deductibility of interest for an accrual method taxpayer turns on meeting a two-part test. First, all events must have occurred which determine both the fact of liability and that the amount of such liability can be determined with reasonable accuracy.[257] Second, economic performance must occur. Here, the business owner–taxpayer is to provide goods or services. Economic performance occurs as the taxpayer provides goods or services to the scrip holder.[258]

As discussed in Chapter 6, the scrip issuer may be a nonprofit organization. Thus, the deductibility of interest is not a problem for this type of scrip issuer. However, if the "discount" does not represent a purchase discount, it constitutes taxable interest to a purchaser of the note or scrip.

Special timing rules exist for "original issue discount" instruments. The term "original issue discount" (OID) connotes a debt instrument issued for money where the instrument's "stated redemption price at maturity" exceeds the instrument's "issue price."[259] An instrument's "issue price" is, generally speaking, the amount of money received by the issuer.[260] An instrument's "stated redemption price at maturity" equals the sum of all amounts payable at maturity, however characterized, excluding interest based on a fixed rate and payable unconditionally at fixed periodic intervals of one year or less during the instrument's entire term.[261] In other words, original issue discount is measured by the difference between the amount paid on redemption and the issue price, that is, the amount the borrower will have to pay the note holder at maturity less the amount the issuer received (borrowed), a difference which is, in effect, compound interest on the issue price during the term of the obligation.

Basically, the Internal Revenue Code: (1) characterizes the OID interest element as ordinary income; (2) requires the holder (the creditor) to include in annual income a portion of the OID allocated to the year at issue;[262] and (3) permits the issuer (the debtor) to take a deduction[263] to the extent that the holder is required to include OID in income.

However, the details of the income tax treatment of OID to a note holder and issuer need not concern us because IRC sections 1272 and 163(e) do not apply to short-term debt instruments, that is, any debt instrument that has a fixed maturity date not more than one year from the date of its issue.[264]

Despite the absence of any definitive judicial or administrative materials dealing with the income tax consequences of a bargain purchase/discount note, practicality may supply an answer. Because these notes are issued in bearer form, it probably is impossible for the Internal Revenue Service to enforce compliance with the reporting of interest income realized and recognized by a noteholder.

The compliance dilemma stems from bargain purchase/discount notes falling under an exception to Internal Revenue Code requirements for the registration of debt obligations. To improve taxpayer compliance in reporting interest received on debt instruments, the Internal Revenue Code provides registration requirements for debt obligations. Most publicly traded corporate debt obligations having maturities of one year or more must be in registered form.[265] An obligation is in registered form if the right to the principal of and the stated interest on the obligation may be transferred only through a book entry, that is, a system by which the owner of an obligation can be identified.[266] However, the term "registration required obligation," which triggers the registration requirement, encompasses all interest-bearing obligations except those obligations: (1) issued by natural persons (i.e., not a corporation); (2) of a type not offered to the public; or (3) having a maturity at issue of not more than one year. Thus, bargain purchase/discount notes which take the form of short-term debt instruments are not subject to the registration requirements, thereby creating a massive compliance problem for the Internal Revenue Service.

Tax Aspects of Local Currency Not Pegged to the U.S. Dollar

Transactions in local currency not pegged to the U.S. dollar, such as an exchange of local currency for U.S. dollars, may result in taxable gain or deductible losses because of fluctuations in the value of the local currency which result in exchange gains or loss. Of particular concern is the characterization of the exchange gains or losses as capital gains (or ordinary income) or capital loss (or ordinary loss). If the local currency is a capital asset, it may be receive capital gains or loss treatment.

Currently, the maximum tax rate on capital gains for individuals equals 28 percent.[267] In contrast, the top marginal rate on ordinary income for individuals if the local currency is not a capital asset equals 36 percent and reaches 39.6 percent with a 10 percent surtax on high-income taxpayers. The 28 percent maximum rate for capital gains only applies to individuals, not corporations.[268] The rate differential between capital

gains and ordinary income provides an impetus for individuals to engage in transactions involving local currency which create capital gains
rather than ordinary income.

A capital gain (or loss) is a gain or loss from the sale or exchange of
a capital asset. Once the amount of the gain or loss resulting from the
exchange of local currency into U.S. dollars is computed,[269] the resulting
gain or loss must be characterized. Characterization turns on the nature
of the property sold or exchanged and on the nature of the taxpayer's
trade or business.

Local currency generally is treated as property, that is, a capital asset.[270] However, if local currency is bought or received incidentally to a
taxpayer's trade or business (e.g., by a currency dealer) it is not a capital
asset and its conversion into U.S. currency results in the realization and
recognition of ordinary income or loss.[271]

Assuming that the local currency meets the definition of a capital asset,
the resulting gain or loss from a sale or exchange into U.S. dollars is
characterized as a capital gain or loss. It is then necessary to determine
whether the gain or loss is short term or long term. Section 1222 of the
Internal Revenue Code defines short-term and long-term capital gains or
losses by reference to the length of time the taxpayer held a capital asset
prior to its sale or exchange. Generally, if a taxpayer holds the asset for
more than the requisite holding period (currently one year), the capital
gain or loss is characterized as long-term.[272] Conversely, if the taxpayer
holds the asset for less than the requisite holding period (currently one
year), any capital gain or loss is characterized as short-term.

A noncorporate taxpayer begins by aggregating all capital asset transactions that occur in a taxable year.[273] If all of these transactions taken
together result in a "net capital gain," then the capital gain preference
comes into play. If a noncorporate taxpayer has no net long-term capital
gain or if her net long-term capital gain does not exceed short-term capital loss,[274] the taxpayer cannot use the special capital gains preference
because net short-term capital gains are not included in the term "net
capital gain"[275] and are taxed in the same manner as ordinary income.

All taxpayers, both individual and corporate, may be limited in their
ability to deduct all of their capital losses in the year incurred. An individual can use capital losses as a deduction, without limitation, to offset capital gains.[276] However, if an individual's capital losses exceed
capital gains, then only $3,000 of that excess can be deducted. Thus, the
maximum amount of ordinary income that can be offset by capital losses
is limited to $3,000 annually.[277] Any capital loss deduction that an indi-
vidual taxpayer cannot currently use is merely postponed, because it
may be carried forward (but not back) indefinitely and treated as a capital loss incurred in a subsequent year.[278]

For a corporate taxpayer, capital losses may be deducted in full to the extent of capital gains but any excess may not be used to offset ordinary income.[279] Subject to certain limitations, a corporation may carry back and carry forward its unused capital loss deductions to prior and subsequent tax years.[280]

CONCLUSION

In short, a local currency system may raise questions under federal and state securities laws and under the federal Internal Revenue Code. However, with the possible exception of Virginia and Arkansas, federal or state currency laws would not restrain a system of alternative paper scrip.

The federal bar to private coinage and to the issuance of fractional paper currency denominated at less than one U.S. dollar per unit remains. We may appreciate the necessity of fractional coinage and fractional paper currency by envisioning the national monetary system without half dollars, quarters, dimes, nickels, or pennies. Moreover, the ability to set finer prices would aid producers in pricing products of varying quality and consumers in choosing between different products. As F. A. Hayek noted:

an [issuer] would clearly also have to provide fractional coins; and the availability of convenient fractional coins in that currency might well be an important factor in making it popular. It would also probably be the habitual use of one sort of fractional coins (especially in slot machines, fares, tips, etc.) which would secure the predominance of one currency in the retail trade of one locality.[281]

For local issuers to create some form of fractional coinage, the 1864 Act prohibiting private coinage should, therefore, be repealed, as well as the imposition of criminal sanctions on the issuance of fractional paper currency with a value of less than one U.S. dollar.

eight

Conclusion

An alternative system of local currencies represents a powerful lever for significant institutional change. It provides the means to democratize the creation of money—the medium of exchange—and thus the exchange process, thereby providing the possibility for human empowerment in an ecologically sustainable manner.

The current systems of credit and money issuance are centralized and tightly controlled, tending to depersonalize access to money and favoring large corporate borrowers or those with well-established credit references and collateral. These institutions, by their very size and nature, discriminate not only against small businesses but also against individuals without capital—the poor, minorities, young families, and single women. The prevailing wisdom is that nothing can be done to counter this bias in favor of the large and the well-established; that it is impossible for locally based, democratically organized groups to issue their own money and control their own credit system. As discussed in Chapter 6, this assumption is not true. It *is* possible to break free of the invisible bonds that restrict local control of what is perhaps the most vital of all existing institutions.

But how will change occur? Is the discussion and analysis of our current plight sufficient? Or, as Milton Friedman concludes, will a time of crisis bring about major changes in monetary and other institutions of our political economy:

On the one hand, we are observers of the forces shaping society; on the other, we are participants and want ourselves to shape society.

If there is a resolution to this paradox, it occurs at times of crisis. Then and only then are major changes in monetary and other institutions likely or even possible. What changes thus occur depend on the alternatives that are recognized as available.[1]

We do not know what the reaction will be if urban and rural communities throughout the United States adopt their own local currency. Continuing education about the values of self-sufficient economies and the growing number of initiatives in small-scale local currency issue will set the stage for a major breakthrough. The present reemergence of local currencies points to the end of centralized economies as they exist today. In their wake will come the building of local communities as people discover the empowerment, the enhanced self-reliance and ecological sustainability and the growth of economic stability provided by community control of currency. This is the challenge for the twenty-first century.

Notes

CHAPTER 1

1. David W. Ehrenfeld, *The Arrogance of Humanism* (New York: Oxford University Press, 1978).

2. Jane Jacobs, *Cities and the Wealth of Nations: Principles of Economic Life* (New York: Random House, 1984), 158.

3. Thomas H. Greco, Jr., *New Money For Healthy Communities* (Tucson, Ariz.: Thomas H. Greco, Jr., 1994), 3.

CHAPTER 2

1. For a general discussion, see Shann Turnbull, "Creating a Community Currency," in *Building Sustainable Communities: Tools and Concepts for Self-Reliant Economic Change*, ed. Ward Morehouse (New York: Bootstrap Press, 1989).

2. John Kenneth Galbraith, *Money: Whence It Came, Where It Went* (Boston: Houghton Mifflin Co., 1975), 19–21.

3. Ibid., 21.

4. For a general discussion, see G. A. Selgin, "The Case for Free Banking: Then and Now," *Cato Institute Policy Analysis*, no. 60 (1985): 2–8.

5. Bray Hammond, *Banks and Politics in America* (Princeton, N.J.: Princeton University Press, 1957), 556; George Trivoli, *The Suffolk Bank: A Study of a Free-Enterprise Clearing System* (Leesburg, Va.: Adam Smith Institute, 1979); Wilfred S. Lake, "The End of the Suffolk Systems," *Journal of Economic History* 7 (November 1947).

6. Selgin, "Case for Free Banking," 4.

7. Hammond, *Banks and Politics*, 627.

8. Arthur J. Rolnick and Warren E. Weber, "Free Banking, Wildcat Banking and Shinplasters," *Federal Reserve Bank of Minneapolis Quarterly Review* (Fall 1982): 10–19; Arthur J. Rolnick and Warren E. Weber, "New Evidence on the Free Banking Era," *American Economic Review* 75 (December 1983); Arthur J. Rolnick and Warren E. Weber, "The Causes of Free Banking Failure," *Journal of Monetary Economics* 14 (October 1984). See also Milton Friedman and Anna J. Schwartz, "Has Government Any Role in Money?" *Journal of Monetary Economics* 17 (1986); Hugh Rockoff, "The Free Banking Era: A Reexamination," *Journal of Money, Credit and Banking* 6 (May 1974); Benjamin Klein, "The Competitive Supply of Money," *Journal of Money, Credit and Banking* 6 (November 1974).

9. For a general discussion, see Milton Friedman and Anna J. Schwartz, *A Monetary History of the United States, 1867–1960* (Princeton, N.J.: Princeton University Press, 1963).

10. *U.S. Statutes at Large, 1789–1873* 12 (1863): 665.

11. Richard H. Timberlake, Jr., *Monetary Policy in the United States: An Intellectual and Institutional History* (Chicago: University of Chicago Press, 1993), 87, n. 7, 433.

12. *U.S. Stats. at Large* 13 (1864): 99.

13. *Act of Mar. 3, 1865, U.S. Stats. at Large* 13:469, 484, as amended by *Act of July 13, 1966, U.S. Stats. at Large* 14:146 and *Act of Mar. 26, 1867, U.S. Stats. at Large* 15:6 and as combined *Act of Feb. 8, 1875, U.S. Stats. at Large* 18 (part 3): 307, 311.

14. Timberlake, *Monetary Policy*, 87.

15. Alfred M. Pollard, Keith H. Ellis, and Joseph P. Daly, *Banking Law in the United States*, vol. 1 (Salem, N.H.: Butterworth Legal Publishers, 1993), 2–19.

16. Paul Salstrom, *Appalachia's Path to Economic History, 1730–1940* (Lexington, Ky.: University Press of Kentucky, 1994), 30.

17. *Resumption Act of 1875, U.S. Stats. at Large* 18: 296.

18. *Act of June 20, 1874, U.S. Stats. at Large* 18: 123.

19. Richard H. Timberlake, Jr., "The Central Banking Role of Clearinghouse Associations," *Journal of Money, Credit and Banking* 16 (1984); Timberlake, *Monetary Policy*, 200–202.

20. Selgin, "Case for Free Banking," 7. For further discussion, see A. Piatt Andrew, "Substitutions for Cash in the Panic of 1907," *Quarterly Journal of Economics* 22 (1980): 477–516; Steven Horowitz, "Competitive Currencies, Legal Restrictions, and the Origins of the Fed: Some Evidence From the Panic of 1907," *Southern Economic Journal* 56 (1990): 6–39.

21. *U.S. Stats. at Large* 38 (1913): 251.

22. Timberlake, *Monetary Policy*, 416.

23. *U.S. Stats. at Large* 48 (1933): 112–113.

24. *U.S. Stats. at Large* 48 (1934): 337.

25. Ibid.

26. Ibid.

27. Franklin D. Roosevelt, *The Public Papers and Addresses of Franklin D. Roosevelt*, vol. 3 (Washington, D.C.: GPO, 1938), 75.

28. "Provisional Regulations Issued Under the Gold Reserve Act of 1934, § 20," *Federal Reserve Bulletin* 20 (1934): 82–85.

29. *Modern Money Mechanics* (Chicago: Federal Reserve Bank of Chicago, 1992), 3.

30. *U.S. Code*, vol. 12, sec. 225a (1988).

31. For a general discussion, see Alfred Broaddus, *A Primer on the Fed* (Richmond, Va.: Federal Reserve Bank of Richmond, 1988), 25–45.

32. U.S. House of Representatives, Committee on Banking and Currency, *A Primer on Money*, 88th Cong., 2d sess., 1964, Committee Print.

33. Ibid.

34. Ibid.

35. J. Whitney Hanks and Roland Stucki, *Money, Banking, and National Income* (New York: Alfred A. Knopf, 1956), 11–14.

36. F. A. Hayek, *Denationalisation of Money: An Analysis of the Theory and Practice of Concurrent Currencies* (Lansing, Sussex: The Institute of Economic Affairs, 1976).

CHAPTER 3

1. For a general discussion, see Paul Wachtel, *The Poverty of Affluence: A Psychological Portrait of the American Way of Life* (New York: Free Press, 1983).

2. Louis Uchitelle, "Job Losses Don't Let Up Even as Hard Times Ease," *New York Times* (22 March 1994): A1; Tamar Lewin, "Low Pay and Closed Doors Greet Young in Job Market," *New York Times* (10 March 1994): A1; Louis S. Richman, "When Will The Layoffs End?" *Fortune* (20 September 1993): 54; Peter T. Kilborn, "Working Is Harder, Not Working Harder Still," *New York Times* (5 September 1993): sec. 4, pp. 1, 4; Louis Uchitelee, "Strong Companies Are Joining Trend To Eliminate Jobs," *New York Times* (26 July 1993): A1; Richard J. Barnet, "The End of Jobs," *Harper's* (September 1993): 47.

3. For a general discussion, see Juliet Schor, *The Overworked American* (New York: Basic Books, 1992); Elinor J. Brecher, "Toll and Trouble: Crisis in the American Workplace," *Miami Herald* (21 March 1993): J1.

4. Paul Goodman and Percival Goodman, *Communitas: Means of Livelihood and Ways of Life* (New York: Vintage Books, 1960), 191, 202–203.

5. For a general discussion, see Lewis D. Solomon, "The Microenterprise Revolution, Job Displacement, and the Future of Work: A Policy Commentary," *Chicago-Kent Law Review* 63 (1987): 71–82; G. Pascal Zachary and Bob Ortega, "Age of Angst: Workplace Revolution Boosts Productivity At Cost of Job Security," *Wall Street Journal* (10 March 1993): A1; Kilborn, "Working is Harder," sec. 4, pp. 1, 4.

6. Christina Duff, "Poor Prospects," *Wall Street Journal* (28 July 1993): A1.

7. E. F. Schumacher, *Small is Beautiful: Economics as if People Mattered* (New York: Harper and Row, 1973), 53.

8. Ibid., 62.

9. For a general discussion, see Lewis D. Solomon, "Humanomics: A Model For Third World Development," *George Washington Journal of International Law & Economics* 25 (1991): 447, 459–465; Emily T. Smith, "Global Warming: The Debate Heats Up," *Business Week* (27 February 1995): 119; William K. Stevens, "A Global Warming Resumed in 1994, Climate Data Show," *New York Times* (27 January 1995): A1; William K. Stevens, "More Extremes Found in Weather, Pointing to Greenhouse Gas Effect," *New York Times* (23 May 1995): C4.

10. Alan T. Durning, " . . . And Too Many Shoppers: What Malls and Materialism Are Doing to The Planet," *Washington Post* (23 August 1992): C3; Kenneth R. Hey, "Business As Usual? Forget It," *Across the Board* 29 (January/February 1992): 30.

11. E. F. Schumacher, *Good Work* (New York: Harper and Row, 1979), 29.

12. Ibid.

13. Jane J. Mansbridge, *Beyond Adversary Democracy* (New York: Basic Books, 1980), 235–248.

14. Alvin Toffler, *Powershift: Knowledge, Wealth, and Violence at the Edge of the 21st Century* (New York: Bantam Books, 1990), 180–181.

15. "Corporate Refugees: After the Pain, Some Find Smooth Sailing," *Business Week* (12 April 1993): 58; Jerry Flint, "Keep a Resume on the Floppy, But Don't Panic," *Forbes* (26 April 1993): 65.

16. Toffler, *Powershift*, 180–189.

17. Gar Alpervitz, "Ameristroika Is the Answer," *Washington Post* (13 December 1993): C3; Frank T. Adams and Gary B. Hansen, *Putting Democracy to Work: A Practical Guide for Starting and Managing Worker-Owned Businesses* (San Francisco: Berrett-Koehler, 1992).

18. Henry Hansman, "When Does Worker Ownership Work? ESOPs, Law Firms, Codetermination, and Economic Democracy," *Yale Law Journal* 99 (1990): 1749; Len Krimerman and Frank Lindenfeld, "Changing Worklife: Grassroots Activism Takes a New Turn," in *When Workers Decide: Workplace Democracy Takes Root in North America*, ed. Len Krimerman and Frank Lindenfeld (Philadelphia: New Society Publishers, 1992), 3–5.

19. Alvin Toffler, *The Third Wave* (New York: Morrow, 1980), 282–305; Goodman and Goodman, *Communitas.*

20. Toffler, "Powershift," *Newsweek* (15 October 1990): 86, 90.

21. For example, see Robert A. Dahl, *After the Revolution?* (New Haven, Conn.: Yale University Press, 1970), 143; Robert A. Dahl and Edward R. Tufte, *Size and Democracy* (Stanford, Calif.: Stanford University Press, 1973).

22. For example, see David Morris and Karl Hess, *Neighborhood Power: The New Localism* (Boston: Beacon Press, 1975).

23. Kirkpatrick Sale, *Human Scale* (New York: Coward, McCann, and Geoghegan, 1980), 471–472.

24. Ibid., 196–198.

25. Ibid., 203.

26. Rudolph Bahro, *Building the Green Movement* (London: GMP, 1986), 17–19, 86–91.

27. Herman E. Daly and John E. Cobb, Jr., *For the Common Good* (Boston: Beacon Press, 1989), 273.

28. Sale, *Human Scale*, 237–238.

29. Dahl, *After the Revolution*, 70.

30. Sale, *Human Scale*, 186–187.

31. Ibid., at 398–399.

32. Ibid., 194.

33. Dahl, *After the Revolution?*, 161.

34. Sale, *Human Scale*, 188.

35. Ibid., at 189.

36. David J. Weston, "Money, Banking and the Environment," *New European* 4 (1991): 35–41.

37. For a general discussion, see Robert Swann, "The Need for Local Currencies," Eighth Annual E. F. Schumacher Lectures (October 1988).

38. New York State, Office of Rural Affairs, *Access to Financial Services in Rural New York: A Report to the Governor and the Legislature* (March 1990), 11.

39. Ibid.

40. For a general discussion, see Jacobs, *Cities and the Wealth of Nations* (see chap. 1, n. 2).

41. Ibid.

42. Ibid., 180.

43. Ibid., 162–163.

44. United States Department of Labor, Bureau of Statistics. *Handbook of Labor Statistics* (Washington, D.C.: GPO, 1989), 475, 481; United States Census Bureau, *Statistical Abstract* (1993), 481.

CHAPTER 4

1. For general discussions, see Michael Linton and Thomas Greco, "The Local Employment System," *Whole Earth Review* 22 (22 June 1987): 104; Heather Wardle, "Haircut Will Cost You 3 Acorns; Britain Latest Country to Take Up Canadian Barter System. *The Gazette* (Montreal) (15 January 1994): 16; "LETS Lets Jobless Work in New Barter System," *Financial Post* (Canada) (17 July 1993): 17; Patricia Orwen, "Barter," *The Toronto Star* (20 June 1993): H1; Bruce DeMara, "Recession Survival Kit: Stretching Your Dollar The Barter Way," *Toronto Star* (10 June 1992): A2; Clive Fewins, "Goodbye ECU, Hello Stroud: A Self-Help Group That Deals in Its Own Currency," *Financial Times* (11 April 1992): XV; Gerrard Raven, "As Pound Sinks, Some Britons Turn To Alternative 'Currencies'," *The Reuter Business Report*, 17 February 1993; Will Bennett, "'Payment in Kind' Is Replacing the Pound; Peck, Link and Pond Gain Popularity As Alternative Currencies," *The Independent* (13 December 1993): 6; Monica Porter, "Return to Tender," *Daily Mail* (1 January 1994): 28; Christopher Middleton, "Greenlets—The Caring Cash Alternative," *Sunday Telegraph* (23 January 1994): 13; John Vidal, "Other Lives: Take a Few Pigs Along to the Pie in the Sky Cafe and Watch Payment Go Bob-Bob-Bobbin' Along," *The Guardian* (12 March 1994): 25; Alan Wheatley, "Bobbins, Acorns, Revive Economy at Community Level," *Reuter Newswire*, 17 June 1994; Nicholas Cole, "Cut Your Household Bills by Turning to the Barter System," *The Guardian* (23 June 1990): 14; Rachel Sylvester, "The Barter Economy Gains Currency," *Sunday Telegraph* (22 May 1994): 10; Annette Brown, "Trade Your Skills!" *Daily Mail* (8 December 1993): MSP; Imogen Edwards-Jones, "Trugs? What A Sterling Idea," *The Independent* (17 March 1993): 23; Rachel Bridge, "How to Mow the Lawn With a Few Bobbins," *Evening Standard* (24 February 1993): 30; Andrew Morgan, "How Britons Barter Their Way Out of Debt—Local Exchange Trading Schemes," *The Observer* (17 January 1993): 10; Kate Cole-Adams, "Bucking The System: In Hard Times, Many Australians Are Avoiding The Cash Economy," *Time* (26 July 1993): 40.

2. Susan Litherland, "Ancient Cash-Free Barter System Enters the Computer Age," *Inter Press Service*, 3 March 1994.

3. Greco, Jr., *New Money*, 168–169 (see chap. 1, n. 3).

4. Linton and Greco, "The Local Employment System," 104; Greco, Jr., *New Money*, 89–91, 120–122 (see chap. 1, n. 3).

5. For a general discussion, see Donnella Meadows, "Ithaca Creates Its Own Money," *Berkshire Eagle* (23 May 1994): A7; Carl Vogel, "Money Makers: Turning Community Talent Into Local Currency," *The Neighborhood Works* (August/September 1993): 14; "An Alternative to Cash, Beyond Banks or Barter," *New York Times* (31 May 1993): 28; Paul Glover, telephone interview by author, 19 July 1994; Franklin Crawford, "Got an Ithaca HOUR? Swap It?" *Ithaca Journal* (31 January 1992): 12C.

6. Michelle Silver, "The Ultimate Barter," *Mother Earth News* (August/September 1993): 32; Crawford, "Got an Ithaca Hour?" 12C.

7. "An Alternative to Cash," 28.

8. Silver, "The Ultimate Barter," 32, 34.

9. Crawford, "Got an Ithaca HOUR?" 12C.

10. E. F. Schumacher Society Newsletter (Spring 1994): 1.

11. Glover, interview.

12. Margaret Stafford, "Alternative Currency Use Is Gaining New Popularity," *Boston Globe* (17 January 1994): 3.

13. "Welcome to the Ithaca Time Zone," *Ithaca Money* (February/March 1994): 1.

14. Silver, "The Ultimate Barter," 32, 35 (Interview with Paul Glover).

15. See generally, Ithaca HOURS, Hometown Money Starter Kit (n.d.).

CHAPTER 5

1. For a general discussion, see Michael Specter, "Capitalizing on Yankee Ingenuity," *Washington Post* (20 May 1991): A1; Tim Fitzmaurice, "Local Currency Is Helping Businesses During Recession," *The Lakeville Journal* (15 August 1991): A2; Susan Witt, "Deli Dollars, Trash Cash and Local Loans: An Interview with Susan Witt," in *Green Business: Hope or Hoax?* ed. Christopher Plant and Judith Plant (Philadelphia: New Society Publishers, 1991), chap. 13, pp. 95–104; Mark J. McGuire, "Making Money the Old-Fashioned Way," *Albany Times Union* (30 August 1992): A1; M. A. J. McKenna, "Short on Cash? This Guy Prints His Own," *Boston Herald* (30 June 1991): 1; Thelma O'Brien, "Scrip Becoming Popular Alternative to Loans," *Berkshire Record* (26 April 1991): B1; Philip Crawford, "Homemade Money Means Another Day, Another Deli Dollar," *International Herald Tribune* (12–13 October 1991): 17.

2. For a general discussion, see Judith Gaines, "Food-Backed Financing: Great Barrington To Begin Trade In Deli Dollars," *Boston Globe* (29 October 1989): 75; Michelle Locke, "Restaurant Issues Its Own Deli Dollars," *Los Angeles Times* (19 November 1989): 23; McGuire, "Making Money the Old-Fashioned Way," A1; "Deli Dollars the Talk of the Town," *Syracuse Herald-Journal* (23 November 1989): BB2; "'Deli Dollars' Gain Currency as a Capitalist Experiment," *Berkshire Eagle* (12 November 1989): A8.

3. Fitzmaurice, "Local Currency Is Helping Businesses During Recession," A2, A12.

4. McKenna, "Short on Cash?" 1, 8.

5. For a general discussion, see Judith Gaines, "'Greenbacks' Tide Farmers Over Winter," *Boston Globe* (28 January 1990): 61; Steve Moore, "South County Farm 'Money' Goes On Sale," *Berkshire Eagle* (22 December 1989): B1; Steve Moore, "Farm Notes Being Used at 2 Farms," *Berkshire Eagle* (23 July 1990): B1; Michelle Locke, "Produce Stands Put Their Trade in Stock," *Philadelphia Inquirer* (7 January 1990): B11; Stephen Fax, "South County Farms Issue Their Own Money," *Berkshire Eagle* (20 December 1989): B1.

6. "2nd Issue of Berkshire Farm Notes," *E. F. Schumacher Society* (Winter 1990–91), 2; Susan Witt, interview by author, Great Barrington, Mass., 8 June 1994. If the notes are distributed to several participating businesses in varying percentages, the parties would, of course, be responsible to the issuer for their specific proportion of the notes.

7. Michael Specter, "Only the Real Money Is Tight," *International Herald Tribune* (21 May 1991): 9; "2nd Issue," 2.

8. Paul Gilkes, "Scrip Novel Solution to Business Slump," *Coin World* 32 (1991): 1.

9. Witt, interview.

10. Ibid.

11. Ibid.

12. Susan Witt, "Print Your Own Currency," interview, *Innovation Group* 1 (Summer 1991): 33; Mark K. Anderson, "Au Courrency," *Valley Advocate* (13 September 1993): 4.

13. Nancy O'Shaughnessy, "Great Barrington Berk-Shares Shopping Promotion Said to Be Generating Late-Summer Enthusiasm, Sales," *Berkshire Record* (28 August 1992): A6; Nancy O'Shaughnessy, "Berk-Shares Going Like Hotcakes," *Berkshire Record* (4 September 1992): A6; Abby Pratt, "Berk-Shares Make Barrington Debut," *Berkshire Eagle* (29 July 1992): D1; "Merchants in Downtown Great Barrington Offering Berk-Shares in Unique Promotion," *Berkshire Business Journal* (September 1992): 8; "It's Berk-Shares Time Again," *Berkshire Record* (30 July 1993): B8; Susan Witt, "Catching the Berk-Shares Fever," *Berkshire Record* (17 September 1993): A6.

14. Susan Witt, letter to author, 14 June 1994.

15. Ibid.

16. Witt, interview.

CHAPTER 6

1. Ralph Borsodi, *Inflation and the Coming Keynesian Catastrophe: The Story of the Exeter Experiments with Constants* (Great Barrington, Mass.: E. F. Schumacher Society and The School for Living, 1989).

2. "The Exeter Experiment," Forbes, 1 February 1974, 45; Borsodi, *Inflation*, 28–32; Frank Donovan, "Exeter's Funny Money Not Meant For Laughs," *Boston Sunday Globe* (1 October 1972): A8; Richard J. Stinson, "The Exeter Affair Or, Has a Nice New England Town Really Beaten Inflation?," *Financial World* 141 (17 February 1974): 28; "The Borsodi Constant: An Inflation-Free Currency," *Mother Earth News* 27 (1974): 82–84.

3. The basket of thirty commodities consisted of: nine metals (gold, silver, aluminum, copper, iron, lead, nickel, tin, and zinc); thirteen food staples (barley, cocoa, coffee, copra, corn, cottonseed, oats, peanuts, rice, rye, soybeans, sugar, and wheat); energy (petroleum); and seven raw materials (cement, cotton, hides, jute, rubber, sulphur, and wool).

4. Borsodi, *Inflation*, 52.

5. "The Exeter Experiment," 45.

6. "Paying With Constants Instead of Dollars," *Business Week*, 4 May 1974, 29.

7. Ibid.

8. "The Exeter Experiment," 45.

9. "Paying With Constants," 29.

10. Ibid.

11. Robert Swann, interview with author, Great Barrington, Mass., 8 June 1994.

12. Robert Swann, *Establishing an Alternative Independent Currency: The Case for Using Forests as a Reserve Currency* (n.p., n.d.).

13. Shann Turnbull, "Creating a Community Currency," in *Building Sustainable Communities: Tools and Concepts for Self-Reliant Economic Change*, ed. Ward Morehouse (New York: Bootstrap Press, 1989), 156–159.

14. *U.S. Code*, vol. 16, sec. 824a–3. For a general discussion, see Joseph T. Kelliher, "Pushing the Envelope: Development of Federal Electrical Transmission Access Policy," *American University Law Review* 42 (Winter 1993): 543; Stanley A. Martin, "Problems with PURPA: The Need for State Legislation to Encourage Cogeneration and Small Power Prediction," *Boston College Environmental Affairs Law Review* 11 (Fall 1983): 149.

15. *The Federal Power Act, U.S. Code*, vol. 16, secs. 796(17)–(18) (1988).

16. Richard Rahn, "Time to Privatize Money? How Good Currency Can Drive Out Bad," *Policy Review* 36 (Spring 1989): 55; Richard Rahn, "Private Money: An Idea Whose Time Has Come," *Cato Journal* 9 (Fall 1986): 353.

17. Lawrence H. White, "What Kinds of Monetary Institutions Would a Free Market Deliver," *Cato Journal* 9 (Fall 1989): 367.

18. For a general discussion, see Lewis D. Solomon and Melissa B. Kirgis, "Business Cooperatives: A Primer," *DePaul Business Law Journal* 6 (1994): 233.

19. Self-Help Association for a Regional Economy, *Proposed Bank Participation in the Berkshare Program* (n.p., n.d.).

20. *U.S. Code*, vol. 12, sec. 2901–2906 (1988). Pollard, Ellis, and Daly, *Banking Law*, secs. 15–48 to 15–59 (see chap. 2, n. 14); Roland E. Brandel and David E. Teitelbaum, *The Community Reinvestment Act: Policies and Compliance* (Englewood Cliffs, N.J.: Prentice Hall Law & Business, 1989 and Supp. 1991); Warren L. Dennis and J. Stanley Potter, *Federal Regulation of Banking: Redlining and Community Reinvestment: Analysis, Commentary and Compliance Procedures* (Boston: Warren, Gorham & Lamont, 1980), chaps. 9–10; Kevin Kane, *A Banker's Guide to the Community Reinvestment Act: Case Studies of 33 Institutions* (Washington, D.C.: Bureau of National Affairs, 1991); Richard Marsico, "A Guide to Enforcing the Community Reinvestment Act," *Fordham Urban Law Journal* 20 (Winter 1993): 165.

21. *U.S. Code*, vol. 12, sec. 2901(a) (1988).

22. *U.S. Code*, vol. 12, sec. 2903 (1988).

23. Some of the factors bank examiners should consider in assessing a bank's conformity with the goals and the guidelines of the CRA are set forth in Federal Financial Institutions Examination Council, *A Citizen's Guide to CRA* (Washington, D.C.: The Council, 1985).

24. *U.S. Code*, vol. 12, sec. 2903(b) (1994). New rules reduce the burden of small banks—those with less than $250 million in assets—to produce loan documentation and other paperwork during CRA compliance examinations. Community Reinvestment Act Regulations, 12 CFR Part 228 (Regulation BB).

25. For example, see Illinois *Compiled Statutes*, chap. 205, secs. 10/3.02, 10/3.071 (1994); Iowa Code, sec. 524.1901 (1992); Massachusetts *Annotated Laws*, ch. 167, sec. 14 (1994); New York Banking Law, sec. 28(b) (1993); Washington *Revised Code*, sec. 30.60.010 (1993); Brandel and Teitelbaum, *The Community Reinvestment Act*, 227.

26. For example, see Arkansas *Code Annotated*, sec. 23–32–1804 (1993); Delaware *Code Annotated*, tit. 5, sec. 163 (1993); Indiana *Code Annotated*, sec. 28–2–13–12 (1993); Iowa Code, sec. 524–1905 (1992); Kansas Statutes Annotated, sec. 9–533 (1992); Michigan Compiled *Statutes Annotated*, sec. 487.430b (1992); Nebraska *Revised Statutes*, sec. 8–902.03 (1992); Ohio *Revised Code Annotated*, sec. 1111.03 (1994); Texas *Revised Civil Statutes Annotated*, art. 342–912 (1994); Vermont *Statutes Annotated*, tit. 8, sec. 1055 (1993); Wisconsin Statutes, sec. 221–58 (1993).

27. Lawrence H. White, *Competition and Currency: Essay on Free Banking and Money* (New York: New York University Press, 1989).

28. Robert Pease, "Promoting Regional Enterprise," *Christian Science Monitor* (3 November 1986): 27; Gary Van Jura, "SHARE Helps Area Businesses Obtain Financing for Small Projects Through Secured Bank Loans," *Berkshire Business Journal* (March 1987): 19; U.S. House Staff Report of the Select Committee on Hunger, *Access and Availability of Credit to the Poor in Developing Countries and the United States*, 100th Cong., 1st sess., 1987, 23; Self-Help Association for a Regional Economy, *Local Investment Means Community Profits* (n.p., n.d.); Self-Help Association for a Regional Economy, *What is SHARE?* (n.p., n.d.).

29. Jane Jacobs, *Systems of Survival: A Dialogue on the Moral Foundations of Commerce and Politics* (New York: Vintage Books, 1992), 160.

30. Charles P. Kindleberger, "Standards as Public, Collective and Private Goods," *Kyklos* 36 (1983): 377.

31. Leland B. Yeager, "Stable Money and Free-Market Currencies," *Cato Journal* 3 (Spring 1983): 305.

32. Rahn, "Private Money."

33. White, *Competition and Currency*, 57–64; George A. Selgin, *The Theory of Free Banking* (Totowa, N. J.: Rowman and Littlefield, 1988), 154.

34. Roland Vaubel, "Competing Currencies: The Case for Free Entry," *Zeitschrift für Wirtscchafts-und Sozialwissenschaften*, 36 (1985): 547, 586, reprinted in *Free Banking: Modern Theory and Policy* 3, ed. Lawrence H. White (Brookfield, Vt.: Edward Elgar Publishing Co., 1993).

35. Hayek, *An Analysis*, 37 (see chap. 2, n. 35). See also F. A. Hayek, *Denationalisation of Money: The Argument Refined: An Analysis of the Theory and Practice of Concurrent Currencies* (London: The Institute of Economic Affairs, 1990).

36. Hayek, *An Analysis*, 37 (see chap. 2, n. 35).

37. White, *Competition and Currency*, 29–34.

38. Hayek, *An Analysis*, 44–45.

39. Ibid., 40–41, 84–85.

40. Ibid., 51.

41. Ibid., 92.

42. Lawrence H. White, "What Kinds of Monetary Institutions Would a Free Market Deliver," *Cato Journal* 9 (Fall 1989): 367; Bart Taub, "Private Fiat Money with Many Suppliers," *Journal of Monetary Economics* 16 (September 1985): 195.

43. Richard N. Cooper, "Is Private Money Optional?" *Cato Journal* 9 (Fall 1989): 393.

44. Selgin, *The Theory of Free Banking*, 151.

45. Roland Vaubel, "Currency Competition versus Governmental Money Monopolies," *Cato Journal* 5 (Winter 1986): 927; Selgin, *The Theory of Free Banking*, 151.

46. Benjamin Klein, "The Competitive Supply of Money," *Journal of Money, Credit and Banking* 6 (November 1974): 423.

47. Selgin, *The Theory of Free Banking*, 151.

48. Hayek, *An Analysis* (see chap. 2, n. 35).

49. Friedman and Schwartz, "Has Government Any Role in Money?" 45–46 (see chap. 2, n. 8).

50. Ibid., 49. White adds: "It is doubtful that a parallel monetary system could gain much of a foothold even in the absence of legal impediments, because of the natural tendency of money users in a region to converge on a common monetary unit. Each trader finds it most convenient to hold the money that he believes others will most likely accept in the near future, which normally is the money they have been accepting in the immediate past, even if that money is depreciating." White, *Competition and Currency*, 64.

51. Milton Friedman, "Monetary Policy: Tactics versus Strategy," in *The Search for Stable Money*, ed. James A. Dorn and Anna J. Schwartz (Chicago: University of Chicago Press, 1987), 374.

CHAPTER 7

1. James W. Hurst, *A Legal History of Money in the United States, 1774–1970* (Lincoln: University of Nebraska Press, 1973), 8–18.

2. Joseph Story, *Commentaries on the Constitution of the United States* (Littleton, Colo.: F. B. Rothman, 1991), sec. 1118.

3. Ibid., sec. 1119. Also see Edwin Vieira, Jr., *Pieces of Eight* (Fort Lee, N. J.: Sound Dollar Committee, 1983), 5–18.

4. U.S. Constitution, art. 1, sec. 10, cl. 1.

5. Ibid.

6. Ibid.

7. Ibid., art. 1, sec. 8, cl. 2.

8. Ibid., art. 1, sec. 8, cl. 5.

9. Ibid., art. 1, sec. 8, cl. 6.

10. Vieira, *Pieces of Eight*.

11. Ibid., 39–40.

12. U.S. Constitution, art. 1, sec. 8, cl. 5.

13. U.S. Articles of Confederation, art. 10.

14. The anticounterfeiting provision, U.S. Constitution, art. 1, sec. 8, cl. 5, re-inforces the Framers' intent to limit "Money" to coin. By distinguishing between "the Securities and current Coin of the United States," the Constitution author-izes the United States Congress to punish counterfeiting "Money" of the United States, composed of "regulate[d]" domestic and foreign "Coin," and "Securities" which are promises to pay "borrow[ed] Money." Vieira, *Pieces of Eight*, 87.

15. U.S. Constitution, art. 1, sec. 10, cl. 1.

16. *Records of the Federal Convention of 1787*, ed. Michael Farrand (1966).

17. *The Legal Tender Cases*, 79 U.S. 457 (1871).

18. U.S. Constitution, art. 1, sec. 8, cl. 5.

19. *U.S. Stats. at Large* 1 (1792): 246.

20. *Annals of the Congress of the United States, 1789–1824* (Washington, D. C., 1834–1856) 2: 2112.

21. Vieira, *Pieces of Eight*, 95–98.

22. Roland P. Faulkner, "The Private Issue of Token Coins," *Political Science Quarterly* 16 (1901): 316, 324; Herbert E. Feavearyear, *The Pound Sterling* (London: Oxford University Press, 1932), 157, 192, 296; Opinion of the Attorney General (1888) 19:98.

23. *Thorington v. Smith*, 75 U.S. 1 (1869).

24. Ibid., 11.

25. *Chapman v. Cole*, 78 Mass. 141 (1858).

26. *United States v. Van Auken*, 96 U.S. 366 (1877).

27. *Hollister v. Mercantile Institution*, 111 U.S. 62 (1884).

28. *Van Auken*, 367–368.

29. *Hollister*, 65.

30. Vieira, *Pieces of Eight*, 28, n. 142.

31. Horace White, *Money and Banking* (Boston: Ginn and Company, 1935), 34.

32. Ibid.

33. Ibid.

34. Ibid. Five-dollar pieces ranged in value from $4.36 to $5. Ibid.

35. *U.S. Stats. at Large* 13 (1864): 120.

36. *Rev. Stat. U.S.*, sec. 5461 (1873).

37. *U.S. Stats. at Large* 35 (1909): 1120.

38. *U.S. Stats. at Large* 62 (1948): 709.

39. U.S. Senate, Special Committee on the Revision of the Laws, 60th Cong., 1st sess., 1908, S. Rept. 10; U.S. House, Committee on the Judiciary, 80th Cong., 1st sess., 1947, H.R. Rept. 304; U.S. Senate, Committee on the Judiciary, 80th Cong., 2d sess., 1948, S. Rept. 1620.

40. *U.S. Code*, vol. 18, sec. 486 (1988).

41. *U.S. Code*, vol. 18, sec. 491 (1995) provides: "Whoever makes, issues, cir-culates, or pays out any note, check, memorandum, token, or other obligation for a less sum than $1, intended to circulate as money or to be received or used in lieu of lawful money of the United States, shall be fined . . . or imprisoned not more than six months, or both."

42. *United States v. Gellman*, 44 F. Supp. 360 (1942).

43. Ibid., 364.

44. *United States v. Roussopulous*, 95 F. 977 (1899).

45. Ibid., 978.

46. *State v. Quackenbush,* 108 N.W. 953 (Minn. 1906).

47. Ibid., 955.

48. *Anchorage Centennial Dev. Co. v. Van Wormer & Rodriguez,* 443 P. 2d 596 (Alaska 1968).

49. Ibid., 598.

50. *Gellman,* 364.

51. *United States v. Falvey,* 676 F. 2d 871 (1982). The court stated that "the primary concern of Congress [in enacting the 1864 act] seems to have been with the prohibition of private systems of coinage created for use in competition with the official United States coinage." *Falvey,* 876.

52. *U.S. Code,* vol. 18, secs. 471–509 (1988).

53. (a) Whoever, being 18 year of age or over, not lawfully authorized, makes, issues, or passes any coin, card, token, or device in metal, or its compounds, intended to be used as money, or whoever, being 18 years of age or over, with intent to defraud, makes, utters, inserts, or uses any card, token, slug, disk, device, paper, or other thing similar in size and shape to any of the lawful coins or other currency of the United States or any coin or other currency not legal tender in the United States, to procure anything of value, or the use or enjoyment of any property or service from any automatic merchandise vending machine, postage-stamp machine, turnstiles, fare box, coinbox telephone, parking meter or other lawful receptacle, depository, or contrivance designed to receive or to be operated by lawful coins or other currency of the United States, shall be fined not more than $1,000, or imprisoned not more than one year, or both.

(b) Whoever manufactures, sells, offers, or advertises for sale, or exposes or keeps with intent to furnish or sell any token, slug, disk, device, paper, or other thing similar in size and shape to any of the lawful coins or other currency of the United States, or any token, disk, paper, or other device issued or authorized in connection with rationing or food and fiber distributed by any agency of the United States, with knowledge or reason to believe that such tokens, slugs, disks, devices, papers, or other things are intended to be used unlawfully or fraudulently to procure anything of value, or the use or enjoyment of any property or service from any automatic merchandise vending machine, postage-stamp machine, turnstile, fare box, coinbox telephone, parking meter, or other lawful receptacle, depository, or contrivance designed to receive or to be operated by lawful coins or other currency of the United States shall be fined not more than $1,000 or imprisoned not more than one year, or both. *U.S. Code,* vol. 18, sec. 491 (1988).

54. Ibid.

55. Ibid.

56. *Gellman,* 364.

57. *Van Wormer,* 597–598.

58. *United States v. Smith,* 318 F. 2d 94 (1963).

59. Ibid., 95.

60. Ibid., 96.

61. *Wholesale Vendors of Texas, Inc. v. United States,* 361 F. Supp. 1045, 1047 (N.D. Tex. 1973).

62. Edward J. Devitt, Charles B. Blackmar, and Michael A. Wolff, *Federal Jury*

Practice and Instructions: Civil and Criminal (St. Paul, Minn.: West Publishing Co., 1987), sec. 52.10).

63. *Craig v. State of Missouri*, 29 U.S. 410 (1830).

64. Ibid., 432.

65. Ibid.

66. *Briscoe v. Bank of Kentucky*, 36 U.S. 257 (1837).

67. Ibid., 314.

68. *Poindexter v. Greenhow*, 114 U.S. 270 (1885).

69. Ibid., 284.

70. *Houston and Texas Central Railroad v. Texas*, 177 U.S. 66 (1900).

71. *Briscoe v. Bank of Kentucky*, 36 U.S. 257 (1837).

72. *Darrington v. Bank of Alabama*, 54 U.S. 12 (1851); *Curran v. Arkansas*, 56 U.S. 304 (1854).

73. *Briscoe v. Bank of Kentucky*, 36 U.S. 257 (1837).

74. *Woodruff v. Trapnail*, 51 U.S. 190 (1851).

75. *Police Jury v. Britton*, 82 U.S. 566, 570 (1872).

76. *The Mayor v. Ray*, 86 U.S. 468, 475, 478 (1873).

77. *Briscoe*, 257 (1837).

78. Ibid., 348.

79. *Act of Feb. 25, 1863, U.S. Stats. at Large* 12: 665.

80. *Act of Mar. 3, 1863, U.S. Stats. at Large* 12: 709.

81. *Act of June 30, 1864, U.S. Stats. at Large* 13: 223, 277.

82. *Act of Mar. 3, 1865, U.S. Stats. at Large* 13: 469, 484.

83. *Act of July 13, 1866, U.S. Stats. at Large* 14: 98, 146.

84. *Veazie Bank v. Fenno*, 75 U.S. 533 (1869).

85. *Act of Mar. 26, 1867, U.S. Stats. at Large* 15: 6.

86. *Act of Feb. 8, 1875, U.S. Stats. at Large* 18: 307, 311.

87. Opinion of the Attorney General (1893) 20: 534.

88. *National Bank v. United States*, 101 U.S. 1 (1879).

89. U.S. Department of Commerce, *Historical Statistics of the United States: Colonial Times to 1970* (Washington, D.C.: GPO, 1975), 1027, 1030.

90. Ibid.

91. *Hollister*, 111 U.S. 62 (1884).

92. Ibid., 65.

93. Ibid.

94. Opinion of the Attorney General (1893) 20: 681.

95. Opinion of the Attorney General (1888) 19: 98.

96. Ibid.

97. *U.S. Stats. at Large* 90 (1976): 1520.

98. *U.S. Stats. at Large* 90 (1976): 1814.

99. U.S. House Committee on Ways and Means, *Tax Reform Act of 1976*, 94th Cong., 2d sess. (1976) H. R. Rept. 94–658, 526; U.S. Senate Finance Committee, *Tax Reform Act of 1976*, 94th Cong., 2d sess. (1976) S. Rept. 94–938, 406.

100. Arthur Nussbaum, *A History of the Dollar* (Boston: Ginn and Company, 1957), 130–131.

101. *U.S. Stats. at Large* 31 (1900): 45.

102. *U.S. Stats. at Large* 48 (1933): 112–113.

103. *U.S. Stats. at Large* 48 (1934): 337, 340.

104. Roosevelt, Presidential Statement (see chap. 2, n. 26).

105. *Perry v. United States,* 294 U.S. 330 (1935); *Nortz v. United States,* 294 U.S. 317 (1935); *Norman v. Baltimore & O.R.R.,* 294 U.S. 240 (1935) (consolidated for review with *United States v. Bankers Trust Co.*).

106. *Norman.*

107. *Nortz; Perry.*

108. *Norman,* 303.

109. *U.S. Stats. at Large* 91 (1977): 1227, 1229.

110. *Par Value Modification Act Amendments, U.S. Stats. at Large* 87 (1973): 352.

111. See n. 108.

112. For example, see Arkansas *Code Annotated* (Michie 1993), sec. 11–4–403; California *Labor Code* (West 1993), sec. 212; Colorado *Revised Statutes,* sec. 8–4–102; District of Columbia *Code Annotated,* sec. 36–102; Indiana *Code Annotated* (Burns 1994), sec. 22–2–4–2; Kentucky *Revised Statutes Annotated,* sec. 244 (1993); Nevada *Revised Statutes Annotated* (Michie 1993), sec. 608.120; Oklahoma *Statutes,* sec. 165.2 (1994); Tennessee *Code Annotated,* sec. 50–2–102; Texas *Revised Civil Statutes Annotated,* sec. 5159b; Vermont *Statutes Annotated,* sec. 343; Virginia *Code Annotated* (Michie 1994), sec. 40.1–29.

113. Florida *Statutes Annotated* (West 1994), sec. 831.26. The Massachusetts statute provides: "Whoever issues or passes a note, bill, order or check, other than foreign bills of exchange, the notes or bills of a bank incorporated by the laws of this commonwealth, of the United States, of some one of the United States . . . , with the intent that the same shall be circulated as currency, shall be punished by a fine of fifty dollars" (Mass. *Gen. L.* ch. 267, sec. 21 (West 1993). A similar fine is imposed on the issuance or passing of a small note; that is, for an amount less than five dollars (Mass. *Gen. L.* ch. 267, sec. 22 (West 1993).

114. Virginia *Code Annotated* (Michie 1994), sec. 6.1–330.52. The Arkansas statute provides: "No person unauthorized by law shall intentionally create or put in circulation, as a circulating medium, any note, bill, bond, check, or ticket, purporting that any money or bank notes will be paid to the receiver, holder, or bearer, or that it will be received in payment of debts or to be used as a currency or medium of trade in lieu of money." The issuer is subject to criminal fine and imprisonment. Arkansas *Code Annotated* (Michie 1994), sec. 4-17-102.

115. Virginia *Code Annotated* (Michie 1994), sec. 6.1–330.49.

116. Vermont *Statutes Annotated* (1993) tit. 11, secs. 921 to 938.

117. Vermont *Statutes Annotated* (1993) tit. 13, sec. 1805.

118. Kenneth E. Scott, "The Patchwork Quilt: State and Federal Roles in Bank Regulation," *Stanford Law Review* 32 (1980): 687; Howard H. Hackley, "Our Baffling Banking System," *Virginia Law Review* 52 (1966): 565.

119. *U.S. Code,* vol. 12, sec. 282 (1988).

120. *U.S. Code,* vol. 12, sec. 1814(b) (1988).

121. *U.S. Stats. at Large* 38 (1913): 251.

122. *U.S. Stats. at Large* 18 (1874): 123.

123. *U.S. Stats. at Large* 64 (1950): 873.

124. *U.S. Code,* vol. 12, sec. 321 (1988).

125. *U.S. Code,* vol. 12, sec. 1814(b) (1988).

126. William H. Schlichting et al., *Banking Law* (New York: Matthew Bender, 1994), sec. 1.05(1)).

127. For a more in-depth discussion of state banking laws, see Scott, "The Patchwork Quilt"; Hackley, "Baffling Banking System"; Schlichting, *Banking Law*.

128. For a more in-depth discussion of state banking laws, see ibid.

129. *U.S. Code*, vol. 12, sec. 110 (1988).

130. *U.S. Code*, vol. 12, sec. 88 (1988).

131. See *U.S. Code*, vol. 12, sec. 221 (1988) (stating that "[w]herever the word 'bank' is used in [title 12 or the Federal Reserve Act], the word shall be held to include State bank, banking association, and trust company, except where national banks or Federal Reserve banks are specifically referred to").

132. See *U.S. Code*, vol. 12, secs. 411–421 (1988).

133. *U.S. Code*, vol. 12, sec. 103 (1988).

134. *U.S. Code*, vol. 12, sec. 104 (1988).

135. *U.S. Code*, vol. 12, sec. 105 (1988).

136. *U.S. Code*, vol. 12, sec. 106 (1988).

137. *Code of Federal Reg.*, vol. 12, part 229 (1994).

138. *U.S. Stats. at Large* 101 (1987): 552, 635.

139. Ibid.

140. *Code of Federal Reg.*, vol. 12, parts 229.30–229.42 (1994).

141. *Code of Federal Reg.*, vol. 12, part 229.2(e) (1994).

142. *Code of Federal Reg.*, vol. 12, part 229.2(z) (1994).

143. *Code of Federal Reg.*, vol. 12, part 229.2(k) (1994).

144. *Code of Federal Reg.*, vol. 12, part 210.2(f) (1994).

145. *U.S. Code*, vol. 12, sec. 342 (1988).

146. *Code of Federal Reg.*, vol. 12, part 210 (1994).

147. *Code of Federal Reg.*, vol. 12, part 210.2(f) (1994).

148. *Uniform Comm. Code*, sec. 4–104(7) (1993).

149. *Uniform Comm. Code*, sec. 3–103(6) (1993).

150. *Uniform Comm. Code*, sec. 1–201(24) (1993).

151. *Uniform Comm. Code*, sec. 3–107 (1993).

152. Sheila O'Heney, "Keeping CHIPS Safe and Private," *ABA Banking Journal* (May 1991): 56.

153. Ibid.

154. Ibid.

155. Massachusetts *General Laws*, ch. 167, sec. 2(25) (Supp. 1994).

156. Georgeann F. Abbanat, Letter to Susan Witt, 6 November 1985.

157. Arkansas *Code Annotated*, sec. 23–32–701(b)(8); Colorado *Revised Statutes Annotated* (West 1993), sec. 11–10–104; Connecticut *General Statutes*, sec. 36–57(i); District of Columbia *Code Annotated*, sec. 26–409; Georgia *Code Annotated*, sec. 7–1–261(1); Indiana *Code*, sec. 28–1–11–2; Kentucky *Revised Statutes Annotated* (Baldwin 1993), sec. 287.210; Louisiana *Revised Statutes Annotated* (West 1993), sec. 6:241(B)(6); Michigan *Compiled Laws*, sec. 487.451(10); Mississippi *Code Annotated*, sec. 81–12–49; Missouri *Revised Statutes*, sec. 362.105; Montana *Code Annotated*, sec. 32–1–107(4); New York Banking Law, sec. 100; Pennsylvania *Consolidated Statutes*, sec. 202(a); Tennessee *Code Annotated*, sec. 45–2–1002; Vermont *Statutes Annotated*, sec. 605(7); Virginia *Code Annotated* (Michie 1993), sec. 6.1–17; West Virginia *Code*, sec. 31A–4–14.

158. *U.S. Code*, vol. 15, secs. 77a–77aa (1988). Other federal securities laws include the Securities Exchange Act of 1934, 15 U.S.C. secs. 78a–78kk (1988), Public

Utility Holding Company Act of 1935, 15 U.S.C. secs. 79–79z–6 (1988), Trust
Indenture Act of 1939, 15 U.S.C. secs. 77aaa–77bbbb (1988), Investment Advisers
Act of 1940, 15 U.S.C. secs. 80b–1–80b–21 (1988), and Investment Advisers Act
of 1940, 15 U.S.C. secs. 80b–1–80b–21 (1988).

159. *U.S. Code*, vol. 15, sec. 77e (1988).

160. *U.S. Code*, vol. 15, sec. 77k (1988).

161. *Bellah v. First National Bank*, 495 F. 2d 1109, 1114 (5th Cir. 1974).

162. For a general discussion, see Thomas L. Hazen, *The Law of Securities Regulation* (St. Paul, Minn.: West Publishing Co., 1990), secs. 2.2–2.5.

163. *U.S. Code*, vol. 15, sec. 77e(b)(2) (1988).

164. Louis Loss and Joel Seligman, *Securities Regulation* (Boston: Little, Brown
and Company, 1989), 339.

165. Ibid., 340.

166. Ibid.

167. *U.S. Code*, vol. 15, sec. 77(b) (1988) (emphasis added).

168. *Reves v. Ernst & Young*, 494 U.S. 56 (1990).

169. *Futura Development Corporation v. Centex Corporation*, 761 F. 2d 33, 40 (1st
Cir.), cert. denied, 474 U.S. 850 (1985).

170. *Exchange National Bank v. Touche Ross and Co.*, 544 F. 2d 1126, 1138 (2d Cir.
1976).

171. *Union Planters National Bank v. Commercial Credit Business Loans, Inc.*, 651
F. 2d 1174, 1181–82 (6th Cir.), cert. denied, 454 U.S. 1124 (1981).

172. *Baurer v. Planning Group, Inc.*, 669 F. 2d 770, 778 (D.C. Cir. 1981).

173. *Exchange National Bank v. Touche Ross & Co.*, 544 F.2d 1126 (2d Cir. 1976).

174. Ibid., 1138.

175. *Reves*, 67.

176. "If the seller's purpose is to raise money for the general use of a business
enterprise or to finance substantial investments and the buyer is interested primarily in the profit the note is expected to generate, the instrument is likely to
be a "security." *Reves*, 66.

177. Ibid., 67.

178. Ibid., 67.

179. Ibid., 66.

180. Ibid., 68, n. 4.

181. Ibid., 67.

182. Ibid., 68.

183. *U.S. Code*, vol. 15, sec. 77(b)(1) (1988).

184. Loss and Seligman, *Securities Regulation*, 900.

185. 50% Cash Back, Inc., Commerce Clearing House, 1991–1992, Federal Securities Law Reporter, 14 November 1991, para. 76,115.

186. *SEC v. W.J. Howey*, 328 U.S. 293 (1946).

187. Ibid., 299.

188. *Teamsters v. Daniel*, 439 U.S. 551 (1979).

189. Ibid., 559.

190. See *Rivanna Trawlers Unlimited v. Thompson Trawlers*, 840 F.2d 236, 240 n.
4 (4th Cir. 1988).

191. *United Housing Foundation v. Forman*, 421 U.S. 837 (1975).

192. Ibid., 850.

193. Ibid., 851.

194. Ibid.

195. Ibid.

196. For example, see *Landreth Timber Co. v. Landreth*, 731 F. 2d 1348 (9th Cir. 1984), *reversed*, 471 U.S. 681 (1985).

197. *Landreth*, 471 U.S. 681 (1985).

198. *U.S. Code*, vol. 15, secs. 77l(2), 77q(a) (1988).

199. Exempted are: Any note, draft, bill of exchange, or bankers' acceptance which arises out of a current transaction or the proceeds of which have been or are to be used for current transactions, and which has a maturity at the time of issuance of not exceeding nine months, exclusive of days of grace, or any renewal thereof the maturity is likewise limited. *U.S. Code*, vol. 15, sec. 77c(a)(3) (1988).

200. For example, see *Holloway v. Peat, Marwick, Mitchell and Co.*, 879 F. 2d 772, 778 (10th Cir. 1989), *cert. denied*, 498 U.S. 958 (1990).

201. *Reves*, 71.

202. Ibid.

203. Ibid., 74.

204. Ibid., 78.

205. Ibid., 73.

206. Ibid.

207. Ibid.

208. Guam *Civil Code*, sec. 45401(1) (1993).

209. Puerto Rico *Laws Annotated*, tit. 10, sec. 881(1) (1993).

210. Alaska *Statutes*, sec. 45.55.130(12); Arkansas *Code Annotated*, sec. 23–42–102(13); California *Corporation Code*, sec. 25019; Colorado *Revised Statutes Annotated*, sec. 11–51–201(17) (West Supp. 1993); Connecticut *General Statutes*, sec. 36–471(13); Delaware *Code Annotated*, sec. 7302(13); District of Columbia *Code Annotated*, sec. 2–2601(12); Georgia *Code Annotated*, sec. 10–5–2(26); Hawaii *Revised Statutes*, sec. 485–1(13); Idaho *Code*, sec. 30–1402(12); Illinois *Revised Statutes*, ch. 815, para. 5/2.1 (Michie 1994); Indiana *Code Annotated*, sec. 23–2–1–1(k) (Burns 1993); Iowa *Code Annotated*, sec. 502.102(14) (West 1993); Kansas *Statutes Annotated*, sec. 17–1252(j); Kentucky *Revised Statutes Annotated*, sec. 292.310(13) (Baldwin 1993); Louisiana *Revised Statutes Annotated*, sec. 51–702(15) (West 1993); Maine *Revised Statutes Annotated*, sec. tit. XV, sec. 10501(18) (West 1993); Maryland *Code Annotated*, sec. 11–101(p)(1) & (2); Massachusetts *General Laws*, ch. 110A, sec. 401(k); Michigan *Compiled Laws*, sec. 451.801(l); Minnesota *Statutes*, sec. 80A.14; Mississippi *Code Annotated*, sec. 75–71–105(l); Missouri *Revised Statutes*, sec. 409–401(l); Montana *Code Annotated*, sec. 30–10–103(19); Nebraska *Revised Statutes*, sec. 8–1101(13); Nevada *Revised Statutes*, sec. 90–295; New Hampshire *Revised Statutes Annotated*, sec. 421–b:2(XX); New Jersey *Revised Statutes*, sec. 49:3–49(m); New Mexico *Statutes Annotated*, sec. 58–13B–2(v) (Michie 1993); North Carolina *General Statutes*, sec. 78A–2(11); Oklahoma *Statutes*, tit. 71, sec. 2(s) & (t); Oregon *Revised Statutes*, sec. 59.015(17)(a) & (b); Pennsylvania *Statutes Annotated*, sec. 102; Rhode Island *General Laws*, sec. 7–11–101; South Carolina *Code Annotated*, sec. 35–1–20(12) (Law Co-op. 1993); South Dakota *Codified Laws Annotated*, sec. 47–31A–401(m); Tennessee *Code Annotated*, sec. 48–2–102(12); Texas *Civil Code Annotated*, sec. 4.A (West 1993); Utah *Code Annotated*, sec. 61–1–13(22); Vermont *Statutes Annotated*, tit. 9, sec. 4202a(10); Virginia *Code Annotated*, sec.

13.1–501 (Michie 1993); Washington *Revised Code*, sec. 21.20.005(12); West Virginia *Code*, sec. 32–4–401(l); Wisconsin *Statutes*, sec. 551.02(13)(a) – (c); Wyoming *Statutes*, sec. 17–4–113(xi).

211. Alabama *Code*, sec. 8–6–2(10); Arizona *Revised Statutes Annotated*, sec. 44–1801(22); Florida *Statutes Annotated*, sec. 17.021(17) (West 1993); North Dakota *Century Code*, sec. 10–4–02(13); Ohio *Revised Code Annotated*, sec. 1701.01(B) (Baldwin 1993); Vermont *Statutes Annotated*, tit. 9, sec. 4202a(10).

212. Alabama *Code*, sec. 8–6–10(9); Alaska *Statutes*, sec. 45.55.140(4); Arizona *Revised Statutes Annotated*, sec. 44–1843.8; Arkansas *Code Annotated*, sec. 23–42–503(9); California *Corporation Code*, sec. 25100(l); Colorado *Revised Statutes Annotated*, sec. 11–51–307(h) (West Supp. 1993); Connecticut *General Statutes*, sec. 36–490(10); Delaware *Code Annotated*, sec. 7309(10); District of Columbia *Code Annotated*, sec. 2–2601(5)(D); Florida *Statutes Annotated*, sec. 517.051(8) (West 1993); Georgia *Code Annotated*, sec. 10–5–8(9); Hawaii *Revised Statutes*, sec. 485–4(10); Idaho *Code*, sec. 30–1434(j); Illinois *Revised Statutes*, ch. 815, para. 5/3(L) (Smith–Hurd, 1993); Indiana *Code Annotated*, sec. 23–2–1–2(6)(D) (Burns 1993); Iowa *Code Annotated*, sec. 502.202(10) (West 1993); Kansas *Statutes Annotated*, sec. 17–1261(i); Kentucky *Revised Statutes Annotated*, sec. 292.400(10) (Baldwin 1993); Louisiana *Revised Statutes Annotated*, sec. 51–708(9) (West 1993); Maine *Revised Statutes Annotated*, sec. 10502(K) (West 1993); Maryland *Code Annotated*, sec. 11–601(10); Massachusetts *General Laws*, ch. 110A, sec. 402(a)(10); Michigan *Compiled Laws*, sec. 451.802(9); Minnesota *Statutes*, sec. 80A.15(g); Mississippi *Code Annotated*, sec. 75–71–201(10); Missouri *Revised Statutes*, sec. 409–402(10); Montana *Code Annotated*, sec. 30–10–104(9); Nebraska *Revised Statutes*, sec. 8–1110(10); Nevada *Revised Statutes*, sec. 90–520(k); New Hampshire *Revised Statutes Annotated*, sec. 421–B:17(g); New Jersey *Revised Statutes*, sec. 49:3–50(10); New Mexico *Statutes Annotated*, sec. 58–13B–26(I) (Michie 1993); North Carolina *General Statutes*, sec. 78A–16(10); North Dakota *Code*, sec. 10–4–05(7); Oklahoma *Statutes*, tit. 71, sec. 401(9); Pennsylvania *Statutes Annotated*, sec. 202(c); Rhode Island *General Laws*, sec. 7–11–401(11); South Carolina *Code Annotated*, sec. 35–1–310(9) (Law Co-op 1993); South Dakota *Codified Laws Annotated*, sec. 47–31A–402(10); Tennessee *Code Annotated*, sec. 48–2–103(10); Texas *Civil Code Annotated*, sec. 6.H (West 1993); Utah *Code Annotated*, sec. 61–1–14(i); Vermont *Statutes Annotated*, tit. 9, sec. 4203a(7); Virginia *Code Annotated*, sec. 13.1–514.9 (Michie 1993); Washington *Revised Code*, sec. 21.20.310(9); West Virginia *Code*, sec. 32–4–402(10); Wisconsin *Statutes*, sec. 551.22(9); Wyoming *Statutes*, sec. 17–4–114(ix).

213. *U.S. Code*, vol. 15, sec. 77c(a)(4) (1988).

214. Alabama *Code*, sec. 8–6–10(8); Alaska *Statutes*, sec. 45.55.140(10); Arizona *Revised Statutes Annotated*, sec. 44–1843(6); Arkansas *Code Annotated*, sec. 23–42–503(8); California *Corporation Code*, sec. 25100(j); Colorado *Revised Statutes Annotated*, sec. 11–51–307(g) (West Supp. 1993); Connecticut *General Statutes*, sec. 36–490(9); Delaware *Code Annotated*, sec. 7309(9); District of Columbia *Code Annotated*, sec. 2–2601(6)(G); Florida *Statutes Annotated*, sec. 517.051(9) (West 1993); Hawaii *Revised Statutes*, sec. 485–4(9); Idaho *Code*, sec. 30–1434(i); Illinois *Revised Statutes*, ch. 815, para. 5/3(H) (Smith–Hurd, 1993); Indiana *Code Annotated*, sec. 23–2–1–2(10) (Burns 1993); Iowa *Code Annotated*, sec. 502.202(9) (West 1993); Kansas *Statutes Annotated*, sec. 17–1261(h); Kentucky *Revised Statutes Annotated*, sec. 292.400(9) (Baldwin 1993); Louisiana *Revised Statutes Annotated*, sec.

51–708(12) (West 1993); Maine *Revised Statutes Annotated*, sec. 10502(J) (West 1993); Maryland *Code Annotated*, sec. 11–601(9); Massachusetts *General Laws*, ch. 110A, sec. 402(a)(9); Michigan *Compiled Laws*, sec. 451.802(8); Mississippi *Code Annotated*, sec. 75–71–201(9); Missouri *Revised Statutes*, sec. 409–402(9); Montana *Code Annotated*, sec. 30–10–104(8); Nebraska *Revised Statutes*, sec. 8–1110(9); Nevada *Revised Statutes*, sec. 90–520(j); New Hampshire *Revised Statutes Annotated*, sec. 421–B:17(m); New Jersey *Revised Statutes*, sec. 49:3–50(9); New Mexico *Statutes Annotated*, sec. 58–13B–26(H) (Michie 1993); North Carolina *General Statutes*, sec. 78A–16(9); North Dakota *Code*, sec. 10–04–05(5); Ohio *Revised Code Annotated*, sec. 1707.02(I) (Baldwin 1993); Oklahoma *Statutes*, sec. 401(8); Oregon *Revised Statutes*, sec. 59.025(1); Pennsylvania *Consolidated Statutes Annotated*, vol. 70, sec. 1–202(e); Rhode Island *General Laws*, sec. 7–11–401(11); South Carolina *Code Annotated*, sec. 35–1–310(8) (Law Co–op. 1993); South Dakota *Codified Laws Annotated*, sec. 47–31A–402(9); Tennessee *Code Annotated*, sec. 48–2–103(7); Texas *Civil Code Annotated*, sec. 561–6(E); Utah *Code Annotated*, sec. 61–1–14(h); Vermont *Statutes Annotated*, tit. 9, sec. 4203a(5); Washington *Revised Code*, sec. 21.20.310; West Virginia *Code*, sec. 32–4–402(9); Wisconsin *Statutes*, sec. 551.22(8); Wyoming *Statutes*, sec. 17–4–114(viii).

215. Loss and Seligman, *Securities Regulation*, 1199–1201.

216. *U.S. Code*, vol. 15, sec. 77c(a)(11) (1988).

217. Loss and Seligman, *Securities Regulation*, 1294–1307.

218. S.E.C. Rule 504(b)(2).

219. S.E.C. Rule 504(b)(1)–(d).

220. *Treasury Reg.*, sec. 1.61–2.

221. *Cumulative Bulletin* 1979–1, Revenue Ruling 79–24.

222. *Treasury Reg.*, sec. 1–446–1(c)(1)(i).

223. *Cumulative Bulletin* 1983–2, Revenue Ruling 83–163.

224. *U.S. Code*, vol. 26, sec. 6045(c)(3).

225. *Treasury Reg.*, sec. 1.6045–1(a)(4).

226. *Treasury Reg.*, sec. 1.6045–1(e).

227. *Treasury Reg.*, sec. 1.6045–1(3)(2)(i).

228. *Treasury Reg.*, sec. 1.6045–1(g).

229. *Treasury Reg.*, sec. 1.6045–1(e)(2)(ii).

230. *Treasury Reg.*, sec. 1.6045–1(f)(1).

231. *Treasury Reg.*, sec. 1.6045–1(f)(2)(i).

232. *Treasury Reg.*, sec. 1.6045–1(f)(2)(ii).

233. *Internal Revenue Bulletin*, Announcement 1983–23.

234. *Treasury Reg.*, sec. 1.6045–1(f)(3).

235. *Treasury Reg.*, sec. 1.6045–1(f)(3).

236. *Treasury Reg.*, sec. 1.6045–1(f)(4).

237. Private Letter Ruling, No. 85–36–060, 12 June 1985; Edgar Cahn and Jonathan Rowe, *Time Dollars: The New Currency That Enables Americans to Turn Their Hidden Resource—Time—Into Personal Security and Community Renewal* (Emmaus, Pa.: Rodale Press, 1992), 78.

238. *U.S. Code*, vol. 26, sec. 6045(c)(3) (1988).

239. *U.S. Code*, vol. 26, sec. 162(a) (1988 and Supp. IV 1992).

240. *U.S. Code*, vol. 26, sec. 212 (1988).

241. *Cumulative Bulletin* 1980–1, Revenue Ruling 80–52.

242. *Treasury Reg.*, sec. 1–446–1(c)(1)(i).

243. *Treasury Reg.*, sec. 1.446–1(a)(1).

244. *U.S. Code*, vol. 26, sec. 448 (1988).

245. *U.S. Code*, vol. 26, sec. 461(h)(4) (1988); *Treasury Reg.*, sec. 1.461–1(a)(2).

246. *U.S. Code*, vol. 26, sec. 461(h)(1) (1988).

247. *Treasury Reg.*, sec. 1.461–4(d)(4)(ii)(A)–(B).

248. *Treasury Reg.*, secs. 1.263(a)(1)–(2), 1.461–1(a)(1)–(2).

249. For example, see *American Lace Mfg. v. Commissioner*, 8 B.T.A. 419, 420 (1927).

250. For example, see *Deputy v. Dupont*, 308 U.S. 488, 497 (1940); *Old Colony Railroad v. Commissioner*, 284 U.S. 552, 559 (1932).

251. For example, see *Professional Services v. Commissioner*, 79 T.C. 888, 915 (1982).

252. For example, see *First National Co. v. Commissioner*, 289 F. 2d 861 (6th Cir. 1961).

253. For example, see ibid.; *Autenreith v. Commissioner*, 115 F. 2d 856 (3d Cir. 1940); *United States v. Virgin*, 230 F. 2d 880 (5th Cir. 1956).

254. Michael Asimow, "The Interest Deduction," *UCLA Law Review* 24 (1977): 749, 772–773.

255. *U.S. Code*, vol. 26, sec. 7701(a)(25) (1988).

256. *Helvering v. Price*, 309 U.S. 409, 414 (1940); *Treasury Reg.*, sec. 1.461–1(a)(1).

257. *U.S. Code*, vol. 26, sec. 461(h)(4) (1988); *Treasury Reg.*, sec. 1.461–1(a)(2).

258. *U.S. Code*, vol. 26, sec. 461(h)(2)(B) (1988).

259. *U.S. Code*, vol. 26, sec. 1273(a)(1).

260. *U.S. Code*, vol. 26, sec. 1273(a)(2).

261. *U.S. Code*, vol. 26, sec. 1273(b).

262. *U.S. Code*, vol. 26, sec. 1272 (1988).

263. *U.S. Code*, vol. 26, sec. 163(e) (1988 and Supp. IV 1992).

264. *U.S. Code*, vol. 26, sec. 1272 (1988).

265. *U.S. Code*, vol. 26, sec. 163(f) (1988).

266. *U.S. Code*, vol. 26, sec. 163(f)(3) (1988).

267. *U.S. Code*, vol. 26, sec. 1(h) (1988). Legislation currently pending in Congress, if enacted, would provide for a maximum tax rate on capital gains for individuals of 19.8 percent.

268. *U.S. Code*, vol. 26, secs. 11, 1201(a)(1) (1988). Legislation currently pending in Congress, if enacted, would provide for a reduced tax rate (25 percent or 28 percent) on capital assets sold by corporations.

269. *U.S. Code*, vol. 26, sec. 1001 (1988).

270. *U.S. Code*, vol. 26, sec. 1221 (1988).

271. *Church's English Shoes*, 24 T.C. 56 (1955), *affirmed on other grounds*, 229 F. 2d 957 (2d Cir. 1956).

272. *U.S. Code*, vol. 26, sec. 1222(3)–(4) (1988).

273. *U.S. Code*, vol. 26, sec. 1222 (1988).

274. *U.S. Code*, vol. 26, sec. 1222(11) (1988).

275. Ibid.

276. *U.S. Code*, vol. 26, sec. 1211(b) (1988).

277. *U.S. Code*, vol. 26, sec. 1211(b)(1) (1988).

278. *U.S. Code*, vol. 26, sec. 1212(b) (1988).

279. *U.S. Code*, vol. 26, sec. 1211(a) (1988).

280. *U.S. Code*, vol. 26, sec. 1212(a) (1988).

281. Hayek, *An Analysis*, 43 (see chap. 2, n. 36).

CHAPTER 8

1. Milton Friedman and Anna J. Schwartz, "Has Government Any Role in Money?" *Journal of Military Economics* 17 (1986): 37, 60 (see chap. 2, n. 8).

Bibliography

Abbanat, Georgeann F. 1985. Letter to Susan Witt, 6 November.

Adams, Frank T., and Gary B. Hansen. 1992. *Putting Democracy to Work: A Practical Guide for Starting and Managing Worker-Owned Businesses*. San Francisco: Berrett-Koehler.

Alpervitz, Gar. 1992. Ameristroika Is the Answer. *Washington Post*, 13 December.

Alternative Currencies: Slip Me a Beak. *The Economist* 327:60.

An Alternative to Cash, Beyond Banks or Barter. 1993. *New York Times*, 31 May.

Anderson, Mark Kendall. 1993. Au Courrency. *Valley Advocate*, 13 September.

Andrew, A. Piatt. 1980. Substitutions for Cash in the Panic of 1907. *Quarterly Journal of Economics* 22: 477–516.

Annals of the Congress of the United States, 1789–1824. 42 vols. Washington, D.C., 1834–56.

Asimow, Michael. 1977. The Interest Deduction. *UCLA Law Review* 24: 749.

Bahro, Rudolph. 1986. *Building the Green Movement*. London: GMP.

Barnet, Richard J. 1993. The End of Jobs. *Harper's*, September, 47.

Bennett, Will. 1993. "Payment in Kind" Is Replacing the Pound; Peck, Link and Pond Gain Popularity As Alternative Currencies. *The Independent*, 13 December.

Borsodi Constant: An Inflation-Free Currency, The. 1974. *Mother Earth News*, 27: 82–84.

Borsodi, Ralph. 1989. Inflation and the Coming Keynesian Catastrophe: The Story of the Exeter Experiments with Constants. Great Barrington, Mass.: E. F. Schumacher Society and The School for Living.

Brandel, Roland E., and David E. Teitelbaum. 1989 and Supp. 1991. *The Community Reinvestment Act: Policies and Compliance*. Englewood Cliffs, N. J.: Prentice-Hall Law & Business.

Brecher, Elinor J. 1993. Toll and Trouble: Crisis in the American Workplace. *Miami Herald,* 21 March.

Bridge, Rachel. 1993. How to Mow the Lawn With a Few Bobbins. *Evening Standard,* 24 February.

Broaddus, Alfred. 1988. *A Primer on the Fed.* Richmond, Va.: Federal Reserve Bank of Richmond.

Brown, Annette. 1993. Trade Your Skills! *Daily Mail,* 8 December.

Cahn, Edgar, and Jonathan Rowe. 1992. *Time Dollars: The New Currency That Enables Americans to Turn Their Hidden Resource—Time—into Personal Security and Community Renewal.* Emmaus, Pa.: Rodale Press.

Census Bureau. 1993. *Statistical Abstract.* Washington, D.C.: GPO.

Cole, Nicholas. 1990. Cut Your Household Bills By Turning To the Barter System. *Guardian,* 23 June.

Cole-Adams, Kate. 1993. Bucking The System: In Hard Times, Many Australians Are Avoiding The Cash Economy. *Time,* 26 July, 40.

Cooper, Richard N. 1989. Is Private Money Optional? *Cato Journal,* 9(Fall): 393.

Corporate Refugees: After the Pain, Some Find Smooth Sailing. *Business Week,* 12 April 1993, 58.

Crawford, Franklin. 1992. Got an Ithaca HOUR? Swap It? *Ithaca Journal,* 31 January.

Crawford, Philip. 1991. Homemade Money Means Another Day, Another Deli Dollar, *International Herald Tribune,* 12–13 October.

Dahl, Robert A. 1970. *After the Revolution?* New Haven, Conn.: Yale University Press.

Dahl, Robert A., and Edward R. Tufte. 1973. *Size and Democracy.* Stanford, Calif.: Stanford University Press.

Daly, Herman E., and John E. Cobb, Jr. 1989. *For the Common Good.* Boston: Beacon Press.

"Deli Dollars" Gain Currency as a Capitalist Experiment. 1989. *Berkshire Eagle,* 12 November.

Deli Dollars the Talk of the Town. 1989. *Syracuse Herald-Journal,* 23 November.

DeMara, Bruce. 1991. Recession Survival Kit: Stretching Your Dollar The Barter Way. *The Toronto Star,* 10 June.

Dennis, Warren L., and J. Stanley Potter. 1980. *Federal Regulation of Banking: Redlining and Community Reinvestment: Analysis, Commentary and Compliance Procedures.* Boston: Warren, Gorham & Lamont.

Devitt, Edward J., Charles B. Blackmar, and Michael A. Wolff. 1987. *Federal Jury Practice and Instructions: Civil and Criminal.* St. Paul, Minn.: West Publishing Co.

Donovan, Frank. 1972. Exeter's Funny Money Not Meant For Laughs. *Boston Sunday Globe,* 1 October.

Duff, Christina. 1993. Poor Prospects. *Wall Street Journal,* 28 July.

Durning, Alan T. 1992. . . . And Too Many Shoppers: What Malls and Materialism Are Doing to The Planet. *Washington Post,* 23 August.

Edwards-Jones, Imogen. 1993. Trugs? What A Sterling Idea. *The Independent,* 17 March.

Ehrenfeld, David W. 1978. *The Arrogance of Humanism.* New York: Oxford University Press.

Exeter Experiment, The. 1974. *Forbes*, 1 February, 45.

Faulkner, Roland P. 1901. The Private Issue of Token Coins. *Political Science Quarterly* 16: 303.

Fax, Stephen. 1989. South County Farms Issue Their Own Money. *Berkshire Eagle*, 20 December.

Feavearyear, Herbert E. 1932. *The Pound Sterling*. London: Oxford University Press.

Federal Financial Institutions Examination Council (U.S.). 1985. *A Citizen's Guide to CRA*. Washington, D. C.: The Council.

Federal Reserve Bank of Chicago. 1992. *Modern Money Mechanics*. Chicago: Federal Reserve Bank of Chicago.

Fewins, Clive. 1992a. In the Country. *The Daily Telegraph*, 29 February at 103.

————. 1992b. Goodbye ECU, Hello Stroud: A Self-Help Group That Deals in Its Own Currency. *Financial Times*, 11 April.

Fitzmaurice, Tim. 1991. Local Currency Is Helping Businesses During Recession. *The Lakeville Journal*, 15 August.

Flint, Jerry. 1993. Keep a Resume on the Floppy, But Don't Panic. *Forbes*, 26 April, 65.

Friedman, Milton. 1987. Monetary Policy: Tactics versus Strategy. In *The Search for Stable Money*, edited by James A. Dorn and Anna J. Schwartz. Chicago: University of Chicago Press.

Friedman, Milton, and Anna J. Schwartz. 1963. *A Monetary History of the United States, 1867–1960*. Princeton, N. J.: Princeton University Press.

————. 1986. Has Government Any Role in Money? *Journal of Monetary Economics* 17: 37.

Gaines, Judith. 1989. Food-Backed Financing: Great Barrington To Begin Trade In Deli Dollars. *Boston Globe*, 29 October.

————. 1990. "Greenbacks" Tide Farmers Over Winter. *Boston Globe*, 28 January.

Galbraith, John K. 1975. *Money: Whence It Came, Where It Went*. Boston: Houghton Mifflin Co.

Gilkes, Paul. 1991. Scrip Novel Solution to Business Slump. *Coin World*, 32: 1.

Glover, Paul, telephone interview by author, 19 July 1994.

Goodman, Paul, and Percival Goodman. 1960. *Communitas: Means of Livelihood and Ways of Life*. New York: Vintage Books.

Greco, Thomas H., Jr. 1994. *New Money For Healthy Communities*. Tucson, Ariz.: Thomas H. Greco, Jr.

Hackley, Howard H. 1966. Our Baffling Banking System. *Virginia Law Review* 52: 565.

Hammond, Bray. 1957. *Banks and Politics in America*. Princeton, N. J.: Princeton University Press.

Hanks, Whitney J., and Roland Stucki. 1956. *Money, Banking, and National Income*. New York: Alfred A. Knopf.

Hansman, Henry. 1990. When Does Worker Ownership Work? ESOPs, Law Firms, Codetermination, and Economic Democracy. *Yale Law Journal* 99: 1749.

Hayek, F. A. 1976. *Denationalisation of Money: An Analysis of the Theory and Practice of Concurrent Currencies*. Lansing, Sussex: The Institute of Economic Affairs.

———. 1990. *Denationalisation of Money: The Argument Refined: An Analysis of the Theory and Practice of Concurrent Currencies*. London: The Institute of Economic Affairs.

Hazen, Thomas L. 1990. *The Law of Securities Regulation*. St. Paul, Minn.: West Publishing Co.

Hey, Kenneth R. 1992. Business As Usual? Forget It. *Across the Board* 29 (January/February): 30.

Horowitz, Steven. 1990. Competitive Currencies, Legal Restrictions, and the Origins of the Fed: Some Evidence From the Panic of 1907. *Southern Economic Journal* 56: 6–39.

Hurst, James W. 1973. *A Legal History of Money in the United States, 1774–1970*. Lincoln: University of Nebraska Press.

Ithaca HOURS. (n.d.). Hometown Money Starter Kit.

It's Berk-Shares Time Again. 1993. *Berkshire Record*, 30 July.

Jacobs, Jane. 1984. *Cities and the Wealth of Nations: Principles of Economic Life*. New York: Random House.

———. 1992. *Systems of Survival: A Dialogue on the Moral Foundations of Commerce and Politics*. New York: Vintage Books.

Kane, Kevin. 1991. *A Banker's Guide to the Community Reinvestment Act: Case Studies of 33 Institutions*. Washington, D.C.: Bureau of National Affairs.

Kelliher, Joseph T. 1993. Pushing the Envelope: Development of Federal Electrical Transmission Access Policy. *American University Law Review* 42 (Winter): 543.

Kilborn, Peter T. 1993. Working Is Harder, Not Working Harder Still. *New York Times*, 5 September.

Kindleberger, Charles P. 1983. Standards as Public, Collective and Private Goods. *Kyklos*, 36: 377.

Klein, Benjamin. 1974. The Competitive Supply of Money. *Journal of Money, Credit and Banking* 6 (November): 423.

Krimerman, Len, and Frank Lindenfeld. 1992. Changing Worklife: Grassroots Activism Takes a New Turn. In *When Workers Decide: Workplace Democracy Takes Root in North America*, edited by Len Krimerman and Frank Lindenfeld. Philadelphia: New Society Publishers.

Lake, Wilfred S. 1947. The End of the Suffolk Systems. *Journal of Economic History* 7 (November): 183.

LETS Lets Jobless Work in New Barter System. 1993. *Financial Post* (Canada), 17 July.

Lewin, Tamar. 1994. Low Pay and Closed Doors Greet Young in Job Market. *New York Times*, 10 March.

Linton, Michael, and Thomas Greco. 1987. The Local Employment System. *Whole Earth Review*, 22 June, 104.

Litherland, Sušan. 1994. Ancient Cash-Free Barter System Enters The Computer Age. *Inter Press Service*, 3 March.

Locke, Michelle. 1989. Restaurant Issues Its Own Deli Dollars. *Los Angeles Times*, 19 November.

———. 1990. Produce Stands Put Their Trade in Stock. *Philadelphia Inquirer*, 7 January.

Loss, Louis, and Joel Seligman. 1989. *Securities Regulation*. Boston: Little, Brown and Company.

Mansbridge, Jane J. 1980. *Beyond Adversary Democracy*. New York: Basic Books.

Marsico, Richard. 1993. A Guide to Enforcing the Community Reinvestment Act. *Fordham Urban Law Journal* 20 (Winter): 165.

Martin, Stanley A. 1983. Problems with PURPA: The Need for State Legislation to Encourage Cogeneration and Small Power Prediction. *Boston College Environmental Affairs Law Review* 11 (Fall): 149.

McGuire, Mark J. 1992. Making Money the Old-Fashioned Way. *Albany Times Union*, 30 August.

McKenna, M. A. J. 1991. Short on Cash? This Guy Prints His Own. *Boston Herald*, 30 June.

Meadows, Donnella. 1994. Ithaca Creates Its Own Money, *Berkshire Eagle*, 23 May.

Merchants in Downtown Great Barrington Offering Berk-Shares in Unique Promotion. 1992. *Berkshire Business Journal*, September.

Middleton, Christopher. 1994. Greenlets—The Caring Cash Alternative. *Sunday Telegraph*, 23 January.

Moore, Steve. 1989. South County Farm "Money" Goes On Sale. *Berkshire Eagle*, 22 December.

———. 1990. Farm Notes Being Used at 2 Farms. *Berkshire Eagle*, 23 July.

Morgan, Andrew. 1993. How Britons Barter Their Way Out of Debt—Local Exchange Trading Schemes. *The Observer*, 17 January.

Morris, David, and Karl Hess. 1975. *Neighborhood Power: The New Localism*. Boston: Beacon Press.

New York State, Office of Rural Affairs. 1990. Access to Financial Services in Rural New York: A Report to the Governor and the Legislature, March.

Nussbaum, Arthur. 1957. *A History of the Dollar*. Boston: Ginn and Company.

O'Brien, Thelma. 1991. Scrip Becoming Popular Alternative to Loans. *Berkshire Record*, 26 April.

O'Heney, Sheila. 1991. Keeping CHIPS Safe and Private. *ABA Banking Journal*, May.

Orwen, Patricia. 1993. Barter. *The Toronto Star*, 20 June, H1.

O'Shaughnessy, Nancy. 1992a. Great Barrington Berk-Shares Shopping Promotion Said to Be Generating Late-Summer Enthusiasm, Sales. *Berkshire Record*, 28 August.

———. 1992b. Berk-Shares Going Like Hotcakes. *Berkshire Record*, 4 September.

Paying with Constants Instead of Dollars. 1974. *Business Week*, 4 May, 29.

Pease, Robert. 1986. Promoting Regional Enterprise, *Christian Science Monitor*, 3 November.

Pollard, Alfred M., Keith H. Ellis, and Joseph P. Daly. 1993. *Banking Law in the United States*. Salem, N.H.: Butterworth Legal Publishers.

Porter, Monica. 1994. Return to Tender. *Daily Mail*, 1 January.

Pratt, Abby. 1992. Berk-Shares Make Barrington Debut. *Berkshire Eagle*, 29 July.

Rahn, Richard. 1986. Time to Privatize Money? How Good Currency Can Drive Out Bad. *Policy Review* 36 (Spring): 55.

———. Private Money: An Idea Whose Time Has Come. *Cato Journal* 9 (Fall): 353.

Raven, Gerrard. 1993. As Pound Sinks, Some Britons Turn To Alternative "Currencies." *The Reuter Business Report,* 17 February.

Records of the Federal Convention of 1787. 1966. Edited by Michael Farrand.

Richman, Louis S. 1993. When Will The Layoffs End? *Fortune,* 20 September.

Rockoff, Hugh. 1974. The Free Banking Era: A Reexamination. *Journal of Money, Credit and Banking* 6 (May): 141.

―――. 1985. New Evidence on Free Banking in the United States. *American Economic Review* 75 (September): 886.

Rolnick, Arthur J., and Warren E. Weber. 1982. Free Banking, Wildcat Banking and Shinplasters. *Federal Reserve Bank of Minneapolis Quarterly Review* (Fall): 6.

―――. 1983. New Evidence on the Free Banking Era. *American Economic Review* 75 (December): 1080.

―――. 1984. The Causes of Free Banking Failure. *Journal of Monetary Economics* 14 (October): 267.

Roosevelt, Franklin D. 1938. *The Public Papers and Addresses of Franklin D. Roosevelt.* 4 vols. Washington, D. C.: GPO.

Sale, Kirkpatrick. 1980. *Human Scale.* New York: Coward, McCann, and Geoghegan.

Salstrom, Paul. 1994. *Appalachia's Path to Economic History 1730–1940.* Lexington: University Press of Kentucky.

Schlichting, William H. et al. 1994. *Banking Law.* New York: Matthew Bender.

Schor, Juliet. 1992. *The Overworked American.* New York: Basic Books.

E. F. Schumacher Society Newsletter. 1994. Spring, 1.

Schumacher, E. F. 1973. *Small is Beautiful: Economics as if People Mattered.* New York: Harper and Row.

―――. 1979. *Good Work.* New York: Harper and Row.

Scott, Kenneth E. 1980. The Patchwork Quilt: State and Federal Roles in Bank Regulation. *Stanford Law Review* 32: 687.

2nd Issue of Berkshire Farm Notes. 1990–91. *E. F. Schumacher Society Newsletter,* Winter.

Self-Help Association for a Regional Economy (SHARE). n.d.a. *Local Investment Means Community Profits.*

―――. n.d.b. *Proposed Bank Participation in the Berk-share Program.*

―――. n.d.c. *WHAT IS SHARE?*

Selgin, G. A. 1985. The Case For Free Banking: Then and Now. *Cato Institute Policy Analysis,* no. 60: 1–15.

―――. 1988. *The Theory of Free Banking.* Totowa, N. J.: Rowman and Littlefield.

Silver, Michelle. 1993. The Ultimate Barter. *Mother Earth News,* August/September, 32.

Smith, Emily T. 1995. Global Warming: The Debate Heats Up. *Business Week,* 27 February, 119.

Solomon, Lewis D. 1987. The Microenterprise Revolution, Job Displacement, and the Future of Work: A Policy Commentary. *Chicago-Kent Law Review* 63: 65.

―――. 1991. Humanomics: A Model for Third World Development. *George Washington Journal of International Law & Economics* 25: 447.

Solomon, Lewis D., and Melissa B. Kirgis. 1994. Business Cooperatives: A Primer. *DePaul Business Law Journal* 6: 233.

Specter, Michael. 1991a. Capitalizing on Yankee Ingenuity. *Washington Post*, 20 May.

————. 1991b. Only the Real Money Is Tight. *International Herald Tribune*, 21 May.

Stafford, Margaret. 1994. Alternative Currency Use Is Gaining New Popularity. *Boston Globe*, 17 January.

Statutes at Large of the United States of America, 1789–1873. 17 vols. Washington, D. C., 1850–73.

————. Vol. 1, p. 246.

————. Vol. 12, p. 665.

————. Vol. 12, p. 709.

————. Vol. 13, p. 99.

————. Vol. 13, p. 120.

————. Vol. 13, p. 277.

————. Vol. 13, p. 469.

————. Vol. 14, p. 146.

————. Vol. 15, p. 6.

Stevens, William K. 1995a. A Global Warming Resumed in 1994, Climate Data Show. *New York Times*, 27 January, A1.

————. 1995b. More Extremes Found in Weather, Pointing to Greenhouse as Effect. *New York Times*, 23 May, C4.

Stinson, Richard J. 1974. The Exeter Affair Or, Has a Nice New England Town Really Beaten Inflation? *Financial World* 141 (17 February): 28.

Story, Joseph. 1991. *Commentaries on the Constitution of the United States*. Littleton, Colo.: F. B. Rothman.

Swann, Robert. 1988. The Need for Local Currencies. Eighth Annual E. F. Schumacher Lectures, October.

————, interview with author, Great Barrington, Mass., 8 June 1994.

————. n.d. Establishing an Alternative Independent Currency: The Case for Using Forests as a Reserve Currency. Great Barrington, Mass., n.p.

Sylvester, Rachel. 1994. The Barter Economy Gains Currency. *Sunday Telegraph*, 22 May.

Taub, Bart. 1985. Private Fiat Money with Many Suppliers, *Journal of Monetary Economics* 16 (September): 195.

Timberlake, Richard H., Jr. 1984. The Central Banking Role of Clearinghouse Associations. *Journal of Money, Credit and Banking* 16: 1–15.

————. 1993. *Monetary Policy in the United States: An Intellectual and Institutional History*. Chicago: University of Chicago Press.

Toffler, Alvin. 1980. *The Third Wave*. New York: Morrow.

————. 1990. *Powershift: Knowledge, Wealth, and Violence at the Edge of the 21st Century*. New York: Bantam Books.

————. 1990. Powershift. *Newsweek*, 15 October, 86.

Trivoli, George. 1979. *The Suffolk Bank: A Study of a Free-Enterprise Clearing System*. Leesburg, Va.: Adam Smith Institute.

Turnbull, Shann. 1989. Creating a Community Currency. In *Building Sustainable Communities: Tools and Concepts for Self-Reliant Economic Change*, edited by Ward Morehouse. New York: Bootstrap Press.

———. 1989. What Everyone Should Know About Banking and Money (Espe-cially Bankers and Economists). In *Building Sustainable Communities: Tools and Concepts for Self-Reliant Economic Change*, edited by Ward Morehouse. New York: The Bootstrap Press.

Uchitelee, Louis. 1993. Strong Companies Are Joining Trend To Eliminate Jobs. *New York Times*, 26 July.

———. 1994. Job Losses Don't Let Up Even As Hard Times Ease. *New York Times*, 22 March.

United States Department of Commerce. 1975. Historical Statistics of the United States: Colonial Times to 1970 (Washington, D.C.: GPO).

United States Department of Labor, Bureau of Statistics. 1989. *Handbook of Labor Statistics*. Washington, D.C.: GPO.

U.S. House of Representatives. 1947. Committee on the Judiciary. 80th Cong., 1st sess., H.R. Rept. 304.

———. 1964. Committee on Banking and Currency. Subcommittee on Domestic Finance. *A Primer on Money*. 88th Cong., 2d sess., Committee Print.

———. 1976. Committee on Ways and Means. *Tax Reform Act of 1976*. 94th Cong., 2d sess., H.R. Rept. 94–658.

———. 1987. Staff Report of the Select Committee on Hunger. *Access and Avail-ability of Credit to the Poor in Developing Countries and the United States*. 100th Cong., 1st sess., 23.

U.S. Senate. 1908. Special Committee on the Revision of the Laws. 60th Cong., 1st sess., S. Rept. 10.

———. 1948. Committee on the Judiciary. 80th Cong., 2d sess., S. Rept. 1620.

———. 1976. Finance Committee. *Tax Reform Act of 1976*. 94th Cong., 2d sess., S. Rept. 94–938.

U.S. Statutes at Large. 1874. Vol. 18, p. 123. *National Banking Act*.

———. 1875. Vol. 18, p. 296. *Resumption Act of 1875*.

———. 1875. Vol. 18, p. 307. *Act of Feb. 8th, 1875*.

———. 1900. Vol. 31, p. 45. *Act of March 14, 1900*.

———. 1909. Vol. 35, p. 1120. *Act of March 4, 1909*.

———. 1913, Vol. 38, p. 251. *Federal Reserve Act*.

———. 1933. Vol. 48, p. 112. *Joint Resolution of June 5, 1933*.

———. 1934. Vol. 48, p. 337. *Gold Reserve Act of 1934*.

———. 1948. Vol. 62, p. 709. *Act of June 25, 1948*.

———. 1960. Vol. 64, p. 873. *Federal Deposit Insurance Act*.

———. 1973. Vol. 87, p. 352. *Par Value Modification Act Amendments*.

———. 1976. Vol. 90, p. 1814. *Tax Reform Act of 1976*.

———. 1977. Vol. 91, p. 1227. *Act of Oct. 28, 1977*.

———. 1987. Vol. 101, pp. 552, 635. *Expedited Funds Availability Act*.

Van Jura, Gary. 1987. SHARE Helps Area Businesses Obtain Financing for Small Projects Through Secured Bank Loans. *Berkshire Business Journal*, March.

Vaubel, Roland. 1985. Competing Currencies: The Case for Free Entry. *Zeitschrift für Wirtscchafts-und Sozialwissenschaften* 36: 547. Reprinted in *Free Banking: Modern Theory and Policy* 3 (1993): 586, edited by Lawrence H. White. Brookfield, Vt.: Edward Elgar Publishing Co.

———. 1986. Currency Competition versus Governmental Money Monopolies. *Cato Journal* 5 (Winter): 927.

Vidal, John. 1994. Other Lives: Take a Few Pigs Along to the Pie in the Sky Cafe and Watch Payment Go Bob-Bob-Bobbin' Along. *The Guardian*, 12 March.

Vieira, Jr., Edwin. 1983. *Pieces of Eight*. Fort Lee, N.J.: Sound Dollar Committee.

Vogel, Carl. 1993. Money Makers: Turning Community Talent Into Local Currency. *The Neighborhood Works*, August/September, 14.

Wachtel, Paul. 1983. *The Poverty of Affluence: A Psychological Portrait of the American Way of Life*. New York: Free Press.

Wardle, Heather. 1994. Haircut Will Cost You 3 Acorns; Britain Latest Country to Take Up Canadian Barter System. *The Gazette* (Montreal), 15 January.

Welcome to the Ithaca Time Zone. 1994. *Ithaca Money*, February/March, 1.

Weston, David J. 1991. Money, Banking and the Environment. *New European* 4: 35–41.

Wheatley, Alan. 1994. Bobbins, Acorns Revive Economy At Community Level. *Reuter Newswire*, 17 June.

White, Horace. 1935. *Money and Banking*. Boston: Ginn and Company.

White, Lawrence H. 1989a. *Competition and Currency: Essay on Free Banking and Money*. New York: New York University Press.

———. 1989b. What Kinds of Monetary Institutions Would a Free Market Deliver. *Cato Journal* 9 (Fall): 367.

Witt, Susan. 1991a. Deli Dollars, Trash Cash and Local Loans: An Interview with Susan Witt. In *Green Business: Hope or Hoax?*, edited by Christopher Plant and Judith Plant. Ch. 13, 95–104. Philadelphia: New Society Publishers.

———. 1991b. Print Your Own Currency. Interview. In *Innovation Group*, 1 (Summer): 33.

———. 1993. Catching the Berk-Shares Fever. *Berkshire Record*, 17 September.

———. 1994. Interview by author, Great Barrington, Mass., 8 June.

———. 1994. Letter to author, 14 June.

Yeager, Leland B. 1983. Stable Money and Free-Market Currencies. *Cato Journal* 3 (Spring): 305.

Zachary, G. Pascal, and Bob Ortega. 1993. Age of Angst: Workplace Revolution Boosts Productivity At Cost of Job Security. *Wall Street Journal*, 10 March.

Index

Act of June 8, 1864, 98
Anticounterfeiting legislation, 95, 99–100
Anticounterfeiting techniques, 78

Banks
  commercial, 5–7, 105
  national, 5, 9–12, 102–103
  note-issuing, federally chartered, 9–10
  state chartered, 10
  wildcat, 9
Banks, involved with local currency not pegged to U.S. dollar, 80–87
  local currency loans, 84–87
Bargain purchase notes (see also Bargain purchase scrip)
  federal income tax
    deduction aspects, 124–125
    income aspects, 123
Bargain purchase scrip (see also Bargain purchase notes)
  benefits, 56–57
  disadvantages, 57–58
  examples of, 54–55

implementation, 58
limitations, 57–58
tax consequences, 123–125
Barter exchanges
  federal income tax
    deduction aspects, 121–122
    income aspects, 117–118
    information reporting requirements, 118–121
Bartering, 37–52
Berk-Shares
  benefits, 60
  description, 59
  implementation, 60–62
Berkshire Farm Preserve Notes, 55–57
Bills of credit
  definition of, 100–101
  monetary-like instruments, 101
  nongovernmental entities, 102
  U.S. Constitution prohibition, 100–102
Bond deposit requirements, 9, 10
Borsodi, Ralph, 68
Business cooperatives, 24–25, 28, 77–78, 92

Centralized monetary system
   impact on inner cities, 31–33
   impact on rural areas, 31–33
Cities, human scale, 28–30
Clearing House Interbank Payment
   System, 108
Clearinghouses, 8, 12, 108
   certificates, 108
   transfer checks, 108
Clearinghouses, involvement with local currency not pegged to U.S.
   dollar, 83–84
Coinage, private, restricted, 95, 97–99
Coinage Act of 1792, 96
Commercial banks, 5–7, 105
Commodities, reserve, 6–7, 8, 70–77,
   90–92
Commodities basket, currency reserve, 75–77
Community Reinvestment Act, 82–83
   implementation of, 82–83
Community reinvestment legislation
   federal, 82–83
   state, 83
Comptroller of the Currency, 103,
   105–107
Constant Project
   commodities basket, 68
   implementation, 68–70
   reserve for, 69
Cooperative organizations, 24–25, 77–
   78, 92
Cordwood, currency reserve, 72–74
Corn Crib, 70–77
Currency, not pegged to U.S. dollar
   (see also Constant Project)
   backing the currency, 70–77
   federal income taxation, 125–127
   implementation, 70
   issuer, 77–79
   problems with, 87–94
   relationship with banks, 79–87
Currency reserve
   basket of commodities, 75–76
   gold, 71
   single commodity, 71–75
Current money, 98–99

Dahl, Robert, 29–30
Decentralization
   economic, 22–25
   political, 25–27
Deli Dollars, 54–56, 58–59
Discount notes (see also Discount
   scrip)
   federal income tax
      deduction aspects, 124–125
      income aspects, 123
Discount scrip (see also Discount
   notes)
   benefits, 56–57
   disadvantages, 57–58
   examples, 54–55
   implementation, 58
   limitations, 57–58
   tax consequences, 123–125
Dual banking system, 105–106

E. F. Schumacher Society, 53–54, 59,
   63, 65
Ecological dilemmas, 20–21, 30–31
Economic institutions
   scale of, 22–25
Ehrenfeld, David, 1
Electricity, currency reserve, 73–75
Employment, decreasing opportuni-
   ties, 18–20
Energy, currency reserve, 73–75
Excessive issuance, local currency, 74,
   89–92
Expanded Berk-Shares Program
   concept, 63–64
   implementation, 64–65
Expedited Funds Availability Act, 107

Federal anticounterfeiting legislation,
   95, 99–100
Federal Deposit Insurance Corpora-
   tion, 105
Federal Housing and Community De-
   velopment Act of 1977, 82
Federal income taxation. See taxation
Federal Reserve Act, 12–13
Federal Reserve Board, 36
Federal Reserve System
   Board of Governors, 106–107

creation of, 12–13
discount rate, 14–15
open market operations, 14–15
reserve requirements, 14–15
Federal Securities Act of 1933
  exempt securities
    nonprofit issuance, 116
    short-term notes, 114–115
  exempt transactions
    intrastate, 116–117
    limited offerings, 117
  registration requirement, 109–110
Fiat money, 14, 35, 88, 94
Forests, currency reserve, 72–73
Fractional reserve banking, 5–7
Fraudulent practices
  local currency issuance, 89–92
Free banking, 5, 7–9
Friedman, Milton, 94, 129

Galbraith, John Kenneth, 7
Glover, Paul, 37, 43, 51
Gold, currency reserve, 71
Gold Clause
  banned, 104
  definition, 103–104
Gold Reserve Act of 1934, 13, 104
Gold Standard Act of 1900, 104
Greenhouse effect, 21

Hamilton, Alexander, 96
Hayek, Friedrich A., 16, 89–91, 93–94,
  127
Housing and Community Development Act of 1992, 83

Independent Arbitrage International,
  69
International Revenue Code
  Section 163(a), 124
  Section 163(e), 125
  Section 448, 122
  Section 1222, 126
  Section 1272, 125
  Section 6045, 120–121
  Section 7701(a)(25), 124
Internal Revenue Service
  Form 1096, 119

Form 1099–B, 120
Letter Ruling 85–36–060, 120
Revenue Ruling 79–24, 118, 149
Revenue Ruling 83–163, 118, 149
Issuance, local currency
  excessive, 89–92
  fraudulent, 89–92
  issuer, currency not pegged to U.S.
    dollar, 77–79
Ithaca HOURS
  benefits, 45–46
  description, 43–45
  disadvantages, 46–47
  impact, 45
  implementation
    create an organization, 47–48
    design the currency, 48
    distribute a barter newspaper,
      50–51
    print the currency, 50
    publicize the program, 51
    publish a barter newspaper, 49–
      50
    recruit members, 48–49
Ithaca Money, 44, 49

Jacobs, Jane, 34
Joint Resolution of June 5, 1933, 13

Kindleberger, Charles P., 87

LANDSMAN Community Services, 42
Legal Tender Laws, 9
LETS, 38–43. *See also* Local Employment and Trading System
Linton, Michael, 37
Loans, local currency, 84–87
Local currency, benefits of
  ecological dilemma, overcoming,
    30–31
  employment opportunities, 35
  feedback mechanism, 33–35
  local economy, revitalizing, 31–33
  noninflationary monetary system,
    facilitating, 35–36
Local currency, not pegged to U.S.
  dollar. *See also* Currency, not
  pegged to U.S. dollar

Local Employment and Trading
    System
  advantages, 38–39
  debit balances, 39
  description, 38–39
  disadvantages, 39
  excessive debit balances, 39
  implementation
    organizational details, 41–42
    recruiting new members, 42–43
  reducing the risk of default
    planning strategies, 39–41

Main Street Action Association, 59, 63
Money market funds, currency re-
    serve, 76
Monopoly, natural, 92–94
Mutual credit, 38–41

National bank notes, 9–12, 13
National Banking Act of 1863, 9–11,
    102
National Banking Act of 1864, 10
National banks, 5, 9–12, 102–103
Natural monopoly, 92–94
Neighborhoods, role in the political
    process, 26–27
New York Automated Clearing
    House, 108
New York City Clearinghouse Associ-
    ation, 12
Nonmember insured state banks, 106
Nonmember noninsured state banks,
    106
Nonprofit organizations
  currency issuer, 77–78
Notes
  issued by national banks, 9–10,
    107–108
  not issued by national banks, tax
    on, 102–103
  privately issued, 7–9
  punitive tax on, 103
  state bank issuance, 9–10, 102–103

Participation
  economic institutions, 23–25
  political institutions, 26–27

Political institutions
  scale of, 25–27
Prosumers, 25, 28
Public good, 87–89
Public Utility Regulating Policies Act
    of 1978, 74

Rahn, Richard W., 88
Regulation CC, 107
Regulation J, 108
Reserve commodities, 6–8
Reserve for currency, 70–77
  commodity basket, 75–76
  gold, 71
  redemption mechanism, 70–71, 76–
    77
  single commodity, 71–75
    cordwood, 72–73
    energy, 73–75
Right livelihood, 19–20, 23
Roosevelt, Franklin D., 104
Rule 504, Securities Act of 1933, 117

Sale, Kirkpatrick, 28–29
Scale, importance of
  economic institutions, 22–25
  political institutions, 25–27
Schumacher, E. F., 19, 23
Scrip corporation, 105
Second Bank of the United States, 7
Securities regulation
  federal, 109–117
  state, 115–116
Security
  defined, 110–111
  evidence of indebtedness, 111–113
  family resemblance test, 111
  Howey definition, 111
  investment contract, 113–114
  note, 111
  stock, 114
Self-Help Association for a Regional
    Economy, 53–55, 58, 84–87. See
    also SHARE
Self-reliance, 27–32
  political economy, role in, 27–30
Self-sufficiency
  agricultural, 29

energy, 24
political economy, 27–30
SHARE, 53–55, 58, 84–87
bank collaboration, 84–87
loans, small business, 84
Societary theory of money, 97
Southern Berkshire Chamber of Commerce, 59, 63
State banks
agents for local currency issuers, 109
State member banks, 105
State law
anticounterfeiting, 104–105
Arkansas, 104–105
employers must pay employees in U.S. currency, 104
prohibition on paying employees in scrip, 104
state banks, act as agents for local currency issuer, 109
Virginia, 104–105
Suffolk Bank of Boston, 8
Suffolk Bank System, 8
Sustainable development, 21–22

Taft Farms, 55
Tax Reform Act of 1976, 103
Taxation
federal income

bargain purchase notes, 123–125
barter exchanges, 117–122
currency, not pegged to U.S. dollar, 125–127
discount notes, 123–125
notes not issued by national banks, 102–103
state chartered bank notes, 9–10, 102–103
Timberlake, Richard H., 13
Time Dollars
income tax aspects, 120
Toffler, Alvin, 25
Tortoriello, Frank, 54–55
Transferring local currency
clearinghouses, 108
Federal Reserve System, limitations on transfer, 107
Treasury Regulations
barter exchanges, information reporting, 118–120

U.S. Constitution
federal monetary powers, 95–96
prohibitions on states, 95–99
Uniform Commercial Code, 108

White, Lawrence H., 88–90
Wildcat banks, 9
Witt, Susan, 54

About the Author

LEWIS D. SOLOMON is Arthur Selwyn Miller Research Professor of Law at The George Washington University Law School. He is the author of twenty-three books including, most recently, *Taxation of Investments* (1994) and *Corporations: Law and Policy* (1994).

ISBN 0-275-95376-9

EAN

HARDCOVER BAR CODE